D0072711

Suburban Dreams

Rhetoric, Culture, and Social Critique

Series Editor
John Louis Lucaites

Editorial Board
Jeffrey A. Bennett
Barbara Biesecker
Carole Blair
Joshua Gunn
Robert Hariman
Debra Hawhee
Claire Sisco King
Steven Mailloux
Raymie E. McKerrow
Toby Miller
Phaedra C. Pezzullo
Austin Sarat
Janet Staiger
Barbie Zelizer

Suburban Dreams

Imagining and Building the Good Life

GREG DICKINSON

THE UNIVERSITY OF ALABAMA PRESS
Tuscaloosa

The University of Alabama Press
Tuscaloosa, Alabama 35487-0380
uapress.ua.edu

Copyright © 2015 by the University of Alabama Press
All rights reserved

Inquiries about reproducing material from this work should
be addressed to the University of Alabama Press

Typeface: Bembo

Manufactured in the United States of America
Cover photograph: Construction site on the outskirts
of Las Vegas, 2007; courtesy of the author
Cover design: Michele Myatt Quinn

∞

The paper on which this book is printed meets the minimum requirements of
American National Standard for Information Sciences—Permanence of Paper for
Printed Library Materials, ANSI Z39.48-1984

Cataloging-in-Publication data is available from the Library of Congress
ISBN: 978-0-8173-1863-5 (cloth) — ISBN: 978-0-8173-8811-9 (ebook)

For Elizabeth Munson and Roger Munson

Contents

Illustrations

Acknowledgments

Much of the initial research that forms the core of this book began during a fall 2007 sabbatical generously supported by the College of Liberal Arts dean, Ann Gill, at Colorado State University. I was also supported by the College of Liberal Arts Professional Development Program, which regularly funded travel to professional meetings and research sites.

As I traveled during this sabbatical across the intermountain West taking pictures, eating at Olive Gardens, attending megachurches, and wandering lifestyle centers, I was hosted by friends and colleagues. In Surprise, Arizona, a former master's degree advisee, Cary Fay Amaro, introduced me to Radiant Church, where she worked and worshiped. In Las Vegas, Nevada, Donovan Conley—who shares interests in place, space, and food—twice toured with me through that city's far-flung suburbs.

I couldn't ask for better departmental colleagues. David Vest and Sue Pendell, department chairs during the course of this project, did all they could to support and encourage my writing. My colleagues up and down the hallways of the Williard O. Eddy Building listened patiently to my endless ramblings about the suburbs. Karrin Vasby Anderson and Carl Burgchardt were particularly helpful conversational partners. I conducted the last round of revisions during a sojourn in the College of Liberal Arts Dean's Office as an associate dean. Dean Ann Gill generously offered additional writing time, and Bruce Ronda and Stephan Weiler, my fellow associate deans, not only asked rigorous questions about my writing, they also helped protect me from the onslaught of e-mails and meetings that is the life of an associate dean.

Over the years, I have taught numerous versions Rhetoric of Everyday Life with unsuspecting graduate students. The readings in the class consistently reflected my obsessions with space, place, materiality, performativity, gender, identity, and many other things. The students came for the ride with me, often steering me in unexpected ways. The seminar has helped produce a number of projects that intersected with my own work in everyday culture. Casey Maugh's interest in natural food grocery stores helped me think about food and suburban space. The work of several master's degree advisees directly influenced my own work: Kyle Cohen's study of northern Colorado housing developments; Jessie Stewart's exploration of Flat-Iron Crossings in Broomfield, Colorado; Elinor Light's engagement with the Fort Collins First Friday Art Walk; Megan Beam's analysis of stores in Old Town Fort Collins and in Centerra Promenade in Loveland all influenced this study. In fact, Megan is a coauthor of this book's chapter 6.

Colleagues and students from around the country have also helped me think about the suburbs. Conversations at St. Thomas University; Christopher Newport University; University of Colorado, Boulder; and University of Nevada, Las Vegas, all shaped the essays in this book.

Many colleagues have responded to arguments made throughout the book: Stephen John Hartnett and Lisa B. Keränen read earlier versions of chapter 1. Joan Faber McAlister read chapter 3, and Giorgia Aiello read chapter 5. All of these chapters are stronger because of their help. I have had amazing conversations with colleagues from across the humanities as I have worked on this project. Conversations with scholars in history, media studies, health communication, environmental communication, geography, and interpersonal communication demonstrated that space, place, and memory have deep resonances across the academy. All have deepened and enriched my thinking about suburbs, families, and the good life.

I also owe a debt of gratitude to my colleagues in the loosely defined field of urban communication. I was able to present many of my initial thoughts about this project at all-day, National Communication Association preconferences focusing on urban communication and sponsored by the Urban Communication Foundation. Often organized by Victoria Gallagher and Matthew Matsaganis, these seminars brought together communication scholars from across the discipline in what were extraordinarily productive cross-disciplinary conversations. My project found a congenial home among social scientists, media ecologists, rhetorical critics, cultural theorists, architects, geographers, urban planners, social activists, and so many others. Although focused on the city, the group listened patiently and responded forcefully to my writing about suburbs.

Eric Aoki has served as a deeply important sounding board. Like me, he was born and raised in the rural West. Like me, he migrated to the great cities of the West Coast. Like me, he has settled into a career as a teacher and scholar at CSU. We talk about cities and towns, food and culture, place and possibility. As a dear friend and a valued coauthor, Eric consistently reframes the work I do, reminding me of powerful connections among people, place, and culture.

Carole Blair—teacher, mentor, colleague, friend—has transformed my work through conversations and the constant excellence of her own writing and thinking. Years ago she sat on my master's thesis committee when I was doing work so different from the work I am doing now and she was just beginning her groundbreaking work on memory and place. Her work, her advice, her encouragement, and the numbers of times she has read essays of mine in one form or another have enabled my scholarship.

But no one has had a more profound influence on my writing and thinking than Brian Ott. Over mid-morning coffees, early evening sandwiches, and late-night beers, we have explored life and love and rhetoric and writing. Our time together made this book—and my life—immeasurably better.

Although all of these people have influenced this work, it goes without saying that this book's infelicities are mine and mine alone.

Finally, my partner Elizabeth Munson has been with me on every step of this journey. She has joined me not just on the journey that resulted in this book, but the one that moved me from rural Washington State into and through graduate school and down the path of teaching, writing, cooking, reading, traveling, and thinking that has formed my life for nearly thirty years. When, during a long hike in Point Reyes, California, at the very beginning of our graduate studies she asked if we could talk about something other than school, she reminded me of all the ways we build a good life. She helped me remember that we always build our good lives with others and that these good lives are projects not destinations. This life we have is good.

Introduction
Rhetorical Constructions of the Good Life

Driving along the E-470 from North Denver toward Denver International Airport I see an apparently weathered sign for a new suburb named Reunion. "Reunion," the sign reads, "A new hometown for the age-old pursuit of happiness." With its referencing of vintage railroad logos and its explicit intersecting of home, town, and the pursuit of happiness, the sign condenses the hopes and fears constitutive of late twentieth- and early twenty-first-century suburbs. At a moment when home in its multiple emotional, material, and national valences is deeply desired and yet seemingly always absent, Reunion offers a visual gathering of family, home, and history. More, however, it sutures these connections with founding national myths of the inalienable rights of life, liberty, and the pursuit of happiness. But the Reunion sign does not stand alone among suburban signs; instead, it is one of many material and symbolic performances through which contemporary suburbs rhetorically construct visions of the good life.

In fact, the postwar suburban landscape has become the material and imaginative hometown of many US Americans. Built into seemingly empty landscapes; absorbing and demanding the products of late modern consumer economy; subject of innumerable television shows, films, novels, advertisements, magazine articles, and critical assessments; and beneficiaries of local, state, regional, and federal largess, the postwar suburb is easily one of the most important sites of individual, communal, and national identity.[1] Even in the midst of the largest housing market decline in decades, ordinary people continue to choose suburbs for their homes.[2] Constructed of concrete and lumber and constituted through rhetorical inducements, the suburbs are symbolic and material enactments of the hopes for and concerns about the contemporary good life.[3]

Of course, the good life—or a vision of happiness—is nearly always at issue in life's big decisions like buying a house or moving to a new neighborhood. But the good life is also at stake in the everyday decisions about how to dress for the day, what to eat, what book to read, or which television show to watch. Made up of big and little decisions and performed in important and seemingly banal actions, the good life is a material and symbolic project, an enactment that is built of enabling and structuring rhetorical resources—that is built of topoi. Topos is, of course, a central concept in rhetorical theory and analysis. Conceptualized as the starting place of rhetoric, as the place that contains necessary rhetorical resources, or as the lines of argument that can structure rhetoric, topos suggests that rhetorical performances are structured by and built out of existing resources. Beyond naming symbolic rhetorical resources, topos also captures the centrality of place in human experience and action.[4] I turn to topos as a key term for this rhetorical study of suburbs and the good life because it so explicitly combines place and argument. Topos will consistently urge consideration of both the material and symbolic rhetorical inducements that shape suburbs and suburban living.

Thinking suburban landscapes topically also provides a complex way of thinking the relationship between structure and agency. Topoi, thought of as already available categories and lines of rhetorical action, indicate that the possibilities of rhetoric are delimited and bounded. Thought of as rhetorical resources, topoi urge consideration of the wide variety of materials out of which landscapes and lives are created. Even as these rhetorical resources organize very specific actions, they do so without determining them, since individuals enunciate these resources in unexpected ways and often combine rhetorical resources into unusual forms as they make and perform their lives.[5] In everyday practices, people enunciate—that is, they say and enact—their lives by taking up the structured resources extant in the places and discourses of which they are a part. But in performing themselves with these resources they never enunciate in the exact way those resources had been previously expressed. It is in these differences that enunciative agency appears. What is more, the topoi used in enunciative action can only be recognized when a specific topos is activated. Thus even as the topos structures possible rhetorical action, this rhetorical action makes and remakes the resource out of which the action is built. In short, topoi serve as foundational inventional materials enabling and structuring—without determining—action.

But the rhetorical tradition focuses on topos more as metaphor than materiality. In spite of the obvious connections to material place encoded into the term, topos is not often imagined as a material place to which rhetors go to find rhetorical resources. Instead, it is a conceptual way of helping rhetors memorize and store common and special argumentative forms. In this sense, topos is related to the architectural mnemonics so important to classical, medieval, and Renaissance rhetorical theory and practice. In fact, Frances Yates argues that "it is probable that the very word 'topics' as used in dialectics arose through the paces of mnemonics."[6] This architectural theory of mnemonics, however, is more than just metaphorical. Instead, it has serious implications for both the construction and material use of place as, for example, Renaissance architects used their rhetorically trained architectural memories to guide them in the design and construction of cities, buildings, and gardens.[7] So also topos—which depends on and founds these mnemonics—is more than metaphorical. Drawing on materialized rhetorical possibilities, designers, architects, and residents make and remake the built environment of suburbs. At the same time, residents and visitors use the material and symbolic rhetorical resources of the suburbs to build, enact, and perform particular versions of the good life.

Over the course of this book I will be writing about the suburbs as late modern spatial topoi. By writing about suburbs as topoi, I will attend to the complex ways the built and symbolic environments work together to offer rhetorical resources out of which people can build their lives. Like topoi, suburbs are constructed in and through time and space, and a careful analysis of the suburbs will attend to the symbolic and material, the temporal and the spatial rhetorical modes and consequences of suburbs. A fully embodied, temporally and spatially rich understanding of topos urges me to engage suburbs not only or even primarily as ideologically loaded landscapes (though they are certainly that), but rather as material landscapes that offer resources—some powerfully positive, others deeply troubling, and always structuring but not determining—out of which suburbanites can dream and enact a very particular good life.

But there is a final layer to my understanding of topos. For I hope this book will offer topoi that, when laced together with the spaces about which I write, will enable a richer, more complex way of living our (suburban) lives. In fact, the purpose of a rhetorical analysis of suburbs is precisely in this impulse. I am less interested in demystifying or debunking suburbs than I am in thinking carefully about how we might engage the suburbs—and more broadly the wide range of spaces of our everyday lives—more carefully, thoughtfully, and rigorously. In this way, then, the book and the suburbs are homologous: the suburbs are built of topoi that shape and guide their construction; they offer topoi useful for residents as they make and enact their (good) lives; they are the topoi of which I compose the book; and finally the book may offer topoi useful in the (re)imagining, (re)enacting, and (re)materializing of the suburbs.

Suburbs are complex topoi. Most obviously, they serve as starting places and lines of reasoning for arguments about the contemporary condition. For example, critics have excoriated and extolled the suburbs as providing the possibilities and opportunities of the good life. For some, the suburbs undermine any hopes of creating the good life, offering instead a denuded image of a richly imagined personal and communal life. Others see in the suburbs a powerfully hopeful opportunity for remaking relations of self, other, and community. And, of course, the suburbs are also topoi for imaginative artists including novelists, essayists, filmmakers, and television producers, all of whom consistently return to the suburbs as grounding for both utopian and dystopian visions of the world. I will take up these texts in the book's first section.

But suburbs also provide a material and symbolic topoi for residents themselves. Certainly films, television shows, books, and essays help suburbanites and others imagine the suburban good life, but the built environment is embedded in the effort to dream and live the good life. The material (and, of course, symbolic and discursive) landscape of the suburbs provides the stage on which, the material goods of which, and the performative values through which suburbanites enact the good life. As I argue in section II, the home and the family, long imagined as the centerpiece of the good life, are made and remade by suburban residential neighborhoods and reimagined in suburban family restaurants. But, as I explore in section III, contemporary suburbs reimagine public life as well. The megachurch's pitch-perfect, popular-culture-infused, nondenominational religious experiences stitch spiritual and communal life into familiar consumer culture forms. These forms are reiterated in recently built lifestyle shopping centers that attempt to recapture small towns and urban downtowns from a fondly remembered past. Both of these archetypal, late modern suburban spaces address the deeply felt need for a value-driven, publicly expressed form of community. The built environment, then, is itself an enactment and manifestation of suburban dreams even as it offers these dreams as powerfully compelling resources—that is, topoi—for a late modern good life. Dreams are dreamed in particular places, shaping responses to and directing the construction of material spaces.[8] The suburban topoi offer materially rich, symbolically complex, and affectively compelling ways of imaging and enacting the world.

While suburbs are indeed complex and offer widely ranging topical resources, it is also possible to identify significant rhetorical themes that bind suburban rhetorics. I call these themes rhetorical spatialities. My attention to rhetorical spatialities draws on growing literatures in rhetoric and across the humanities and social sciences emphasizing the central role space plays in everyday life.[9] In fact, leading mid- and late-twentieth-century scholars of everyday life like Pierre Bourdieu, Michel de Certeau, Michel Foucault, Henri Lefebvre, and more recently Meaghan Morris recognized space as a crucial element in the lives of ordinary people and consequently offered spatial analysis as a powerful entrée into the analysis of everyday life.[10] Spatial analysis demands attention to the ways everyday performances are constrained and enabled by life's material conditions; the modes by which power and resistance are arrayed across discursive and material landscapes; the means by which bodies come into contact, identities are performed, and communities are developed and dissolved. *Rhetorical spatialities*, however, takes these interdisciplinary impulses and turns them into a distinctly rhetorical project. Gathering together the recent attention to space with the ancient understanding of topoi, rhetorical spatialities will focus attention on how landscapes—and the people who inhabit and thus make and remake them—embody, enact, and urge values, beliefs, and actions. Material and discursive landscapes, in this view, are "meaningful, legible, partisan, and consequential," and rhetorical analysis will attend carefully to these characteristics of the spaces.[11]

While the suburban topoi and the rhetorical spatialities they help construct are nearly infinite, close attention to specific suburban landscapes suggests three broad and broadly intersecting rhetorical spatialities: memory, locality, and safety. Memory, locality, and safety are rhetorical because they are at once resources for compelling rhetoric and are themselves rhetorical effects. They are also spatialities because memory, locality, and safety shape space even as they are apprehended and performed spatially. Take one brief example. United States suburban housing developments draw on a particular US pastoral vision by referencing agricultural images and buildings through their location in and citations to what was once productive farmland, their frequent inclusion of farmers' markets, and their consistent referencing of an older way of life situated between city and country.[12] The use of the pastoral is clearly rhetorical—that is, it is an affectively powerful aesthetic that is meaningful, legible, partisan, and consequential.[13] More, however, a spatialized rhetoric for the pastoral is directly performed in and on the land. Even more specifically, it embodies a rhetorical spatiality of memory as it draws on old images of an ideal America, of locality as it roots suburbs and suburbanites into a particular land and vision of the land, and of safety as the pastoral implies a comforting homogeneity of residents and relationships.[14] This argument about the pastoral will weave in and out of the book and will find its fullest development in chapter 3. It is sufficient at this point, however, to simply indicate that nearly all of the suburban enactments and materializations that occupy my argument will, to varying degrees, engage these intersecting rhetorical spatialities. For now, I will outline the concerns these three controlling themes address.

Memory

Suburban dreams and constructions are frequently made compelling through powerful appeals to memory. Suburban films often situate narratives in nostalgic longings for a small-town past, lifestyle centers reimagine early twentieth-century urban downtowns, chain restaurants like Olive Garden or Macaroni Grill embody (admittedly thin) memories of Italianicity, and domestic architecture continually places homes in some vaguely executed European or American past. And so the mnemonics of contemporary suburbs are varied and diverse, taking as their explicit and implicit content a wide range of memory possibilities. As diverse as these memories seem to be—vacillating between small town and downtown or between uninflected American and ethnically limned familial identities—nearly all of these suburban memories circulate around themes of home and images of local contexts that root suburban subjectivity into stable renderings of time and place and do so in part to create a sense of personal and familial safety.

Memory is deeply connected to space and, more specifically, to home. Recent memory studies demonstrate not only that memory is rhetorical but also that "memory places are especially powerful rhetorically."[15] In fact, the connections among space, memory, and rhetoric (and, as indicated above, topos) go back to the very beginnings of Western literacy, as the earliest forms of rhetorical mnemonics relied on carefully developed memories of temples and other striking buildings.[16] These mnemonics were not simply techniques to foster recall of textual passages, but were linked directly to the development and enrichment of the soul and, by implication, the enactment of a virtuous life.[17] But not only ancients twined together memory, place, soul, and the good life. In Renaissance gardens and theaters, designers drew on rhetorical mnemonics as they imagined and built spaces for the better enactment of emerging understandings of citizenship.[18] Or (to move far too quickly), Freudian psychoanalysis is, at least partly, a project that links memory and soul and—in the conceptualization of the uncanny—demonstrates spatial dimensions.[19]

This connection between space, soul, and memory animates the early pages of Gaston Bachelard's pathbreaking *The Poetics of Space*. Asserting that memories are essentially spatial in nature, Bachelard writes, "The finest specimens of fossilized duration concretized as a result of a long sojourn, are to be found in and through space. The unconscious abides. Memories are motionless, and the more securely they are fixed in space, the sounder they are."[20] The originating memory-space of the human is the house where life begins well, "enclosed, protected, and warm in the bosom of the house."[21] Through dreams, the imagination, and the functions of memory humans create their houses and, not coincidentally, themselves. These houses secure the individual and make possible the imaging of a good life.[22] Memory, then, is often powerfully connected to, triggered by, and enacted in space, and few spaces are more fecund sites of memory than the house.

This powerful relation among memory, self, and house partially explains the ways house and home have served as a locus of modernity's deeply held spatial anxieties. As I will argue in chapter 1, modernity is characterized not only by shifting spatial, economic, and cultural conditions but is also marked by a series of anxieties that are connected to space, circulate around the home, and frequently involve memory and memory loss. Nostalgia—which in the seventeenth century was considered a serious medical pathology— is the archetypal form of this anxiety. Expressing the felt loss of a fondly remembered home, nostalgia encapsulates many of the concerns embodied in modernity and late modernity, most specifically modernity's intense desire for the home. Nostalgia and, more broadly, memory, becomes not only a desire for a lost object but also is itself an object of desire.[23] The longing for home expresses itself in a pining for something lost and in a whole host of performances and constructions that turn present and future homes into objects of desire. From the mass-reproduced sublimity of Disney's Main Street to the banality of the Reunion billboard, home, nostalgia, and memory are objects of desire.

Locality

Houses and their landscapes—which in the contemporary United States are suburban—are spaces that encode the possibilities of memory, working against the dispersal of the subjectivity along globalizing and (apparently) deterritorializing networks of contemporary culture. Together, home and memory create a powerful place-making logic that can help suburbanites establish themselves in place and time, and do so through a rhetoric of locality. Locality, as I will argue in the next chapter, is a rhetorical construction that draws on wide-ranging and often disparate aesthetic, symbolic, affective, and material resources to carve out a meaningful space/time that at once acknowledges the distancing forces of globalization and the deep desire to know exactly where (and when) we are. Because it helps establish where in the world we are, locality nearly always depends on material instantiations that are recognizably place-based. For example, suburban lifestyle centers—the most recent form of suburban shopping centers—will often use locally sourced rough-hewn stone or geographically reminiscent brick. While building with local materials and forms is one way of producing locality, a second less obvious way to create locality is by connecting space to familiar but not local spaces. Olive Garden, for example, consistently signals its connection to Tuscany while residential landscapes will draw on English cottages or French country homes to locate themselves. Regardless, locality materializes an effort to position a space and its users in a recognizable place. Combining locality's ability to create recognizable place with memory's time-binding properties, suburbs strive to situate themselves and suburbanites into a comforting place and time. Suturing landscapes and people into familiar place/time relations is absolutely central to the success of contemporary suburbs, since broader cultural forces consistently work against this very sense of rootedness.

Safety

Memory's and locality's ability to help situate individuals in time and place is centrally connected to a final suburban obsession: safety. For many suburbanites, safety serves as a major reason to move to and stay in suburban neighborhoods. This sense of safety is produced dialectically. For well over one hundred years, US political and cultural discourse has framed the city as a site of decay and crime. As Steve Macek argues, from the 1970s to the present much discussion of the contemporary city expresses and produces a "moral panic" that "infected the general public, particularly the suburban middle class," convincing them that the city creates and houses deeply disturbing race and class conflicts.[24] Against this imaging of the city as a site of risk, the suburbs create the appearances of safety. Built behind gates and walls, advertised as secluded and private, protected by private security forces, and serviced by the pseudo-public spaces of lifestyle centers and malls, suburbs offer what I will call the affective aesthetics of safety. Setha Low's anthropological work demonstrates that while gated communities are no safer than the neighborhoods surrounding them, the residents of these communities believe themselves to be safer even as they are obsessed by encroaching risk.[25] The belief in suburban safety relies, then, on an aesthetic that materializes and symbolizes the hope of safety. Memory and locality are central to this aesthetic, for the powerfully localizing imagining of home draws on and creates a sense of safety even as it situates residents in a clearly delimited time and space.

The Space/Time of Suburbs

As the forgoing discussion of memory, locality, and safety suggest; time and place are deeply interwoven in suburbs. So to they are woven into the book itself. In fact, the constantly shifting place of suburbs in the US moral, economic, and material landscape raises important theoretical and methodological issues. Perhaps the most central of these theoretical and methodological issues is how critics can best engage the encoding and enacting of memory in material place when both memory and place are in constant flux. The shifting suburban landscapes and imaginaries of the last decade raise this problem of memory, place, and time to a flashpoint. In a recent *New York Times* Op-Ed, Christopher Leinberger argued that far-flung, outer-ring suburbs, like the ones I am studying, are a dying relic of the very recent past. Created in a time of irrational exuberance, and founded on deeply unsustainable economic, environmental, and social practices, these outer-ring suburbs seem a less compelling landscape of the good life compared to old inner-ring suburbs and even older urban neighborhoods. Empty nest baby boomers are looking for smaller homes in more walkable neighborhoods, while millennials are looking to cities and older suburban downtowns to meet lifestyle needs. Making matters worse for recently built suburbs, the oversupply of new suburban homes along with the mortgage crisis of the last few years have so depressed home prices in these developments that some are worth less than what it would cost to replace them.[26]

At the same time, strong home prices in inner-ring suburbs (like Pasadena) and in gentrifying city neighborhoods (like Denver's Capitol Hill), indicate a cultural and economic shift from new suburbs to old suburbs and from suburbs to cities. Over the last decade residents of cities like Denver, Portland, and Phoenix consistently voted to increase funding for alternative transportation, including light rail, express bus lanes, and bike trails, suggesting an erosion of the car's prominence in the metropolitan landscape.[27] Of course, not everyone agrees with this analysis, and suburbs remain a popular and important destination for individuals and families.[28] Ten years after beginning to write about the suburbs, I write this introduction in a moral and economic landscape radically altered by suburban-mortgage-fueled recession. What a difference a decade makes.

Writing about contemporary popular culture is always a risky endeavor.

On the one hand, as Meaghan Morris argues, the analysis almost always comes too soon.[29] Written in the midst of or immediately following the maelstrom of cultural transformations, *Suburban Dreams* seems to come too soon to level considered and thoughtful judgment of either the present of suburbs or the suburbs of the immediate past. Over the course of the decade I have been writing this book, suburbs experienced the peak of the housing bubble and the depths of the bubble's burst and, with housing prices modestly increasing and housing starts in suburbs rising slowly, experiencing a modest suburban rebound. Surely it is too soon to understand these shifts, and an exploration of the suburban good life of the turn of the twenty-first century is, at best, provisional. At the same time, with writers like Leinberger already pronouncing the death of these suburbs, the essays written here come too late to offer moral or heuristic lessons about the suburban good life during the boom. The good life, it seems, has changed its mailing address, (re)settling in cities and inner-ring suburbs. The timing of a book like this is always, almost necessarily, wrong.

I am confronted with this conundrum not only because I am writing about the near past but also because I am writing about the built environment that casts social, cultural, and economic mores into concrete and stone. One of the paradoxes of writing about the materialities of popular culture is that these materialities are both more and less permanent than other forms of popular culture. A television show, once completed, is nearly always available in nearly unchanged form; a speech may be archived in print or audio or video recording; a movie preserved on DVD and Blu-ray. But houses in foreclosure, neighborhoods abandoned, buildings repurposed, remodeled, or torn down are fundamentally different from their original forms and purposes, and their consequentiality can seem unrecoverable. And so writing about suburbs (or, for the matter, cities and other places) is always too late; by the time the writing is done the place has changed. And so even writing about the immediate past is a bit like writing history without the years and decades that is often the historian's luxury. This too lateness, then, is an inherent consequence of the attempt to write the spatiality of rhetoric and, to be frank, is a consequence of the growing effort to write the materiality of rhetoric more generally.[30] Rhetoric's materiality depends, in a crucial way, on both the present and on presence.[31] Writing about materiality not only shifts registers (translating the a-signifying rhetoricity of materiality to the signifying arguments of criticism) but shifts time (from the present of the critical encounter to the constant deferrals of the critical text). Thus writing into being the materiality of television, public address, or film founders on the same conundrum as the one I have faced in writing about ever-shifting concrete landscapes of contemporary suburbia.

Rather than arguing against engaging rhetoric's materiality, this conundrum can actually be seen as a reason to take materiality seriously. The most apparent reason to seriously engage ever-shifting landscapes is because these kinds of shifts are central to our experience of daily life. In fact, the vagaries of life are the precise problem the spatial topoi of memory, locality, and safety respond to. I cannot hope, as a critic, to stop this change for the convenience of academic writing. That said there are at least four methodological consequences of thinking seriously about suburbs as material and symbolic rhetorical enactments. First, as Carole Blair argues, being there matters; that is, rhetorical engagement with rhetoric's materiality demands that the rhetorical critic go to the site of the rhetorical enactments investigated.[32] This book depends on hours, days, and weeks spent in the spaces about which I write as well as a careful reading of attendant literatures. This analysis cannot be accomplished in the study, the office, or the screening room. This *being there* enacts a doubled materiality since being there makes it possible for the critic to engage in the concrete materialization of rhetoric and also involves the critic's own embodied engagement with rhetoric.

Second, and consequently, being there matters because rhetoric's materiality is apprehended sensually through the practices of seeing, hearing, tasting, touching, and smelling. It takes serious effort when attending to public, material places to ignore the physicality and sensuousness of rhetoric and focus exclusively on the symbolicity of a rhetorical site. The heat of a summer's day in Phoenix or the chill of a winter's afternoon in Denver alters the rhetorical enactments of lifestyle centers: the fire pit in Centerra Promenade in Loveland, Colorado, offers a differently positioned, rhetorically produced sense of place than does a similar feature in suburban Phoenix.

These first two methodological considerations—that being there matters and that being there engages all of the senses alerted to rhetorical consequentiality—meant limiting analysis to only a few suburban landscapes. I spent significant time over the course of the last ten years in three major suburban locations: the suburbs of Denver and along Colorado's suburbanized Front Range, suburban Phoenix, and suburban Las Vegas. I chose these landscapes for personal and scholarly reasons. If a careful spatial analysis requires regular and committed attention to the actual spaces, then I needed to choose landscapes I could regularly visit. Living in Fort Collins, Colorado—itself mostly suburban in form—I was close to the suburbs that surround Denver, making these obvious landscapes for attention. As I expanded my research toward other suburbs that stretch across the Mountain West, my attention was drawn to the rapidly growing suburbs of Phoenix and Las Vegas. These suburbs share some characteristics with those of Denver. The climate is arid and the urban and suburban development is recent. But, where Las Vegas and Phoenix were consistently among the fastest-growing Western and national suburbs, the suburbs of the Colorado Front Range were more controlled in their growth, and the state was more restrained in its recession. Regardless, I have not surveyed the wide variety of post–World War II suburbs splayed across the country or even along the vast Sunbelt that stretches from Florida to California. And so I cannot make a claim of generalizability, even as I consistently check my own findings against those reported in the growing scholarly suburban literature.

Although the first two considerations engage issues of materiality, the third methodological concern urges me to resist opposing rhetoric's materiality and symbolicity. Instead, materiality and symbolicity are entwined and enmeshed. Where much rhetorical criticism and theory overemphasizes the symbolic—often to the extent of ignoring or denying materiality—the best work engaging rhetoric's materiality refuses the polarity of symbol and material. Indeed, symbols always and necessarily depend on rhetoric's materiality, for they are always mediated through material forms. For this reason I am consistently shifting between the symbolic and the material. The book's form moves from the more familiar territory of symbolicity toward less familiar material groundings of analysis.

Finally, materiality is oddly fleeting. The landscapes I studied in this book are different today than when I started the project, turning the apparent fixity of the suburban landscapes into a mirage. The fleetingness of rhetoric's materiality returns me to the first two lessons of being there and embodiment, for our presence already changes the rhetoric even as the rhetoric changes us. Rhetoric's materiality demands of the critic and the theorist a serious commitment to presence, to embodied possibilities and risks, to an engagement with "permanence and change."[33] Of course, the fleetingness of materiality in general and of the suburbs in particular does not mean that the present project is meaningless or useless. Critically accounting for the materiality of rhetoric, even as we shift time and affect/effect registers to do so, can have moral and heuristic consequences. For Barry Brummett, "The ultimate goal and justification [for rhetorical criticism] is pedagogical: to teach people how to experience their rhetorical environments more richly."[34] By attending to suburbs as an environment that is rendered materially and symbolically, this rhetorical criticism can help suburbanites—that is to say, me and many like me—experience our rhetorical environments more richly and more concretely.

What follows, then, is a heuristically attuned rhetorical criticism. I am on the lookout less for the ideology of particular places, more for the resources—the topoi—the places offer their residents and visitors for making, performing, and imaging the good life. I explore the power of memory and locality to situate suburbanites into time and place and do so through my own fully embodied experiences of those places. Because, however, memory and locality are always shifting, because the needs others and I bring to the places and because of the needs and desires the places seek to create are constantly changing, the memories and places are not exactly the ones that readers of the book experience; my desires and places, my grounding memories and localities are not yours. But we may not be that different either. At the very least, all of us negotiate our daily lives in the midst of material and symbolic landscapes, at once flung across the flows of globalization and located in time and place through memory and geography. The book that follows, I hope, offers topoi for fully engaging the places of our daily lives. It may do so by offering insights into landscapes readers are intimately familiar with—perhaps from frequent visits to the local lifestyle center or regular meals at Olive Garden. But it may also offer ways of thinking about our daily, banal spaces more generally. We can move, I trust, analogically from reconstructed old towns in lifestyle centers to the Old Town in which I actually wrote this book; from the sacred spaces of particular megachurches to the material and symbolic practices of a local church, mosque, synagogue, or temple. Our hopes and fears, our ways of being good, our chances at happiness are built and enacted in the buildings and institutions of our daily lives. In so many houses—suburban or urban, town or country, large or small, old or new—are located the hopes built of and built into home. These hopes for and topoi out of which are built a located and locatable good life will be the focus of the rest of the book.

I. Imaging the Suburban Good Life

Everyday Practices, Rhetoric, and the Suburban Good Life

> Suburbia is the site of promises, dreams, and fantasies. It is a landscape of the imagination where Americans situate ambitions for upward mobility and economic security, ideals about freedom and private property, and longings for social harmony and social uplift.
>
> —Dolores Hayden

In the years following World War II, more and more US Americans dreamed their good lives in the bedrooms of their new suburban homes. These new dreams of the suburban good life—first imagined in the early part of the twentieth century and fully realized in the suburban boom of the last sixty years—remade the country both spatially and culturally. Imaging the nation as composed primarily of suburbs demanded new ways of understanding what it meant to be American.[1] Indeed, the postwar era drew increased attention from scholars and pundits concerning the meaning of this spatial transformation. Critics regularly argue that this shift from city to suburb is negative. With neither the diversity nor richness of the city nor the simplicity or purity of the countryside suburbia is often imagined as a place of banality and anomie.[2] Suburban communities, critics often assert, are based more on homogeneity than on passionate commitments to people and place. Insular, unchallenging, environmentally unsound, and culturally deadening, suburbs, these critics argue, are a wasteland.

And yet people keep moving to the suburbs. Many US Americans across the spectrum of ethnic and class differences continue to choose suburbia as a nearly ideal place to make a life.[3] Even as popular and academic critics excoriate suburbia, individuals settle into new suburban homes, shop at the latest lifestyle centers, choose their evening's meal from the new row of restaurants, and worship in megachurches; they move in, settle down, and make a life. Are the critics correct that suburbanites are duped by a powerful and ideologically wily commodity culture that fosters and depends on suburban living and are seduced by the promise of community-built comforts of homogeneity?[4] Or are residents who keep choosing suburbs right when they suggest that far from being soulless, deadening, and devoid of community, their new hometowns fulfill the hopes for a good life in an increasingly difficult world?[5] Perhaps there is some space between these poles. Perhaps there are good reasons for choosing suburbs as the place to perform a good life even as suburbs depend on unsustainable practices and enforce racial, ethnic, and class-based exclusions.[6] It may be the case that suburbanites understand the difficulties of making community in a commodified space and recognize the deadening potential of block after block of look-alike houses and nonetheless, or, perhaps therefore, choose suburbia as the place to stake their claims to the good life.[7]

I will argue throughout this book that suburbs offer compelling dreams of the good life while responding to real difficulties and important challenges. Indeed, my contention is that suburbs embody, perform, and construct the good life within a world nearly overwhelmed with tenuous and contested understandings and enactments of the good life. Even as suburbs offer their own visions of the good life, they are also deeply felt responses to a series of modern spatial anxieties. These anxieties circulate around confounding difficulties of home and city and are constitutive of and constituted within the rapid changes of modernity. Modernity, with its world-altering and nearly cataclysmic changes, fostered the spatialized anxieties of nostalgia, the uncanny, and agoraphobia. Each of these anxieties circulates around and troubles the idea of home. Nostalgia is the (sometimes disabling) desire for a childhood home. The uncanny is the fear of homes made unhomely or haunted. And agoraphobia is literally the fear of the marketplace that forces its sufferers to stay home. While taking the home as a central figure, these anxieties are also often linked to the city, as the rise of the modern city serves as a material and symbolic location for life-altering changes of modernity. It is in these cultural, social, political, and economic contexts that postwar suburbs are built. In fact, postwar suburban dreams I am focusing on in this book are deeply linked to the urban nightmares crucial to postwar politics and imagination.[8] Against these anxieties and nightmares, the suburbs comprise, extend, and challenge rhetorical constructions of the good life that entangle memory and locality with the hopes and dreams of home.

In this chapter and the next, I trace the historical, cultural, and visual framing for the suburban built environment I will analyze in sections II and III. I begin this chapter with a consideration of the long rhetorical and philosophical conversation about creating a communal and public good life. The good life, I am going to suggest in the first part of the chapter, is a rhetorical project that is symbolic and material and depends on a rich and ancient sense of ethos or a sense of dwelling together.[9] And yet, as I argue in the second part of the chapter, the spatial anxieties characteristic of modernity and late modernity produce difficulties surrounding home and threaten to turn dreams of a safe and comforting home into nightmares and thus impinge on the hopes for a suburban good life. Although modern spatial anxieties—and particularly anxieties located in both the home and the city—make imagining and enacting the good life difficult, I will suggest in this chapter's conclusion that memory and locality provide meaningful rhetorical resources out of which suburbs strive to imagine and construct a rhetorically appealing landscape. Appeals to home and history are affective and effective rhetorical inducements that can draw residents away from the concerns performed by modern spatial anxieties even as these appeals enact particular material and symbolic visions of the suburban good life.[10]

The Suburban Good Life

As both the site of and response to the anxieties of the present, suburbia is a material and symbolic landscape of constitutive of the contemporary good life. Even as suburbanites continue to express their fears and anxieties within and about suburbia, for many residents the suburbs remain the best hope for finding comfort in a difficult world. It is in this sense that we can turn to the suburban built environment to begin analysis of the forms of the good life at the turn of the twenty-first century. In fact, just as philosophers debate about the relation between pleasure, goods, and projects and the good life, suburban theorists, planners, builders, designers, and residents also perform these debates. Suburbia's worth, for example, can be judged in terms of its ability to foster something that feels like community, to encourage the moral growth of its residents, or to tie residents to region and nation.[11] Within these debates, suburbia's worth depends on its ability to "order" life, to create an overall good life, to foster not just present pleasure, but long-term and life-wide goodness.[12] Others judge suburbia on much more immediate questions of pleasure and pleasurable goods. These debates hinge on judgments of suburbia's ability to offer the commodity goods and worthwhile projects that maximize individual, familial, and community pleasure.[13] Regardless, as home to a majority of US Americans and as the site of recent explosive growth, it is within suburban landscapes that we must look for the building of the contemporary good life.

While it is not my intention to trace a fully developed theory of the good life, what I do want to suggest is that the problem of the good life is one that has both rhetorical and spatial dimensions. Crucial to this understanding is a basic assumption that the good life is not a completed result, a resting place, or a final consequence of beliefs or action. Instead, a good life is a practice, a performance, or a striving. A good life is not something one has or attains; it is something one tries to do. Following Plato, David Russell argues that "the key to happiness is found not in the goods or even the projects that form the 'ingredients' of a person's life, but in the agency of the person herself that gives her whole life direction and focus, and which therefore determines her happiness."[14] The good life is one, then, that is directed toward a particular goal—happiness—and happiness comes from the interweaving of the pleasurable goods and projects. The good life is a performance that combines theory that imagines some sort of ultimate good and practice that enacts some imperfect version of the good constrained by the contingencies of everyday life.[15] The actualized practice of the hoped-for good life is rhetorical action; that is, action that constitutes and materializes the good life within the difficulties of day-to-day practice.[16] Crucially, images, imaginations, and hopes for the good life motivate us in our daily practices and performances. While we may not be explicitly referencing well-conceptualized contours of the good life when we make everyday decisions, these decisions and actions are often structured by implicit theories of goodness and, at the same time, reveal and enact whatever principles of the good life we in fact believe.

What is more, this enactment of everyday lives—lives that are more or less structured by principles of what it means to live a good life—must have a space of their appearance. As a number of twentieth-century theorists have argued, analysis of the everyday or of everyday practices inevitably involves analysis of the spaces of those practices.[17] Indeed, as both Henri Lefebvre and Michel de Certeau argue, everyday practices and space (or place) are co-constitutive. For Lefebvre, space is always a social product, constructed and brought into being by the (often banal) movements and gestures of people.[18] For Certeau, individuals carve agency out of the structures of place. This carving out he variously calls tactics, enunciations, or walking rhetoric.[19] But we can reach further back in Western thinking to recognize the connection between the striving for the good life and the construction of space. Isocrates, for example, places the polis as the central achievement of humans, an achievement made possible by rhetoric.

In short, the good life is never simply an individual performance or an individually ordered life but is also always lived in relation to others. The organization of the good life in relation to others results in cities and in citizenship. Building the polis, or "making the city," is a practice, a result, and a staging ground for the performance of the good life.[20] Making cities and suburbs is always a moral act and is guided by images and imaginations of the good life. The good life, then, needs its space of appearance and enactment. For the ancients, the city served as this stage, while for many of us today, suburbs are the scenes of our enactments of the good life. These enactments are not only emplaced, they are very distinctly rhetorical. Most obviously, cities are built of brick and stone but also of and by rhetoric. Rhetoric is necessary to compel and create the cooperative action necessary to building the city and is characteristic of city dwelling. This building of the city, though, is much more than simply organizing the material resources to put roofs over citizens' heads; it is the creation of citizenship itself.

The polis, politics, rhetoric, and the good life circulate around the ancient concept of *ethos*. While in fifth century BCE ethos means character, according to Charles Chamberlain its earlier meaning is "the places where animals are usually found."[21] Meaning something like animal haunts or habitat, ethos indicated the place where an animal belongs, its natural habitat, and, in the case of domesticated animals like horses, was imagined as the place to which these animals long to return. This early meaning of ethos includes more, however, than a sense of place but also of habit, for the horse desires not simply to return to its ancestral pasture but to its natural way of being and acting. In this ancient meaning of the word, place (the place an animal belongs) and performance (the habits that best describe the animal in its natural setting) are commingled.[22]

Over the course of several hundred years, ethos shifts from this idea of a natural haunt toward character, but, as Chamberlain argues, the new form of character retains some of its older meaning. The word begins to expand in meaning, including not only the haunts and habits of animals but also to embrace the natural setting and ingrained behaviors of humans, and then, under the influence of Plato, Isocrates, and Demosthenes, ethos moves into the human soul. Chamberlain suggests that this shift from pasture to soul retains the sense of ethos as the "center of belonging."[23] Finally, it is this idea of ethos as a center of belonging that influences the political meaning of the word: cities, states, constitutions, and the groups of people named by and contained within these institutions can be said to have ethos or character. From the natural spaces and habits of animal belonging to the richly textured meaning of the ethos in the writings of Plato, Aristotle, and other Greeks, ethos brings together space and habit, individual and collective, and finally rational and irrational—as some habits are not easily tamable and are intractable in the face of reason.[24]

It is possible to imagine rhetoric as the mode that brings together space and habit, sutures individual and collective, and negotiates between the rational and irrational. The ethos of rhetoric can "transform space and time into 'dwelling places' [that] define the grounds, abodes or habitats, where a person's ethics and moral character take form and develop."[25] Ethos, then, is a distinctly spatialized concept. It does not simply imply that rhetoric happens in or at some place; ethos is also constitutive of the place creating places that are good or potentially good. This goodness of place involves its aesthetics, its materiality as place-in-time, and also its ability to foster communing or dwelling together. This version of ethos moves us away from simply a mode of proof (or a way of arguing toward some other goal), but is, itself, a goal of rhetoric. The ethos of rhetoric offers evidence or argument for a position but at the same time creates the conditions under which consideration of how to live is possible.

Creating the conditions for individuals to discuss and enact the good life, ethos looks very much like the rhetoric necessary for creating the polis. Just as political rhetoric creates the polis-city and, thus, citizens, ethical rhetoric invites or calls into being dwelling places and inhabiting individuals who strive for ethical action. As Michael Hyde writes, "The call of the human being, of conscience, calls on us to be rhetorical architects whose symbolic constructions both create and invite others into a place where they can dwell and feel at home while thinking about and discussing the truth of some matter that the rhetor/architect has already attempted to disclose and show forth in a specific way with his or her work of art."[26] Here we see again the hope for home, or better, a feeling of being at home. And this home-ness provides the rhetorical structures for discussing and creating visions of the good life. In response to the agoraphobia and unhomeliness of the present, suburbs offer images of safe and secure homes as the landscape for imagining new forms for the good life.

But as rhetorical architects, suburbanites—builders, designers, and most particularly residents—do not simply create symbolic constructions but material ones as well. Houses, parks, shopping malls, restaurants, and churches are, without a doubt, symbolic. They are also material. These spaces bound and constrain, enable and restrict with walls, sidewalks, medians, curbs, doors, windows, and gates.[27] The built environment—and suburbs in particular—offer compelling ethical rhetoric because they create both symbolic and material dwelling places—homes—for individuals and communities to stake claims to the good life. While the history of Western philosophy and city building indicates that the good life and the built environment have long been inextricably linked, the particular contours of these links are constantly and consistently shifting. Contemporary suburbs rhetorically construct their claims to the good life within very particular historical, material, cultural, and social conditions. Crucially, post–World War II suburban builders and residents create the good life within the context of the deep and profound changes that mark modernity and late modernity.

Urbanization, Modern Spatial Anxieties, and the Longing for Home

The good life characterized by a rhetoric of ethos suggests the importance of places and practices in creating, performing, and arguing for visions of the good life. For many in the West, home—like the soul—serves as a place and practice that most clearly materializes visions of goodness and comfort. Even as the good life takes home as a central setting, modernity's rapid temporal and spatial shifts place the home—and other sites of security— under strain. Indeed, modernity's cultural, economic, and social changes create psychic disruptions that circulate around the home. Perhaps the most far-reaching of these disruptions is encoded in the complexity of nostalgia.

First identified in the seventeenth century, patients presenting with nostalgia were said to "lose touch with the present" through a longing for the past and for home.[28] Svetlana Boym locates the discovery of nostalgia in the same moment when ideas of history and time were undergoing "radical" changes.[29] For example, eschatological time was lost; the idea that the "end of time was near" began to fade and, in its place, infinity of time began to open up.[30] Even as theologians rationalized time, philosophers, mapmakers, and architects increasingly rationalized space. For example, Renaissance explorers produced new, rationalized, and more abstract maps to make sense of the geographies they had experienced. These shifts in time and space in the Renaissance and early modernity begin to create the distinction between the local and universal. Nostalgia inserts itself into this increasingly abstract world: "What is crucial is that nostalgia was not merely an expression of local longing, but a result of a new understanding of time and space that made the division into 'local' and 'universal' possible."[31] European voyages and explorations of the globe along with migrations within and beyond Europe of early modernity all fostered the distinction between the local and the universal.

Nostalgia became even more prevalent in the eighteenth century. Soldiers in Napoleon's empire-building expeditions were particularly susceptible during their long marches hundreds of miles from home. The increased movement across space, along with time and space rationalizing technologies such as clocks, and, in the nineteenth century, railroads and railroad schedules, time zones, time-clock work in factories, all undermined the ability to "assimilate the past into the present" even as the future seemed ever more expansive.[32] Nineteenth-century modernity, especially as expressed in the rise of the great European and US cities—London, Paris, Vienna, Chicago, New York—contributed to the increasing sense of spatialized and temporalized abstractions. These cities, seemingly built of whole cloth and magnets for migrations from the agricultural hinterlands to these new technologized and abstracted spaces, emphasized spatial anxieties. These debilitating longings were not only for a specific home—the original form of nostalgia—but "for being at home in the world," a sense that became "hopelessly fragmented," according to Georg Lukács, "in the modern age."[33] The first of the modern spatial anxieties, nostalgia morphs into a generalized longing for and anxiety about the possibility of being at home. In this sense, nostalgia is entangled with a second important spatial anxiety: that of the uncanny.

The first identification of the uncanny was by German writers who named the discomforts of uncanniness with the word *unheimlich*, which literally meant the unhomely. The uncanny, as Anthony Vidler argues, expressed anxieties about new, real conditions in the nineteenth-century city.[34] In this city, individuals are torn from their roots in time and place. Writing in the early nineteenth century, Benjamin Constant asserts that "individuals, lost in isolation from nature, strangers to the place of their birth, without contact with the past, living only in a rapid present, and thrown down like atoms on an immense and leveled plain, are detached from a fatherland they see nowhere."[35] Neatly encapsulated here is a strong sense of loss and longing. The loss spans both time ("without contact with the past") and place ("isolation from nature, strangers to the place of their birth"). Increasingly, time and place, history and geography become abstracted and fluid. This new fluidity prompts cultural, social, and spatial estrangement, an estrangement that is deeply disturbing, since home is central to a comforting and unified sense of self and exhilarating since the new urban spaces, new cultural possibilities, and rapidly changing economic relations offer immense opportunities.[36]

Karl Marx and Friedrich Engels, writing in 1848, capture this doubled sense of estrangement and excitement: "All that is solid melts into air," they write, "all that is sacred is profaned."[37] New economic relations destroy the feudal and patriarchal relations that had settled workers into the land and familiar social relations. Searching constantly for new outlets, the bourgeoisie remake the world even as they have "stripped the sanctity from the professions" and "reduced [family relations] to purely monetary ones."[38] Estranged from their labor, their families, and their homes, nineteenth-century westerners confronted a world where familiar ways lay in waste and new modes of being become "outmoded before they can ossify."[39] Written in a nostalgic tone and drawing on the force of the uncanny, the *Communist Manifesto* captures, in nearly poetic terms, the profound concerns and the revolutionary possibilities of modernity.

This loss of tradition in the nineteenth century expressed itself as a hunger for and a deep concern with memory. Richard Terdiman, writing about nineteenth-century struggles over memory in Europe, points to the work of sociologist Ferdinand Tönnies, who conceptualized a distinction between gemeinschaft and gesellschaft as an explanatory model for the changes of modernity. Those embedded in gemeinschaft lived in communities based on traditional village ways. In the modern city, on the other hand, people lived outside of the tradition and community, what Tönnies called gesellschaft. For Terdiman, this binary system was a response to the perceived deficiencies of the present through an invocation of an idealized past. More than descriptions, these oppositions are "modalized by affects of loss or lamentation."[40] The desires for memory and the lamentations of its loss are encoded as a shift from rural to urban living. The city and its cultural, technological, and demographic changes became the spatial manifestation of the loss of structuring memory. Crucially, this lamentation is not for just any past but for a past when memory functioned meaningfully, when the institutions of tradition were stable and useful. At base, the desire and recollection of gemeinschaft is a desire for memory itself, for gemeinschaft's comforts are those provided by institutions of memory. Thus the duality of gemeinschaft and gesellschaft is a complex systemization of a "nostalgia for memory," encoded into the seeming neutrality of social science.[41] The sense of loss entailed in the discussion of gemeinschaft and gesellschaft is one way that "all that is solid melts into air," as the social relations that bound people to each other and, often, to the land, melted into the abstractions of modernity. Crucially, gemeinschaft and gesellschaft signified shifting social relations that caused and were caused by changing spatial conditions.

This loss of tradition connected to radical spatial shifts gave rise in the nineteenth century to the specifically spatialized anxieties of agoraphobia and claustrophobia. Agoraphobia comprised a particular concern to nineteenth-century theorists. Literally the irrational fear of the marketplace, agoraphobia named a host of intersecting anxieties urbanites felt at the ever expanding space of the modern city. Linked to Pascal's horror of the vacuum, agoraphobics were overwhelmed by fear and anxiety when confronted by the long, wide streets or the massive plazas characteristic of the modern city. Architect and critic Camillo Sitte, in his analysis of Vienna's empty spaces of the Ringstrasse, argued that agoraphobia is a distinctly urban and modern anxiety.[42] "Agoraphobia is a very new and modern ailment," Sitte writes in the late nineteenth century. "One naturally feels very cozy in small, old plazas and only in our memory do they loom gigantic, because in our imagination the magnitude of the artistic effect takes the place of actual size. On our modern gigantic plazas, with their yawning emptiness and oppressive ennui, the inhabitants of snug old towns suffer attacks of this fashionable agoraphobia."[43] Sitte locates this new ailment, literally a dis-ease—in vast city spaces. Fashionable new city plazas—emptied of familiar forms and built on a scale once unimaginable—call forth fashionable new ailments like agoraphobia. More, connected to the rising medicalization of psychology (it is not a mistake that Freud is practicing in Sitte's Vienna), agoraphobia is also available to fashionable ways of thinking about the human mind and body. "Snug old towns" offered vestiges of families, familiar sights, and were spaces that resisted modernity's anxieties and lay outside the grasp of nineteenth-century medical discourse.

The entire city, then, became the locus of modernity's discontents; it became responsible for the anxieties of individuals and communities. Indeed, the city was increasingly envisioned by architects, planners, and psychologists not only as ill but also as the epicenter of estrangement and nervousness. "The Great City," Anthony Vidler writes, "was seen to shelter a nervous and feverish population, overexcited and enervated, whose mental life was relentlessly antisocial, driven by money."[44] This relentless drive for money characterized both the modern city and agoraphobia. In many nineteenth-century accounts the commerce and capitalism of the modern city are imagined as the cause of the agoraphobic's anxieties and fears. "In this context agoraphobia, the anxiety and immobility occasioned by the space and scope of streets, by the appurtenances and avenues of traffic, is an anticommercial condition—literally, fear of the marketplace."[45] The city becomes the locus of spatialized anxieties not only because it is a new and unfamiliar kind of space but also because it is constructed within the context of the new and unfamiliar set of economic conditions of modern capitalism.

The discourses of agoraphobia thus articulate a set of intertwining concerns. Agoraphobia and other spatialized anxieties including nostalgia and the uncanny serve as modes for thinking the new social and spatial relations of the capitalist, nineteenth-century city. As Vidler argues, "the extension of the individual psychological disorders to the social conditions of an entire metropolis was on one level no more than metaphorical hyperbole. On another level, however, the 'discovery' of these new phobias seems to have been a part of a wider process of remapping the space of the city according to its changing social and political characteristics."[46] The city—as a spatial and social organization—became locus and object of the anxieties produced by the rapid changes of modernity.

While it is easy to see the shifts of the nineteenth century and these articulations in discourse exclusively through the lenses of anxiety and fear, we need to also recognize that the very same spatialized changes that foster modernity's special anxieties also offer possibilities and pleasures. Large cities in Europe and the United States attracted millions of residents in part because of the economic benefits of the city. As hard as life was on the factory floor and in the tenement dwellings, the city offered far more possibility for economic and social advancement than did the poverty of the rural landscape.[47] In fact, for centuries, the density of cities has produced enormous economic gains for individuals and societies. The very technological, economic, and social changes that raised anxiety to a flashpoint were also the factors that made cities grow. Ports—and the diversity they encouraged—fostered the growth of New York, Philadelphia, and Boston. This growth created density and powerful economic incentives produced by individuals rubbing shoulders, sharing ideas, and building new businesses.[48]

More than money drew people from the hinterlands to the cities, however. The city afforded newfound freedoms and pleasures. For women in particular and the working classes more generally, the nineteenth- and early twentieth-century city was a place of hardship but also of remarkable social and cultural freedom and possibility.[49] As Patricia Pringle argues, "modernity finds spatial manipulation pleasurably fascinating."[50] An immense range of new movement, perceptual, and entertainment technologies offered embodied and spatialized pleasures never before available. Steampowered amusement rides, bicycles and roller skates, the expansion of sports to women and the middle classes, the invention and improvement of eyeglasses and binoculars, and the development of photography and cinema all radically remade the body's relation to space, and often did so in ways that were at once frightening and enthralling.[51]

Whether imagined as pleasurable or frightful, nineteenth-century urbanism, capitalism, and technology radically remade space and time, shifting ways of seeing and ways of feeling. Certainly the city as a landscape of opportunity, a place where people and ideas, goods and commerce intersected, made many wealthier and offered enormous cultural and social opportunities. At the same time, the profound spatial shifts of modernity raised deep anxieties that drew on and recreated long-held concerns about cities and often articulated preferences for the rural and pastoral landscapes. Modernity's spatial anxieties affectively express these contradictions between the expanding opportunities and horizons and the recognition of radically changing social, economic, and spatial landscapes. These shifts of modernity remake ways of imaging and building "the good life," a remaking that was not finished in the nineteenth century but continues to this day.

Modernity to the Present

If we are considering shifting relations among individuals, time, and space, it is better to imagine postmodernity as an intensification of rather than a radical break from the experiences of modernity, indeed, where many call the present postmodernity others refer to the present as late modernity or super modernity.[52] Regardless of the name, the last forty years can be characterized by dramatically shifting constructions and experiences of space. Building on the changes of modernity, our current moment is marked by massive migrations; new transportation and communication technologies; shifting national, international, and transnational economic and political relations; all of which shrink and expand space. On the one hand, the differences among spaces are diminished. Cities around the globe become more and more homogenous.[53] Increasingly, Boulder looks like Berkeley, and Las Vegas can be found in Shanghai.[54] What is more, geographic location is weakening as a factor in determining our interpersonal, communal, political, and economic relations.[55] In the contemporary moment, Anthony Giddens argues, "place becomes increasingly phantasmagoric, that is to say, locales are thoroughly redefined by and shaped in terms of social influences quite distant from them. . . . The 'visible form' of the locale conceals the distanciated relation which determines its nature."[56]

At the same time, however, our everyday spaces are increasingly atomized. We desire to become "located" in smaller and more tightly defined geographies, a desire often expressed in the deeply etched distinctions of class and race within late modern US American landscapes.[57] As space simultaneously expands and shrinks, it can no longer serve—if it ever really did—as a stabilizing experience or location for individual or collective identity.[58] In late modernity, and in particular in the late modern suburb, it is all too easy to "lose our place in time," making difficult and ever more complex the weaving of personal and social identity into time and space.[59]

Despite the place- and time-destroying logics of late modernity, localness has not disappeared.[60] Instead, as I will argue throughout the rest of this book, the local continually returns to the scene and does so in at least two ways. First, the local is a central part of mass suburban developments, since, even in the abstractions of mass-built housing, the local landscape has some consequentiality in the building of the homes and the design of buildings. Second, and more importantly, as I will demonstrate in the following chapters, the local continually (re)appears through constant and continual efforts to create a sense of the local, offering to residents the possibility that these new suburbs are, in fact, rooted in history and geography, in time and place. In Centerra Promenade, for example, the building materials and landscaping consistently work to situate the northern Colorado lifestyle center in the image of local towns and is oriented toward the mountains. Meanwhile, chain restaurants like Olive Garden and Macaroni Grill connect their suburban locales to rural Italy, and the developments surrounding them almost obsessively refer to the earth and to a pastorally imagined nostalgia. I term these material-semiotic efforts to create a sense of the local a *rhetoric of locality*. Locality, as Jessie Stewart and I have argued elsewhere, is "a visual and material rhetoric that offers users a sense of location, or a sense of where [we] are in the world."[61] As a direct response to the abstractions of postmodernity, and more specifically as a response to the desire for locating oneself in space and time, suburbs offer a range of rhetorics of locality.[62] Residential developments, chain restaurants, megachurches, and lifestyle centers each in their own way work to root suburbanites in time and place, to offer a sense of community and of home in a world where both institutions seem fragile.

Indeed, by the 1990s, as Marita Sturken argues, contemporary US culture is marked by intensified fear and paranoia. Reactionary, right-wing political groups most clearly articulate this paranoia, but contemporary paranoia and fear also find full expression in mainstream political and cultural discourse. The paranoia of the 1990s intersected, in the post-9/11 world, with a fear of terrorism to make fear a dominant motivating emotion. Surrounding issues of home and domesticity, political and popular discourse increasingly responded to this culture of fear with a desire for comfort. Across consumer culture, comfort is for sale and, according to Sturken, is a fundamental way US Americans have responded to particular tragedies like the Oklahoma City bombings and multiple attacks of 9/11. Buying teddy bears, furnishing homes with muted colors, and wearing NYPD T-shirts all serve as affective (if not directly effective) responses to these fears. Moreover, the last two decades were marked by building practices that Nan Ellin has called the architecture of fear. Using architectural appeals to nostalgia, retribalization, escapism, and spiritual (re)turn, contemporary architectural practices—especially those that seem more domestic like the building of suburbs—work to respond directly and affectively to strongly felt fears and anxieties.[63] This culture of fear and comfort and its architectural and consumer responses is at once political and depoliticizing. It is political in that it is useful for politicians making arguments for election and in favor of or against particular policies or justifying wars. At the same time, domesticating comfort offers its warmly affective response to fear as a sufficient personal and collective response to the challenges we face in the present. As Sturken argues, the teddy bear—the archetypal item of comfort in the post–Oklahoma City bombing era—"doesn't promise to make things better; it promises to make us feel better about the way things are."[64] In the following analysis I will consistently return to these entanglements of fear and comfort.

Crucially, the suburbs will work to locate individuals into comforting relations of time and place and will often do so through appeals to memory. As a direct response to the ease with which we "lose our place in time," many late modern spaces directly call on older, nostalgic forms as attempts to locate individuals within a cherished past and familiar place.[65] Suburbanites can use the offered memory images as a way of imaging and imagining the good life within suburbia. In fact, as I will argue in the following chapters, memorialized images of community, connection, safety, and stability are all prevalent resources for imagining and striving for the good life within contemporary suburbia. Even as the information age undermines the security of deeply held memorized relations among people and places, memory images offer the possibility and hope for reconnection. These memory images guide and structure the arguments, buildings, and performances of the suburban good life.

Becoming a Suburban Nation

Perhaps the underlying memory image within contemporary suburbs is that of home. The centrality of the image of home is by now unsurprising. If some of the fundamental characteristics of modernity and postmodernity are the constellation of anxieties expressed in agoraphobia (fear of public spaces/desire for home), the uncanny (a sense of homelessness), and nostalgia (a return to and hope for rootedness in time and place), then images of home can offer powerful responses to present anxieties. It is precisely within these anxieties that the Reunion sign with which I began the introduction makes sense: it neatly encapsulates the complex weaving of past, present, and future along with powerful assertions about how this weaving places home (and town) at the center of the building of a good life. Not only, however, does this sign respond to present concerns about home and town, past and future, but it also draws on a long history of suburban building.

One way of understanding the growth of suburbs in the United States over the last 150 years is to place suburban growth precisely into the context of modern urban anxieties. That suburbs are only a response to the urban anxieties, however, oversimplifies the factors that determined their growth. What I will argue throughout this book is that the particular form of suburbanization—and the good life represented, materialized, and enacted in these forms—are a direct response to these anxieties. Nonetheless, it is worth tracing interlocking factors that moved the United States from an urban to a suburban nation. Over the last 150 years a whole range of economic, political, technological, and cultural shifts have made suburbs appear as an obvious way of making a good life. A brief history of US suburbanization will reveal the complexity of the creation and maintenance of suburban living.

Economically, the growth of suburbia depended on a series of shifts, perhaps the most important of which was industrialization, and with industrialization the growth of the middle class. Industrialization served to radically shift cities. The rise of factories as major employers drew large populations to cities. Indeed, the nineteenth century is spatially marked as the moment when the majority of people in many industrialized nations lived in cities rather than in the country. Factory owners paid poorly and demanded long hours. Factory workers lived in abysmal conditions. By the middle of the nineteenth century, major industrial cities in the United States were experiencing a spatial crisis as the population of poor, often non–Anglo-American workers exploded. For the city's middle class, this spatial crisis created a push to leave the city behind. The tenements that housed the working poor were figured as incubators of moral and physical disease.[66] Proponents of suburbia claimed that the suburbs offered distance between the tenements while providing the middle class with an investment (home ownership) to protect them against economic insecurity.

This mid-nineteenth-century industrialization offered opportunities for rural poor as they moved to the city for new and better-paying jobs. These same economic shifts funded an increasingly well-to-do middle class. The growing middle class had the economic means to build and buy new homes on the outskirts of cities, pushed there by their fear of the new urban scene. This growing market for suburban homes—along with the pressing need to reduce the cost of shipping factory-made goods from factory to market—fostered transportation systems that allowed greater distances between home, work, and shopping. Trolley systems—originally powered by horses and mules and then by electricity—ferried workers and shoppers from the city center to the new suburbs. The rapid change in transportation technologies—from electric trolley to buses to cars—democratized the suburbs, making suburban living available to more and more people.[67]

These economic and technological shifts intersected with Anglo-American beliefs about individualism, property ownership, and capitalism. In the United States, these ideas coalesced, according to John Archer, into an ideal of the "self-made man." An owner of property, deeply committed to rural values, and able to care for himself through independent action, the nineteenth-century ideal of the self-made man articulated with new suburban developments. Suburban developments, Archer argues, "could incorporate and sustain certain beliefs about household domesticity (gender roles and household upkeep), morality (rural values), and identity (as formed in part through spatial practice)."[68] Set in a pastoral scene, each suburban home had its own plot of land, space for a garden, and a house designed to offer men respite from the difficulties of everyday urban life and women spaces to fully develop their domestic skills.

Finally, in the late nineteenth century, local, regional, state, and federal governments began to interest themselves in home ownership, suburban development, and spatial reform. For example, it was only in the late nineteenth century that local, regional, and state governments started to build and maintain roads at taxpayers' expense. Indeed, the first urban/suburban transportation systems were private, for-profit enterprises. Developers made significant profits by buying land, building houses, and building the transportation systems from city to the house. Each part of this transportation and development system offered potential income to developers since the suburban residents paid fares to ride the trolley to and from the city. As government leaders became more interested in suburban development as an engine for economic growth and to create morally upright landscapes, they began to fund and maintain roads.[69]

Government support of the suburban development underlies the success of this spatial transformation. In the 1920s, government insured and sponsored banking systems focusing on home loans, new insurance regulations, and tax credits to builders worked together to support a suburban growth spurt.[70] But probably no single government subsidy was as important as the federal government's remarkable expenditures on the interstate system in the 1950s. These new freeways, which were both the result of and a sign of government subsidies for suburban development or suburban sprawl, combined with the postwar economic growth that funded house building, home buying, and car purchases, to transform the United States into a suburban rather than urban nation.[71]

Finally, even as a set of economic and technological transformations pulled residents from the cities to the suburbs, discourses of and about the city pushed individuals—especially whites—out of the city and into seemingly safer and certainly more homogeneous suburbs. For many social theorists and political commentators from the late nineteenth century to the present, the city breeds all manner of undesirable social relations. Out of these socially produced relations, Steve Macek argues, conservative writers were able to create a "moral panic." The city became articulated as a nearly incurable site of crime, drug use, and sexual perversions. This antiurban discourse draws on Victorian urban writing to argue that the city dweller is a savage, a human in name only. Of course, this discourse was politically motivated. It responded to African American migrations from the rural south to urban north and justified disinvestment in the cities. At the same time, these disinvestments helped produce the deepening poverty of the city, a rising culture of social protest intersected the urban riots of the late 1960s to early 1970s, riots perhaps best symbolized by the Watts riots in Los Angeles in 1965. Responding to police brutality, the relentlessness of the poverty of South Central Los Angeles, and the profound segregation of the city, residents in Watts rioted for five days. By the end of the riots over thirty people were dead, hundreds injured, and millions of dollars of property destroyed. The Watts riots, and the dozens of other urban riots across the nation, fed into the rising moral panic about the city.[72] By making the city a site—even a cause—of social, cultural, and political degeneration, neoconservatives could argue against the kinds of investments in infrastructure and social and cultural programs that could maintain the health of cities.[73]

While Macek focuses on the ways this discourse worked to destroy the city, it is essential to understand that it is at the very time of the rising moral panic about the city that suburban growth exploded. Even as cities are imagined as sites of anxieties in the nineteenth century and of social and moral ills in the twentieth century, the suburb is offered as a panacea to the sick city, a curative to restore balance and (homogenized) harmony. At the same time as popular culture imagines the city as crime-ridden, nonwhite space, these same culture industries picture a suburban life that is white, stable, secure, and safe. Amy Kenyon, in her exploration of popular culture representations of suburbia in the immediate post–World War

II shift to suburbs, argues that televisual and cinematic portrayals of the suburb configure suburbs in relation to the city: every suburban vision included anxiety about the city. For example, film noir and a series of films about juvenile delinquency figure the city as a site of sin and (suppressed, but present) evils of race and class. Meanwhile, other films imagined escaping to the suburbs as a mode of salvation from the crime and degeneracy of the city, while small town films helped fuel the desire to leave the city.[74] In short, white, middle-class Americans are pushed from the city by shifting race relations and the moral panic perpetrated by popular culture.

At the same time, the suburbs were material realizations of new dreams. Dominant discourses dreamed ourselves to be American, and, in the postwar years, dreamed ourselves to be suburban. These postwar suburban dreams included deep commitments to and desire for the development of rich and meaningful communities, the building of aesthetically pleasing homes and neighborhoods, and a sense of safety in a world that seemed increasingly risky. The construction of the suburban built environment, for example, quite clearly expresses these twined dreams as culs-de-sac; gates, walls, and yards at once signify the center of community and at the same time work assiduously to eliminate and marginalize nonresidents. Hidden behind the walls and excluded by the gates are the social exclusions upon which postwar suburbs were built. As Becky Nicolaides argues, the idea of suburban community produced racial and economic inequality. "In producing racial and economic inequality and doing so in a context of community vitality, suburbia has transformed the community ideal from a positive source of human fulfillment and acceptance into a destructive tool of exclusivity and inequality."[75] Suburban dreams, then, are complicated, offering at once respite, community, and connection and often building these hopes on exclusions and inequalities.[76]

By the twenty-first century suburbs have become the decentered center of US life. Suburbs are not only sites of dramatic population growth, they are central to much of the US economic growth as well. No longer are suburbs only residential enclaves, they also house the high-technology, service, and information industries typical of the US post-Fordist economy.[77] Always imagined as a hybrid space between city and country, past and present, suburbia now houses the industries, cultural conditions, and social structures characteristic of our contemporary era. Not only does suburbia provide the space for these late modern ways of being, it depends on them as well. The technologies and epistemologies of the information age found, fund, and foster suburban growth.

Suburbia confronts us with and comprises the space where we confront the possibilities and difficulties of the contemporary condition. Just as the rapid growth of the modern city in the nineteenth century engendered a set of urban anxieties, the postmodern suburb raises a host of concerns—concerns that rather than being wholly new are best understood as intensifications of the difficulties and opportunities offered by the modern city. Whereas the modern city began to tear the bonds of time and place in the nineteenth and early twentieth century, the suburbs, with their cookie-cutter homes, instant landscaping, and bland, ahistorical public spaces like the mall only increased this sense of placeless and spaceless existence.[78] And so the suburb became the site of US Americans' hopes for a new and better community and it also became the site of the anomie and fragmentation characteristic of postmodernity.

Not surprisingly, this postmodern suburban moment is marked by its own set of anxieties. Agoraphobia, for example, which originated in the anxieties fostered by the massive squares of the nineteenth century, finds different locales in the twenty-first century. Where the giant plaza was the site of agoraphobia in the nineteenth-century city, "Today, the 'stage' for this inscrutable display is the blank expanses or urban freeways that circle through the center of our cities and the big-box architecture of the suburban shopping mall so saturated with commodities that its emptiness is only experienced viscerally."[79] Agoraphobia—along with a majority of US Americans—has moved from the city to the suburbs traversing modernity's highways.

But the unhomely has moved as well. The dangers and disruptions of the city that pushed people into the suburbs return with a vengeance in the suburban landscape. As Setha Low argues, contemporary suburban dwellers are nearly obsessed with danger and safety, others and community. The suburbanites she interviewed desire connections with neighbors and community. And yet enacting this desire is curbed by deeply seated fears of others, crime, and poverty. Many US American suburbanites struggle with the "dilemma of how to protect themselves and their children from danger, crime, and unknown others while still perpetuating open, friendly neighborhoods and comfortable, safe homes."[80] Low here captures the heart of the difficulties and triumphs of suburbia—the fear of others and crime matched by the hopes for community and home. In this sense, suburbia at once offers a response to and houses yet another of modernity's anxieties—that of the sense of the unheimlich or the unhomeliness. And here, finally, is the crux of the matter: even as the agoraphobic feels anxiety in the public spaces of the present and turns toward home for comfort, contemporary uncanniness marks the house itself as a site of anxiety. Suburbs, then, are freighted with deeply held hopes and profoundly felt—and contradictory—anxieties. It is in this contradictory condition where suburbs house compelling hopes and powerful anxieties that suburbs stake claims to the good life.

Twining Together Memory and Locality

And they stake these claims to the good life through grounding memories. Modern spatial anxieties raise questions about our rootedness in both time and place. Because the city was often imagined as the constitutive site of anxieties, post–World War II suburbs are offered as responses to the difficulties imagined and built into the city. But, built of whole cloth, suburbs could not only be other than cities, they also need to offer imaginative and material resources that could directly respond to anxieties about our unrootedness in place and time. Brand new suburbs designed outside of the strictures of either time or place are not well suited to the problems raised by modern spatial anxieties. Rhetorically constructed memories can bridge this gap between the desire for a new and cleansed nonurban space and the need to drill our personal and communal identity into place and time.
✝Memory has the obvious advantage of suturing us into a time, offering an image of the past relevant to the present. Building or rebuilding space within the contexts of memory is not new. For example, drawing on ancient mnemonics, and inspired by the architectural theorizations of Alberti, fifteenth-century Italian Renaissance architects and planners rebuilt Rome, created formal gardens, and imagined memory theaters, all for the purpose of connecting individuals to remembered and structuring social relations.[81] These landscapes of memory—imagined and materialized—depend on three important memory relations for their rhetorical force: memory/space, memory/style, and memory/identity.[82] All three are spatial invocations of memory. They employ style to induce memory. And the memories induced serve to create or center identity. In Rome, the memories served to stabilize the identity of the Christian church and, just as importantly, to center each visitor as a Christian.[83] The imagined memory theater located individuals in suddenly knowable cosmic and spiritual relations.[84] The Renaissance garden served to center the citizen within himself. The memories invoked allowed the visitor to maintain his identity as a citizen through continued civil behavior.[85] All of these designs were created—and often understood—by architects, planners, and patrons steeped in rhetorical training, a training that had maintained an allegiance to all five of the

rhetorical canons, including that of memory.[86] While not the first time that memory, place, style, and rhetoric are linked, these Renaissance memory places clarify theses relations in powerful ways.[87]

The vicissitudes of these relations of the five centuries following the redesign of Renaissance Rome could fill the rest of the book. What is important for my purpose is that modernity and late modernity ushers in a powerful (re)turn to memory in the built environment. Since at least the 1980s, cities, suburbs, and countries are building more and more places of memory. Following the success of Maya Lin's Vietnam Veteran's memorial, the United States is experiencing an explosion of proposed and completed memorials in Washington, DC, and across the country. At the same time, postmodern architecture and city planning turn to memory for inspiration in designing new spaces and redesigning the urban landscape. The outburst of memorials and urban spaces devoted to images of the past arrives at the very moment when lived memory seems more difficult to experience. Drawing on a wide range of mnemonics, suburbs work to link themselves to early moments of place-making strategies. Images of Europe, references to real or imagined agricultural pasts, design details referring to nineteenth-century cities and small towns work to connect brand new suburbs to remembered and comforting aesthetics.

But as these examples suggest, memories can also root us in place. Many of the mnemonics not only refer to previous moments in time but also to particular places. Olive Garden and Macaroni Grill aim to connect restaurant goers to a warmly remembered—even if never directly experienced—Italy. Many suburban homes suture residents into Craftsman style houses of the early twentieth-century Midwest and West or older Colonial styles of the East Coast. Lifestyle centers simultaneously refer to surrounding cities cleansed of their disturbing detritus and nostalgically rendered small town main streets. Suburbs are offering memories of past times and places as a way of locating suburbanites in history and geography. As such, memory is a fundamental mode by which locality is constructed. In fact, if locality is the rhetorical means by which we can situate ourselves in the world, memory is one of the specific ways this situating can occur. Situating us in both time and place, suburban memory places offer powerful responses to the anxieties and unrootedness of modernity. Suburban landscapes respond to the deep desire for place and past through a twining of locality and memory.

And it is precisely through this twining of locality and memory that suburbs offer rhetorical and material constructions of the good life—constructions designed to offer comfort and shelter in response to the spatial anxieties characteristic of modernity, the culture of fear developed over the late twentieth century, and the moral panic about the city. Fundamentally, the comforts suburbs offer are those made available through rhetorics of memory and locality that circulate around home, which is, itself, a place deeply embedded in both cultural and personal memory, a place imagined as most secure and yet also a place of private and social anxiety—in short, the home is a site of dreams of the good life and the nightmares that haunt us.

I will argue throughout this book that suburban landscapes create memory spaces and images of locality that strive to bulwark suburbanites against the haunting of the nightmares and work to embed us in dreams of the good life. In the face of the storms of the universe, Gaston Bachelard writes, "Come what may the house helps us to say: I will be an inhabitant of the word, in spite of the world."[88] The (suburban) house—a powerful location of memories—offers us the possibilities abiding in the world, of imaging a good life even in the maelstrom of the everyday, and of building roofs and walls, roads and bridges that will suture the resident into time and place.[89] In the next chapter, I take up representations of these homes, exploring the visual imaginary of suburbia offered in turn-of-the-century suburban films. As I will argue, each of the houses and the houses' residents face threats, usually the threat of banality and anomie. These films offer the possibility of risky and powerful emotional connections across difference while, in the end, returning the protagonists back into the comforting bosom of the suburban family. Directly confronting the criticisms of suburbs I outlined at the beginning of this chapter, the films consistently and constantly offer suburban homes, embedded in memory, as affectively powerful dwelling places for surviving life's storms.

Imaging the Good Life
Visual Images of the Suburban Good Life

> The city in our actual experience is at the same time an actually existing
> physical environment, and a city in a novel, a film, a photograph, a city
> seen on television, a city in a comic strip, a city in a pie chart, and so on.
> —Victor Burgin

Few films in the last twenty years as carefully capture the contradictory
visions of suburban life as does *Pleasantville* (1998).[1] The film opens with
images of a fictional, 1950s television show, *Pleasantville*. The televisual clips
introduce the audience to the perfect nuclear family, the perfect house, and
the perfect life all filmed in crisp black and white. The film's viewers are
then jolted into the present. Images of a contemporary suburb constructed
out of look-alike, beige, stuccoed homes marching up the barren hills of
California fill the screen. Students in the high schools are disengaged from
their education, a disengagement fostered by teachers who drone apocalyp-
tically about the future. The film's magical conceit is this: siblings from the
present dystopic suburb travel through their television set into the black-
and-white perfection of the fictional TV town of Pleasantville. In sharply
marking this contrast between the twined banalities and anxieties of the
contemporary suburb and the imagined simplicity of the 1950s at the beginning of the film, *Pleasantville* engages its audience in a crucial contemporary question: what constitutes the good life in contemporary suburban
living? In so doing, this film offers a crucial introduction to the suburban
topoi that will guide the critical analysis of contemporary suburbs.

In this chapter I argue that *Pleasantville* and a constellation of recent
suburban movies help produce a spatial imaginary of nostalgically tinged
suburbs that place individuals into the bosom of imperfect but loving and
white families while remaking home and away, self and other on founda-
tions of security and comfort. Functioning as a rhetoric of ethos, the films
create suburban dwelling places that map particular contours of suburbia.
Through this mapping of suburban dwelling places, the films also strive
to produce a suburban imaginary that is white, heterosexual, paradoxically
devoted to risk and safety, and bounded both spatially and discursively. In
the first section of the chapter I will introduce the idea of the spatial imaginary, arguing that the spatial imaginary is aesthetic, affectively charged,

socially structured, and draws on and produces the built environment. In the second section of the chapter, I turn to a thematic reading of selected suburban films to trace the contours of a spatial imagination of suburbia demonstrating that, at least within the specific instances of the suburban spatial analysis I attend to, suburbs are secured through nostalgically tinged memory, circumscribed by whiteness, devoted to heteronormative families, and expressive of a deep desire for home. In the final section of the chapter I will consider the ways spatial visions engage us in ethical deliberations and explore how these films embody and produce topoi for reading the suburban built environment within the context of the modern spatial anxieties I detailed in the previous chapter.

Spatial Imaginary

By the spatial imaginary, I mean the ways imaginative texts like novels, poetry, magazine articles, nonfiction books, and especially visual texts like photographs, films, and television programs—in short, the elements of what Victor Burgin calls *mediatic space-time*—engage, construct, and are constructed by spatiality.[2] The spatial imagination can be thought of as similar to mental maps about which Yi-Fu Tuan wrote in the mid-1970s. Mental maps, he writes, "Are imaginary worlds. They depict attractive goals that tempt people out of their habitual rounds."[3] For Tuan, mental maps are built of experiences of more or less real places as well as photographs, stories, letters, conversations, and purely fanciful combinations of memories and experiences. Further, these maps express affectively powerful goals that can compel human spatial action. By way of example, Tuan writes about the "quintessential human migration [that] occurs when people deliberately abandon one home in favor of a distant and unseen goal. In the nineteenth century many Europeans left their homes for remote parts of the world of which they had no direct experience. They did not go blindly: the move was a calculated risk. They had images of their new homes based on hearsay, letters from relatives, and immigration literature. Indeed these attractive images were a cause of their desire to move."[4] For Tuan, mental maps are a kind of spatial imaginary built of aesthetically compelling material and imaginary texts that are culturally structured and have affective and material consequences.

Tuan's discussion of mental maps introduces four significant dimensions of the spatial imagination: (1) The spatial imagination is built of and manifests in wide-ranging sites of spatial aesthetics; (2) these spatial aesthetics encode and constitute affective responses to space, as the images indicate not only what may exist but also how to respond to real and fictional spaces; (3) while the spatial imaginary is embodied in particular individuals, it is socially ordered out of culturally available and structured aesthetic and affective possibilities; and (4) rather than existing apart from or in contrast to actually occurring spaces, the spatial imagination is built out of and frames the perception of material spaces even as it motivates the construction of spaces.

First, the spatial imagination is aesthetic and in part built of mediated images even as the spatial imagination takes actual spaces as their content, context, and inspiration. On the one hand, imaginative texts like photographs, paintings, novels, films, and television shows have consistently taken the built environment as a primary or secondary subject. The photographs of Alfred Stieglitz or Jacob Riis, the films of film noir, or a novel like Theodore Dreiser's *Sister Carrie* all take the city as a subject or an actor in crucial spatial dramas as well as an object of analysis. At the same time, our experience of the city as an aesthetic environment is always constructed via these imaginative texts. Writing of representational space (one of the triad of conceptual space, representations of space, and representational space), Lefebvre asserts that representational spaces are "space[s] as directly lived through its associated images and symbols, and hence the space of 'inhabitants' and 'users.' . . . [Representational space] overlays physical space, making symbolic use of its objects."[5] Thus material space is available for the production of imaginary texts even as imaginary texts are resources through which we experience space itself.

Second, while this experience is certainly a rational, objective, and semiotic experience—we recognize particular built forms based on our past experiences with similar buildings and representations of space[6]— the spatial imaginary also produces affect. Engaging rhetoric's affectivity points us toward the ways rhetorical enactments encourage affiliation, attachment, and investment and urges us to understand how and why some enactments and performances stick and how and why others do not.[7] This stickiness of rhetorical enactments cannot be explained exclusively through a decoding of rhetoric's semiotics or symbolism but rather demands that we attend to the wide range of aesthetic modes by which rhetoric becomes fully and corporeally meaningful. Indeed, affect movingly connects bodies to texts. Brian L. Ott, writing about affect in film, argues that affect is corporeal and involves an embodied continuum that moves from our "experiencing body (i.e., immediate sensations of movement, color, and sound, for instance) to, on the other end, our body of experience (i.e., our body's memory of previous sensations)."[8] Thus the spatial imaginary engages affect and in so doing engages fully embodied rhetorical interactions.[9]

These relations among spatial aesthetics, affect, and the body can be particularly important in a moment of spatial anxiety.[10] Modernity's anxieties are spatial, embodied, and affectively powerful and, as I argue in this and the following chapters, have aesthetic manifestations. Our modern anxieties over place demand that we attempt to get back into place, an attempt that is always connected to both affect and the imagination. "As Freud, Bachelard, and Proust all suggest," Edward Casey writes, "to refind place—a place we have always already been losing—we may need to return, if not in actual fact then in the memory or imagination, to the very earliest places we have known, and even this return may not prevail against episodes of place-panic that holds us in their grip more than we may care to admit."[11] The nostalgia in *Pleasantville* and *The Truman Show* and deep sense of the uncanny in *Little Children* and *American Beauty* are powerful because they imagine material connections among affect, space, and bodies. These material connections are created through mnemonic images that trigger deeply seated memories of securely built homes.

Third, these affective and aesthetic experiences are not only individually structured but are also socially ordered.[12] Writing about affect's cultural importance, Lawrence Grossberg uses a tellingly spatial and embodied metaphor asserting that affect "anchors" individuals into the social order. Organized and structured, affect—and affectively compelling rhetorics—positions us in a particular place in a social order and, perhaps more importantly, urges powerful investments in and attachments to social organization.[13] Images and imaginations of home, for example, urge audiences to connect in compelling ways to a very specific spatial and social order that has been produced over time, is productive in the present, and helps produce imaginations of the future. Like other topoi, the spatial imaginary functions individually as an individual may fantasize about or imagine a particular world, and also functions socially as it encodes a social ordering of our aesthetic, affective, embodied relations to spatiality. Like Lefebvre's representations of space, the spatial imaginary is ordered and leads to "knowledge, to signs, to codes, and to 'frontal relations.'"[14]

Fourth, Lefebvre at once recognizes the difference between representations of space (or conceived space) and representational space (or lived space) even as he refuses to accept them as separate.[15] Indeed, like representations of space, spatial representations are deeply symbolic and absolutely imaginary. Representational spaces he defines as "embodying complex symbolisms, sometimes coded, sometimes not, linked to the clandestine or underground side of social life, as also to art (which may come eventually to be defined less as a code of space than as a code of representational spaces)."[16] Within representational lived space, space as built and space as conceived come together. In his example of the medieval village, Lefebvre writes that "representational spaces, for their part, determined the foci of vicinity: the village church, graveyard, hall and fields, or the square and belfry. Such spaces were interpretations, sometimes marvelously successful ones, of cosmological representations."[17] Space as lived, built, and imagined, intersects.

Similarly, the spatial imaginary is different but not separate from material place.[18] In the first place, the spatial imaginary directs our attention to aesthetic elements in actually occurring spaces. Previous experiences of spaces and of representations of spaces urge us to see space in particular ways and to attend to specific aesthetic elements and ignore others. Meanwhile, the spatial imaginary structures and triggers affective experience enabling the aesthetic and affective attachments we have to new spaces. As Victor Burgin argues, "The city in our actual experience is at the same time an actually existing physical environment, and [is] a city in a novel, a film, a photograph, a city seen on television, a city in a comic strip, a city in a pie chart, and so on."[19] Finally, the spatial imaginary intersects with the plans for and production of actual places, as we bring to our homes, neighborhoods, malls, lifestyle centers, and churches an already embodied and structured imaginary. At least since the early Renaissance, city planners and architects drew on sophisticated spatial imaginaries (which, not coincidentally, were framed by rhetorical theories and practices of memory) to create cities out of (imagined) aesthetics rooted in history for the purpose of triggering memories, producing affective relations to the city, and creating and recreating embodied relations to the space.[20]

The spatial imaginary, then, is aesthetic, affective, socially structured, and is interlaced with the built environment. As such, the spatial imaginary is also entwined with our hopes for the good life. Indeed, as Tuan suggests about mental maps, it is our spatial imaginary that allows us to judge the ethos of a place, comparing our experience in the present time and place to past experiences and to future dreams and plans. The ethos of rhetoric can, according to Michael Hyde, "transform space and time" into dwellings and homes that "define the grounds, abodes or habitats, where a person's ethics and moral character take form and develop."[21] The rhetorical art, seen from this perspective, is "architectural." It creates spaces in which rhetors and audiences can "feel more at home with others and [their] surroundings."[22] This architectural art is an everyday practice that relies on spatial stories (or topoi) that enunciate lines of connection and of boundaries.[23] These stories locate individuals with regard to (and often in resistance to) larger structures, providing ways of imagining an everyday life that is aesthetically, polemically, and ethically rich.[24] Suburban films are spatial stories—instances of a suburban imaginary and enactments of suburban topoi—that strive to create dwelling places in the world responsive in meaningful ways to the concerns of everyday life. These stories engage audiences in the most important of ethical questions: what might be the good life in suburbia? The spatial imaginary is a fundamental mode by which the good life is thought, structured, and produced. The films under investigation are constitutive elements of the suburban spatial imagination.

This suburban imaginary is constituted in part by the range of spatialized anxieties I outlined in chapter 1. It is into this context of late modern suburban anxiety that the films under investigation here have their effects and their affects. The films strive to create communal dwelling places, boundaries, and domains that are, in Hyde's language "stimulating and aesthetically, psychologically, socially, and perhaps theologically instructive."[25] Indeed, these films teach us much about the values desired of and encoded in everyday suburban life. The films mark the contours of the good life within suburbia, pointing to the (im)possibilities that border ideal suburban living as the films struggle with seeming contradictions within (white) suburbia.[26] In the films, suburbia is imagined as a bland landscape devoid of deeply felt emotions or passionately committed relationships. Yet suburbia, in part because of this blandness, is also imagined as a place of safety and as a dwelling place or home that offers security and acceptance. The struggle in these films becomes one of offering passionate commitments and emotionally engaging relationships while maintaining the safety of familiarity and the security of a risk-free environment.

Often, like suburban spaces themselves, the films negotiate these contradictions through appeals to memory. As we will see, *Pleasantville* and a wide range of other suburban films draw on deeply held and often nostalgic memories. By appealing to (and, at times, rejecting) these nostalgic memories, the films choose safety and security, offering images of white heterosexuality leavened with a just a bit of danger and risk offered by seemingly aberrant sexuality and the authenticity of other racial and ethnic identities. If successful, audiences incorporate the films into their memories and their spatial imaginations. The films become resources for managing and organizing in the world, for mapping suburbia, and thus useful as strategies of self-location. In this sense, the films may mark the contours and limits of the good life within suburbia, teaching viewers what suburbia looks like, what it feels like, and how it ought to be built and enacted. In short, investigating suburban films as crucial elements of a suburban spatial imagination can generate an understanding of the visual and rhetorical topoi brought to bear on suburban living and will begin to mark the possibilities and limits of the suburban good life.

Constructing the Suburban Spatial Imaginary

Since the spatial imaginary is created out of complex weavings of intertextual relations, we can turn to texts about suburbs to begin to guide us in our understanding of built space.[27] At the end of the twentieth century, Douglas Muzzio and Thomas Halper argue, suburbs became a "cinematic fixation."[28] This welter of suburban films indicates the ways suburbia became a crucial issue for many audiences. At the same time, the number of films about suburbs suggests the importance of tracing the intersections and diversions among the films. For the purposes of my argument, I am taking *Pleasantville* as prototypical of the films that take suburbia as their theme. Focused as it is on the differences between present suburbia and nostalgically held TV memories of 1950s suburbs, *Pleasantville* takes up visual and ethical concerns about contemporary suburbia as its central thematic. And yet *Pleasantville* does not fully develop a suburban, spatial analysis by itself. Instead, a constellation of other films develops and makes more complex the issues raised by *Pleasantville*. I will draw on readings of other related films to more carefully limn the boundaries of cinematic suburbia. I turn attention in particular to *American Beauty* (2000), *Edward Scissorhands* (1990), *Far from Heaven* (2002), *In the Land of Women* (2006), *Little Children* (2006), and *The Truman Show* (1998), all of which explored visual and relational life in the suburbs and many of which, like *Pleasantville*, engaged images of suburbia through the lenses of memory.[29] In *American Beauty*, Lester returns to nostalgic memories of his high school years to reimagine a better suburbia. *Edward Scissorhands* is told as a long and nostalgic flashback and is set sometime in the 1970s. In *In the Land of Women*, Carter, the movie's central character, returns from Los Angeles to his grandmother's suburban home in hopes of finding himself. *Little Children*'s narrative is stitched together by an omniscient narrator who already knows the story and, thus, places the action in the immediate past. *Far from Heaven* is set in the 1950s and is a nostalgic homage to the melodramatic films from that time period. *The Truman Show* uses memory-tinged New Urbanist architecture and city planning as its visual framework.[30] Finally, nearly all of these suburban films appear to be, in some way, critical of suburban life. At the same time, they are emphatically not rejections of suburbia but rather invent revised visions of suburbia that offer the safety and homogeneity of the suburbs made more meaningful through nostalgic invocations of the past and more tantalizing with just the slightest hint of racialized and/or sexualized danger. Careful investigation of these films will begin to indicate the aesthetics and affective commitments of the suburban spatial imagination.

White Picket Fences

The fantastical idea that forms the basis of *Pleasantville* is one reason the film is a compelling text to help me think about the ethos of the suburban imagination. The film is framed as a comparison/contrast argument about suburbia. Images of present suburban life are sharply contrasted with the suburbia of the past. One avenue into these contrasts is through the film's suburban aesthetics. While the images of the contemporary suburb are in color, the colors are washed-out and beige: the California hills are the sandy colors of the desert, the houses are in earth tones, the school yard is paved and unrelieved by green grass. Compare this vision to that of the first images of Pleasantville. The film's color is black and white, and yet the images seem sharper, more focused, somehow more appealing. Just as importantly, the images are those of the idealized, archetypal suburban aesthetic. The streets are well maintained and cars drive by slowly. Large trees provide shade and visual interest. The houses are well kept and fronted by steps and porches. Neighbors connect over the fences and homeowners devote time to yard work. Perhaps most importantly, each house is surrounded by well-kept yards behind white picket fences.

The single family home set in its own manicured lawn is fundamental to the suburban aesthetic. In *Pleasantville*, both contemporary and 1950s suburbs emphasize the house with a yard. These houses are nearly always placed along clean, well-maintained, quiet, tree-lined streets.[31] In *American Beauty*, the film opens with a panoramic shot from above of the trees that serve as a canopy to the street on which the Burnhams live. Viewers will see Lester Burnham and the film's other characters walk, run, garden, and drive on these apparently peaceful streets. In fact, nearly all the films examined here open with exterior shots that focus attention on the streets, landscaping, and the houses themselves. In the opening of *The Truman Show*, audiences get a close-up of the brick street when Truman Burbank gets out of his car to investigate a light that fell out of the sky onto the road. The first vision of the *Edward Scissorhands* suburb focuses on pastel ranch-style houses as an Avon lady drives her 1970s-era Dodge Duster along the gently winding streets.

The house and street serve as one element in the visual vocabulary of the suburbs, one that is directly tied to a second element. Filmic suburbs separate residential space from commercial and civic space, creating a distinctly different visual sense from mixed-use urban scenes. This separation encourages and is represented through individual transportation from home to school, work, or shopping. The automobile seems nearly as important as the houses in defining suburban space in general and particular characters' place within the space.[32] Viewers are drawn, early on, into the movie town of Pleasantville through the immaculate convertibles of the 1950s. Lester Burnham demonstrates his rebellion against the straitjacket life he has been leading by trading in his Toyota Camry for a 1970 Pontiac Firebird. In *Edward Scissorhands*, all the men, in their Fords, Chevys, and Dodges, drive home in the evening and out to work in the morning at the exact same time.[33]

More central yet to the visual vocabulary of the suburb are the well-kept lawns. Bordered by white picket fences, the lawns are green, the flowers are perfect, and the shrubs and trees are tall and healthy. What is more, the movies consistently show that these immaculate yards take work. Audiences see Bud's neighbors in Pleasantville watering and mowing their lawns.[34] Truman Burbank—the unwitting "star" of his own television show—works in his front yard in plaid shorts. Edward Scissorhands uses his scissor hands to dress up his adoptive family's yard and the neighbors' yards with animal topiaries fashioned out of the ubiquitous shrubs. In fact, Edward's acceptance into the neighborhood, in spite of his physical oddities, is initially fostered by his ability to artfully trim the neighborhood's bushes. *American Beauty* introduces Carolyn Burnham—unfulfilled real estate agent, mother, and wife of the narrator—as she is pruning one of her perfect red roses.

While the Burnhams' lawn is perfect (so perfect that it prompts a neighbor to ask for advice on growing roses), the new next-door neighbor's yard is composed of a dying lawn and unpruned plantings, and it is not bordered by a white picket fence.[35] This provides the visual clue that the new neighbors themselves may be morally corrupt—and, in fact, the son is a drug dealer, the mother is agoraphobic and obsessive about cleanliness, and the father is sexually attracted to Lester and homophobic, abusive and, in the end, a murderer. Yards, it becomes clear, are more than pleasurable visual additions to a house, they are modes by which moral and civic worth can be expressed and measured.[36] As Cynthia Girling and Kenneth Helphand argue, "Even in the seemingly prosaic suburban yard/garden, Edenic characteristics are present: peacefulness, innocence, and idealized nature, a place where the world is both useful and good to look at."[37] In each of the films, yards indicate the moral worth of the neighborhoods. Further, they consistently reinforce gendered norms, as lawns and lawn care have consistently been marked as masculine.[38] These yards, drawing on gendered and class norms, offer visions of safety and stability. Even as a critique of suburbs is leveled, this visual landscape of Edenic yards, well-painted houses, and the white picket fence remains undisturbed and unquestioned.

Finally, filmic visions of the suburbs are marked by the presence of whiteness and the nearly complete absence of nonwhite faces and non-Anglo-American cultures.[39] In *The Truman Show*, when Truman Burbank first appears on the steps of his house, he is greeting his neighbors, including a handsome African American family, a family that appears only as neighbors to be greeted in the morning. But, as is the case with the rest of the films, this couple does not become a significant portion of the narrative. In *American Beauty* the only African Americans we see are men playing basketball, and in *Little Children* we see a black police officer on a touch football field and again in uniform. The suburbs of *Edward Scissorhands*, *In the Land of Women*, and *Pleasantville* appear to be exclusively white.[40]

This is not to say that films ignore diversity. The conceit of *Pleasantville* is that the black and white residents of Pleasantville become "colored" as they have strong, emotional experiences that allow them to become fully human or true to themselves. Edward Scissorhands explores the desire for—and ultimate rejection of—difference. The dramatic tension in *Far from Heaven* turns on the romantic relationship between white homemaker Cathy Whitaker and black gardener Raymond Deagan, along with Cathy's husband's closeted homosexuality. Thus even as race and nonnormative sexuality are expelled from these visions of suburbs, race along with desiring and performing sex outside of white heteronormativity serves as one mode of providing affectively real experiences within a setting that is visually figured as safe but boring.[41]

Torpor, Danger, Authenticity, and Nostalgia

In fact, most of the suburban films addressed here turn on this dialectic between suburban safety and the desire for a real, authentic, or passionate emotional life. Where the white picket fence and the perfectly tended yard represent safety and serenity, they also imply conformity and control. The extraordinarily green yards, constantly flowering annuals, the ever-growing trees seem—in their very liveness—to cover over and compensate for a deadness of the homes' residents. When, in the opening scenes of *American Beauty*, Carolyn Burnham pricks her finger on a rose bush, the sharpness of the thorn and the drawing of blood points to the hidden dangers of the garden's beauty while, as the film makes clear, the life she gives to the garden is completely repressed in the rest of her existence. Thus even as the yard, in its beauty and control bordered by the visual and material framing of the picket fence, draws on the deep desire for pastoral living, it also hides the repressions and deeply flawed interior lives of the suburban residents.[42]

More than simply hiding repressions, however, suburbia is also figured in these films as the site and cause of these repressions. The enforced normality of the suburbs distances, abstracts, even makes impossible access to true feelings, deep emotions, or passionate experiences. This desire for denied passion is summed up by Sarah in *Little Children* when, near the end of the movie's second act, she asserts that "it's the hunger" that motivates being alive. This hunger—and its satiation—names Sarah's motivation for the torrid affair she is having with her neighbor and fellow stay-at-home parent Brad.

Little Children opens with the sounds of children playing filtered through an echo chamber intercut with the ticking of dozens of clocks. A camera speeds by the tops of the mature trees that line the suburban streets that will serve as the film's landscapes. The shots shift from the verdant outdoors to an interior stuffed with porcelain figurines of children and the incessantly ticking clocks. These opening scenes, taken together, set a tone of unending time, where children play but are frozen in time like the figurines, tethered to the metronomic clocks, and heard from a distance. As we soon learn, these images of clocks, figurines, and the sounds of children playing as if in a dream (or a nightmare) represent the inner life of Sarah while immediately introducing us to homes that are uncanny and unhomely.

We first meet Sarah in an idyllic park (which serves as the publicly available version of the pastoral scene) on a perfect day as children play (their voices no longer heard through the distancing effect of an echo chamber). The camera first sees children playing, then shifts its attention to middle-class white mothers criticizing a woman they know for returning to work too quickly. The camera pans to a woman who is sitting on the ground a little apart from the others. A man's voice intones in a voice-over, "Smiling politely to mask a familiar feeling of desperation, Sarah reminded herself to think like an anthropologist. She was a researcher studying the behavior of typical suburban women. She was not a typical suburban woman herself.""[43] The camera pans in and catches her pensive look. Sarah and her child Lucy do not interact with the other mothers or children in the park. Sarah only comes to the park, the voice tells us, because if she did not come she might go crazy spending too many hours alone with her "unknowable" child. Her desperation, we learn, is that of being married to a unfulfilling man (caught, early on in the film, masturbating to online porn in his home office), of having to respond to the constant demands of her child, and of giving up on her PhD studies in literature for an unexplained reason (though we suspect it is to get married, have a child, and move to the suburbs).

We learn about her giving up on her graduate education—and most fully understand the ways suburbia has deadened her—at the end of the movie's second act. She is invited to join a book club by an older woman with whom she takes evening walks. The book for the night is (of course) *Madame Bovary*. Not only are the regulars—all older women—at the reading group but so too is Mary Ann, the most censorious mother of the group we met at the park.[44] Near the end of the discussion of the book—a discussion in which Mary Ann labels Emma Bovary a slut—Sarah is invited to share her response to the book. Her friend, who invited her to the reading group, authorized the speech she is about to give by saying that Sarah has a PhD in literature, a PhD that Sarah reminds her, she has not yet earned.

She begins her interpretation by saying that when she first read the book in graduate school she did not understand Emma Bovary and, thus, did not like the book. But in this new reading, framed by the suburban-induced torpor, Sarah gains a new understanding of and empathy for Emma.[45] Emma, Sarah asserts, is trapped, married to the wrong man, and deeply unhappy with her lot. In a pointed exchange with Mary Ann, she argues that Emma's struggle is noble and feminist:

Sarah: Oh she fails in the end, but there is something beautiful and even
    heroic about her rebellion. My professors would kill me for even
    thinking this, but in her own strange way Emma Bovary is a feminist.
Mary Ann: Oh that's nice, so now cheating on your husband makes you
    a feminist.
Sarah: No, no, no, no. It's not the cheating. It's the hunger. The hunger
    for an alternative. And the refusal to accept a life of unhappiness.

What Sarah identifies with is the hunger, the desire, the passion, and Emma's refusal to constantly deny her own passions. Sarah's vision of Emma has radically changed from the days of graduate school. She suggests that the standard reading of Emma's life is only as a failure. But from within Sarah's more recent lived experience of a deadening, stultifying, soul-killing suburban and heteronormative landscape, suddenly Emma's struggle appears noble and feminist. Feminism and, more broadly, a meaningful human life, are at least partly about deeply felt hungers and desires and a willingness to risk much for a full expression of that desire.[46]

What is at stake here is not so much a reading of *Madame Bovary* but rather a vision of the good life. Sarah, in this instance, takes up with Callicles in Plato's dialogue on rhetoric and the good life, *The Gorgias*. For Callicles—the one character that Socrates never fully overcomes—the good life is experienced in the nexus of deeply held desires and the power to fulfill these desires. Similarly, for Sarah suburbia and the heteronormative family deaden her to her own only partially repressed desires. Her illicit affair with Brad offers her the risky possibilities Emma experienced, presenting her with the chance to feel and feel strongly for the first time in years.

But as powerful as these emotions are for Sarah, the film's audience is asked to experience the passion at a distance. In *Little Children* the distancing technique is that of the voice-over. Sarah's life (and those of the other main characters) cannot speak for itself. Instead, a declamatory voice consistently names their experiences and, in the end, draws for the audience the moral of the story. While I will return at the end of this chapter to the distancing techniques nearly all of the films employ, what is crucial for my purposes now is the way the voice-over places the narrative in the immediate past. The narrator could not, of course, know the unfolding of the story unless the story was already completed. Thus while the film is not immediately apparent as a memory text it relies in its narrative form on a sort of nostalgia, a gauze-like imaging of the story told through the scrim of the voice-over, seen through the dappling of old oak trees and the hazy sun-filled attic where Sarah and Brad rapturously conduct their affair.

This constellation of imagining the suburbs as stultifying and of nostalgia as a powerful response links *Little Children* to the other films addressed here. Most broadly, the films install nostalgia for a past that was more authentic and at the same time safer than the present. As the analysis has already suggested, however, these two modes of nostalgia—where the past was more authentic and the past was safer—are often at odds with each other.

Authenticity through nostalgia is a central theme of *American Beauty*. As the film opens, Lester Burnham, in voice-over, describes himself as sedated, and, "in a sense, dead already." The movie is the story of Burnham's reawakening. Lester's first moment of happiness comes when he shares a joint with a neighbor who becomes both Lester's dealer and Lester's daughter's boyfriend. As they get high, Lester describes high school summers flipping burgers, smoking marijuana, and having sex. It was, he says, the best time of his life. Thus begins his (nostalgic) awakening. With this newfound understanding of himself, Lester takes a job at a burger joint, settles into a pot habit, begins working out in the garage, and buys a red Pontiac Firebird, the car he has "always wanted. And now I have it. I rule." And, of course, he seduces and is seduced by Angela, his daughter's best friend from high school, an "all-American beauty." While at the final moment Lester chooses not to have sex with Angela, their attraction to each other completes Lester's high school fantasy of drugs, rock and roll, fast cars, and sex. The blandness of present suburban life—the color tones of the movie run from white to ecru with the exception, of course, of Angela's red, red lips, and the red rose petals that cover her naked body in Lester's masturbatory fantasies—is countered with a fantasy of a better suburbia. In this better suburb, middle-aged men get stoned, get laid, and work out in their garages with Pink Floyd playing in the background.[47] In Lester's fantasy he risks little while nostalgia installs an older, better, sexier, and profoundly patriarchal, white, and heterosexual space.

Lester's sedation and subsequent waking relies on nostalgia. However, the theme of sedation or loss of authentic self runs in opposing directions. In *Pleasantville* the present is fraught with overwhelming danger that leads to both angst and boredom.[48] As Setha Low suggests, highly controlled suburbs are responses to the anxieties produced within globalization. Yet these new, often gated, communities foster the anxiety to which they are responses.[49] It is in this context that visions of past (and better) suburbs make sense. This relation between the profound anxieties within contemporary society and the safety of warmly remembered suburbia is perfectly encoded near the beginning in *Pleasantville*. Cutting between images from the TV show *Pleasantville* and David's present life, *Pleasantville* creates a dialectic between an anxiety-ridden and profoundly boring present and a safe and secure past. The film's viewers first see a TV promotional for a Nickelodeon-style cable channel *Pleasantville* marathon. The following scene takes the audience into the high school classrooms where teachers drone to bored students about how difficult the present is and the future will be—incomes are going down and global temperatures are going up, the teachers warn. These utopic and dystopic visions coalesce as David watches the *Pleasantville* intro (dad comes home from work, is met by his beautiful homemaker wife and two chirpy, perfect teenagers) while trying to ignore his mother's argument with her ex-husband over weekend parental duties. The contrast is clear: Pleasantville is good, safe, warm, and loving; present-ville is fractured, unsafe, and scary.

But *Pleasantville* is more deeply instructive than this simple dialectic suggests. The movie demonstrates that while the safety of the 1950s suburban past may be a desirable escape as a TV show, it is not acceptable for "real life." David's and his sister's transportation back to Pleasantville profoundly transforms the town's people, transformations that are signified by residents who begin to change from black and white to Technicolor. The film seems to suggest that having sex is the key to becoming colored. Yet, as Jennifer points out midway through the movie, while she is having more sex than anyone, she nonetheless remains a study in gray tones. It becomes apparent that the residents remain black and white as long as they repress their true emotions. They take on color as they take the risk of powerful, personal emotions. The 1950s show—as a TV show—is a powerful counter to the difficulties of the present in proffering safety, security, and certainty in response to the contemporary trauma. However, this safety, when taken alone, is just as numbing to the spirit as is the fragmentation and fear of the present.

Nonetheless, *Pleasantville*, far from arguing against nostalgia (as some critics have suggested), argues for nostalgia, but a nostalgia that is leavened with a hint of danger or risk; for it is risk, the movie suggests, that leads to full human emotions.[50] As it becomes clear to David's Pleasantville girlfriend that there is life beyond Pleasantville's borders, she asks him "what's it like out there?" "It's louder," David responds, "scarier I guess, and it's a lot more dangerous." "Sounds fantastic," she replies. This dialectic between "a lot more dangerous" and "sounds fantastic" is precisely what is at stake in these movies.[51] The movies critique the deadening effects of the safety of suburbia, and yet, while the danger "sounds fantastic" from inside Pleasantville, it is, at its best, a danger always contained within safe, larger boundaries that remains unquestioned. For the film's audiences, the danger is all the more fantastic because while danger is frightening it has been objectified, thus the fear is experienced and contained.

The danger and risk that foster authentic experience are nearly always coded in complex intersections between race and sex. The film offers racial difference as a key to authentic emotionality and passionate relationships, but offers this difference within the safety of whiteness. The awakening of the residents of Pleasantville is signified most obviously by their gaining color, and for many, experiencing sexual passion is the key to becoming colored. This coloring of the residents of Pleasantville becomes obviously racialized as the black and white residents strive to ostracize the newly colored folks raising signs against people they call coloreds and making rules against colored behavior and music. The film remembers the 1950s' struggle over racial equality, and yet black citizens are completely absent from this suburb, and those liberated from Pleasantville's strictures are all white.

But black and white individuals coming alive and becoming colored is racialized in more subtle ways: the music of the coloreds is that of nascent rock and roll and jazz. As characters become colored the film consistently shifts from "white" to "black" music.[52] Perhaps the most telling of these shifts comes near the end of the film's second act. David, having been named a hero for putting out a fire in a tree, arrives for work at the soda fountain. The soda shop is filled with teenagers who demand an explanation for how David knows about fire (an unknown to Pleasantville residents—including the firefighters). David's explanation—and the growing realization among the town's residents that there is a world outside of Pleasantville—is set to Dave Brubeck's "Take Five." As Krin Gabbard points out, Brubeck's music—especially "Take Five"—was popular in the 1950s and introduced bebop to a broadening (whiter) audience. The teenagers at the soda fountain press David with more questions, including about the library books they are just beginning to read. One boy asks David about how *Huck Finn* ends. As David begins to tell the story of Huck and Jim (and as the words magically appear on the page), the music shifts from Brubeck to Miles Davis's "So What."[53] The shift to Davis's "So What," writes Gabbard, serves as a "signifier of profound transformation. . . . As black music, the Miles Davis recording carries with it an aura of the forbidden and the transgressive that *Pleasantville* needs as it moves the narratives of the civil rights movement to a small town devoid of African American faces."[54]

Finally, these shifting musical/skin tones are reinforced in *Pleasantville* through visual art that is inspired by the music and the awakening of emotions. This art, produced by the formerly repressed owner of the soda shop, is somewhere between modernist and pop art. Most provocatively it is painted, like graffiti, on the side of a commercial building. By offering David's telling of Huck's and Jim's story as the realization of individual freedom; a soundtrack that associates black music with passion and feeling; and urban, modernist, graffiti as honest and authentic visual expression; *Pleasantville* uses racialized and sexualized differences to assert authentic emotionality and connectedness. But these racialized possibilities remain always screened as the characters become colorized versions of whiteness.[55]

This connection between modernist art, jazz, race, and sex is made most explicit in *Far from Heaven*. Produced as an homage to 1950s melodrama and drawing on a nearly complete range of suburban visual vocabulary, the movie explores the repressions of the 1950s. The story revolves around the perfect suburban couple, Cathy and Frank Whitaker, and their black gardener, Raymond Deagan. Cathy is an ideal wife and mother. However, she leads an unfulfilled life (unfulfilled in part because Frank does not desire to have sex with her) and begins a relationship with Raymond. She meets him in her garden, then at the opening of a modern art show at the Hartford art museum. This second meeting cements Cathy and Raymond's relationship. Raymond is intelligent, caring, kind, and a good father—many characteristics that Frank no longer possesses, if he ever did. Finally, after Frank hits her, out of his own sexual frustrations, Cathy goes with Raymond to a restaurant in a black neighborhood of Hartford. They have drinks and dance to a jazz combo. Of course the relationship is doomed. When the town begins to talk of Cathy and Frank's relationship (they are seen together at the restaurant), Cathy is ostracized from society, Raymond is run out of town (by both the whites and the blacks, he indicates) and Cathy is left alone with her son, daughter, and black maid.

Raymond is the voice of reason about both race and how to live life. She desires to come see him in Baltimore. Raymond decides that her coming will not work. "I'm not sure that would be a wise idea. . . . I've learned my lesson about mixing in other worlds. I've seen the sparks fly, all kinds." With tears in her eyes, she turns to go. Raymond touches her shoulder; she grabs his hand but keeps her back turned. Raymond blesses their parting: "Have a proud life, a splendid life. Will you do that?" She nods, he kisses her hand, and she leaves. The sparks Raymond has seen fly are the powerfully positive sparks of romantic and sexual attraction. But this illicit attraction caused even greater sparks—the sparks of racial conflict—that are far more dangerous and uncontrollable than Raymond is willing to risk. This moment expresses in fairly precise form what Thomas DiPiero calls the hysteria of whiteness.[56] Cathy, rejected by her husband and searching for an identity, a self that feels real and right, turns to Raymond. But he, wiser than she in the ways of race, reaffirms the irreconcilability of their differences. He recollects, for her, her whiteness, restitching her into the white space of suburbia even as he moves to the not-white space of the city.

The dialectic between danger and safety gets recoded throughout these movies. Edward Scissorhands, after his initial success in integrating into suburban life, is chased out of town, back up the hill to the castle where he lives alone. Near the end of movie, while the suburbanites are chasing Edward, Peg, the suburban mom, Avon lady, and Edward's surrogate mother, says to her daughter Kim: "You know, when I brought Edward down here to live with us, I didn't think things through, and I didn't think about what could happen to him, or to us, or to the neighborhood. And now I think that maybe, it might be best if he goes back up there, because at least there he's safe, and we just go back to normal." Formally, this functions in the exact same way as the ending of the relationship between Cathy and Raymond in *Far from Heaven*. The risky Other is expelled from the suburb. The white suburb is too dangerous for the Other, and, at the same time, the Other is far too disturbing to the suburb. For the rest of her life the white woman left behind longs for this real experience. Indeed, *Edward Scissorhands* begins and ends with Kim, the daughter who fell in love with Edward, telling Edward's story to her grandchild. As with Cathy, Kim gave up this chance of love, this moment of authenticity, because the risks of difference were too profound.

Finally, in *The Truman Show*, as Truman stands on the liminal edge between his created world and the "real" world, Christof, the creator of the television show, and Truman engage in a conversation about safety and truth. Christof says:

C: I am the creator of a show that gives hope and joy to millions.
T: Then who am I?
C: You are the star.
T: Was nothing real?
C: You were real, that's what made you so good to watch. . . . There's no more truth out there than the worlds I created for you . . . but in my world you have nothing to fear.

As in *Pleasantville*'s black-and-white TV suburb, Truman's TV home is safe and comfortable. This safety is at once desirable and, at the same time, terrifyingly boring.

The Truman Show is the one film discussed here that does not return its characters to the comforts of home. Truman finally escapes his hermetically sealed life. His escape is shown on live television. The film cuts between Truman finding the door out, hesitating, and finally deciding to leave, and the television show's audiences, including security guards, bar patrons and workers, and a female former character on the show who had begun to awaken Truman's wonder about an outside world (conflating, again, sexuality and honest emotionality). The movie's theater audience identifies with the television audience who identifies with Truman as he escapes the simulacra of his world. The film's audience is asked to respond as do the television's audience: by cheering Truman on but staying at home.

The Truman Show's critique of simulacra is itself proffered through simulacra. And this, I want to suggest, is precisely the ethical nub of these movies. As the theater audience cheers the television audience cheering for Truman's escape from his plastic world, the film's audience can experience, in some small way, and at some significant distance, their own escape. And in seeing Truman's individual triumph over simulacra, the audience's audience can begin to imagine (without being called on to enact) an escape from their own plasticized, televised world. What these films offer along with a critique of suburbia is a mediated experience of authenticity and memory that can assuage the conflicts surrounding life in the suburbs. In experiencing the risky sexual and racial relations within the films, audiences can partially overcome their own torpor. If audiences accept the narrative arc of most of these films, then they can risk authentic emotions, they can cross boundaries of diversity, but as with *American Beauty's* Lester and *Pleasantville's* David they return to the safety of their carefully controlled and designed suburbs, and into the bosom of their imperfect but beautiful families.

"Perverse" Spaces

There is one final difference that runs through many of these films and has remained just below the surface of my text: the difference of homosexuality.[57] *American Beauty* and *Far from Heaven* depend on homosexuality to generate the narrative tensions within the films. *American Beauty* begins and ends with images of (male) homosexuality. The only seemingly well-adjusted family on the Burnham's block is the gay couple that lives next to the Burnhams. The movie famously ends with Colonel Frank Fitts shooting Lester in the back of the head just as Lester has returned to the heart of his family. Frank shoots Lester after fantasizing that his son is having an affair with Lester and after himself kissing Lester. Viewers are invited to understand Frank as a repressed homosexual. This repression is portrayed as the psychic center of a dysfunctional family and of Frank's violent abuse of his son, abuse that becomes most troubling after Frank believes he sees his son performing fellatio on Lester. Within these scenes, the garage—the prototypical masculine space, and located adjacent to, but not embedded in the domestic space of the home—becomes the site of deeply disturbing perversity.

In *Far from Heaven*, Cathy desires a blissful normalcy with her husband, Frank, but he is unable to fulfill her needs. He is emotionally and physically distant and clearly on his way to alcoholism. Viewers learn over the course of the movie that Frank is a closeted homosexual. Again, the repression of this "perverse" sexuality is read as the roots of Frank's inability to carry on a positive family life. And, as in *American Beauty*, this homosexuality is nearly always placed outside of the domestic sphere of the suburban house. In *Far from Heaven*, Frank's office, urban bars, a Miami Beach hotel room, and an urban flat contain the homosexuality that undermined the heterosexual suburban utopia of Cathy and Frank's perfect family. Just as the black man is banished to the city spaces of Baltimore, Frank's homosexuality is lived outside of the heterosexist space of suburbia. In the end, Cathy is left alone in her vast and echoing suburban home, abandoned by her (gay) husband, her (black) lover, and her (racist, heteronormative, and homophobic) friends.

These images of real and fantasized homosexuality depend on a larger epistemological, visual, and geographical imagination of homosexuality as, quite materially, marginalized.[58] Intriguingly, of course, the image of the closet is a crucial mode of (spatially) thinking the marginalization of homosexuality. The closet as metaphor and space directly raises the image of domesticity, an image crucial to the suburban imagination just as the closet serves as a foundational epistemology within the Western imagination.[59] This epistemology of closeted sexuality intersects with deeply spatialized struggles over sexuality.[60] George Chauncey, for example, details the shifting sexual landscapes of New York City through the twentieth century. The visibility of homosexuality in public spaces and in particular neighborhoods shifted over the century and across space. These shifts were not linear or progressive. In New York, homosexuality was more visible and accepted before World War I, was forced underground between the wars, and in the post–World War II years became again more visible.[61] Part of this new visibility came through the struggle for gay rights, which is partly a struggle over the performance of sexuality in space; of creating what Gordon Brent Ingram calls "queerscapes."[62] No matter the particular contours of these changing borders, by "policing of the gay subculture the dominant culture sought above all to police its own boundaries."[63] These boundaries involve conceptualizations of the public and private and the urban and the suburban.[64] These films, in imagining homosexuality at the margins and heterosexuality at the center of suburban domestic space and in figuring homosexuality as disturbing to the normalcy and safety to the heterosexual suburban family, produce within the suburban spatial imaginary these very boundaries.

Suburban Dreams, Perverse Spaces, and the Ethos of *Pleasantville*

Thus these stories formulate spatialized boundaries between city and suburb, black and white, homosexual and heterosexual, bad and good. While passionate, authentic emotions lie in the first of the binary, the films return us, always, to the second term. The ethos of these films creates a suburban spatial imaginary in which safety, comfort, and normalcy are structured within the white heterosexist spaces of suburbia. More, however, the films point to the edges, the apparently unsayables, of contemporary life. Crossing over into this dangerous territory, these films seek to create the human subject in the suburb through the imagining of the sublimity (and thus the unsayability) of same-sex, cross-racial, cross-generational, and even cross-species (in *Edward Scissorhands*) sex. The audiences of the films, addressed at a distance, are witness to a failure of discourse and to an imaging of the possible and the impossible.

In fact, as with *The Truman Show*, the films nearly always place the audience at a distance from the impossibilities the films proffer. *American Beauty*'s Lester is already dead, as we know from the opening sequence. *Edward Scissorhands* is told as a long and nostalgic flashback. *Far from Heaven* is set in an idealized past. *Pleasantville* is set in this same past but is even more removed, as this past is mediated both by the film and the film's television show. In each case, audiences are invited to experience a mass-mediated form of perverse sublimity. But even this apostrophic address of the mass media is not enough to insulate the viewers from the risky borders proffered by the films. And so, the films nearly always add yet another layer of distance—whether of time or simulacra—between the audience and the perverse honesty within the narrative arcs. Thus these films represent something like the sublime aesthetics of which Nathan Stormer has been writing. "Sublime aesthetics," Stormer writes, "enact a strange variant of one of the oldest commonplaces, the possible and the impossible. Ultimately, through the apostrophic play of possibility and impossibility, the spectator is reconfigured into the rhetorical topography of humanism."[65] Put differently, in viewing the impossibilities of crossing over from the banality of suburbia into the sublime authenticity of Otherness, viewers are reconfigured into the rhetorical topography of the suburbs.

If the audiences accept the narrative arc of most of these films, then they can risk authentic emotions, they can cross boundaries of diversity, but as with *American Beauty*'s Lester, *Pleasantville*'s David, *Far from Heaven*'s Cathy, *Edward Scissorhands*'s Kim, or *Little Children*'s Sarah and Brad, they always return to the safety of their carefully controlled and designed suburbs, and into the bosom of their imperfect but beautiful families. In this suburban movement between the impossible and the possible these films construct a very particular spatial imaginary of suburban space as white, heteronormative, and patriarchal. This ethical appeal creates seemingly safe dwelling places within a deeply fragmented world, a world of fear and longing. But just as crucially, these films help construct a suburban subject whose boundaries and borders are marked by the profoundly threatening impossibilities of perverse sex. In the economy of these films, it is this risky sexuality that inspires authentic emotional responses. Through desiring an Other that, as we have seen, is ultimately rejected, the white suburbanite finally takes on a fully embodied suburban subjectivity. As is so often the case, the suburban subject creates and depends on a passionately desired and expelled Other.[66]

Tied together in these movies (as in suburbia itself), then, are profoundly difficult contradictions, the most fundamental of which is that between the risks of deeply felt emotions and passionately held human attachments on the one hand, and the safety and security of living a normal and socially accepted life on the other. In these films, passionate desire is filtered through nostalgic longing, a longing that returns the narratives back to center. The nearly unbridgeable differences, as enriching and disturbing as they can be, are, in the end, rejected in favor of the nostalgically limned suburb. In most cases, the return to normalcy is celebrated because of the lessons learned in the trip to the wild side. David, the hero of *Pleasantville*, returns to his suburban home of the 1990s better able to cope with this familiar world because of the lessons learned from the 1950s. The teenager has grown and is able to comfort his divorced mother. "There is no right house, no right car," he tells her, and this, he suggests, is the way it ought to be.[67] Lester, just before he is shot, returns to the bosom of his family, realizing that as difficult as his life has been, it has been good. In his final voice-over, after the audience sees him shot, Lester says, "I can't feel anything but gratitude for every single moment of my stupid little life." At the very end of *Little Children*, as we see Brad being enveloped by his wife and Sarah spooning her child and both returning to their heteronormative homes, the male narrator's voice-over asserts, "You couldn't change the past. But the future could be a different story." In short, the films offer audiences escapes from the boredom of suburban life but return the audience to that very same suburb, the same relationships. The journey through the risk of racialized difference and sexualized passion returns the characters back home—wiser, perhaps, and chastened, and able to tell "a different story"—but home nonetheless.

More broadly, however, these films offer a suburban ethos or a dwelling place in which the suburban good life is imagined. These films' architectural rhetoric, however, is not purely metaphorical. Instead the films offer images of dwelling places—houses, yards, streets, towns—that at once draw on and offer the potential of creating the houses, yards, streets, and towns audiences desire. With suburbia becoming the decentered center of everyday life in the United States, understanding this imagination becomes central to understanding much about many people's everyday lives and desires.

I have focused on several films central to construction of a suburban spatial imaginary, tracing the aesthetic and affective contours of that imaginary. The suburban aesthetic, as I have argued, is built of detached homes, lovely yards and gardens (or not, if we are to understand the homeowner as uncommitted to suburban values), white picket fences, and white residents. Moreover, the films consistently envision these aesthetics as rooted in some form of memory. Told from the immediate future, set in the immediate or more distant past, or moving between the past and present, the movies urge an aesthetic response to the present that draws from the well of memory. More specifically, I have suggested that the visual aesthetics install forms of nostalgia as a response to the difficulties of the films' presents. All of these aesthetics, including that of nostalgia, guide the building and understanding of recently built suburbs.

But, as I argued in chapter 1, nostalgia is not only or even primarily an aesthetic mode; instead, it is also an affective mode. A name of an anxiety over the loss of home and homeland and of an aesthetic and affective response to this anxiety, the suburban imaginary is shot through with nostalgia. These films consistently oscillate between the excitement of adventure and risk in engaging new and different others, while at the same time expressing longings for old and perhaps forgotten homes and habits. What is more, the films create aesthetic and spatial dimensions of an affective suburban landscape, as nonnormative sexuality is consistently shunted out of the homes' domestic spaces into attics, basements, garages, urban apartments, while the domestic space of kitchen and living room are the sites of the films' most important lessons. David reminds his mom as they sit in the kitchen that the right home and the right car are not around the corner, while Lester's epiphany about his love for his family comes as he is looking at a family photo and sitting at the kitchen table. Over the course of the next two chapters in particular I will explore how this spatial imaginary of home is materialized in suburban developments and chain restaurants.

Meanwhile these affectively compelling aesthetics are socially organized. The anxieties the films raise and address are, of course, culturally familiar and have a long history. By the mid-1990s and even more in the aftermath of the conflagration of the 9/11, anxiety, fear, even paranoia have become constitutive of the US American affective state. These anxieties circulate around the home both as a location of the anxieties and a safer refuge against terror imagined lurking outside the home's doors.[68] At the same time, as memory texts, these films appeal to well-recognized visual tropes of suburbia—the yard, the fence, the single family home—while loading these tropes with moral and affective weight. Ill-kept yards indicate an unhomely home and dysfunctional residents, while urban apartments, black jazz clubs, and adjacent cities contain dangers and excitements that lure and repulse.

And so, finally, the suburban spatial imaginary can also have spatial and material consequences. Homes and neighborhoods are built and understood within the aesthetic and affective registers that produce and are produced by these films. Famously, *The Truman Show* was filmed in Seaside, Florida, a prime example of New Urbanist suburban design. Meanwhile, within the film's narrative the television show is funded by constant product placement—indeed, everything seen in the village is for sale in the Truman catalog. At once a critique of the interlacing real and televisual life and a product of that interlacing, *The Truman Show* and the other films here provide topoi for reading the built environment of suburbia. The films offer audiences—and rhetorical critics—glimpses into the hopes and fears of suburbia, the possibilities and contours of the suburban imaginary, and the chance for creating dwelling spaces rich enough to support the good life. The spaces of dwelling take up the rest of the book. Over the next four chapters, I will explore the material, built environment of suburbia looking, in part, for the ways material suburbs draw on, resist, refine, and redefine the suburban topoi traced here. In the next chapter I write about residential neighborhoods of recent suburbs where we will see the ways that the narratives of danger offered in the films are nearly completely repressed in the building of the suburbs while the hope for safety and security—in its many valences—takes center stage.

II. Home and Kitchen: Building Safe and Authentic Space

3
Housing the Good Life
Residential Architecture and Neighborhoods

> Come what may the house helps us to say: I will be an inhabitant of the
> world, in spite of the world.
>
> —Gaston Bachelard, *The Poetics of Space*

In *The Poetics of Space*, Gaston Bachelard takes the house and the home as a
founding image of the human understanding. Always spatialized, the subject
relies on and requires a house as a fundamental imagined structure and experience. This house provides a framework for engaging the greater world
and the security necessary to building a daily, meaningful life.[1] Early in
Bachelard's phenomenological meditation on space, he reflects on the relationship between houses and storms. The storm is chaotic, frightening,
powerful, sublime, and exterior. The house is a haven in the storm; its walls
and roof keep out the storm, creating an interior space of stillness, comfort, and security. In the center of real and imagined storms, "the house
helps us to say: I will be an inhabitant of the world, in spite of the world."
From the security of the house, the subject can make plans for essaying
into the world, for within the comfort of the house, the good life is imaginable and possible.

If the house is the material grounding for the subject's move into the
world, it should also be central to understanding the suburban materializations of the good life. As the previous chapter's argument indicates, the
house organizes the suburban imagination, offering a cultural, visual, and
material place that can secure personal, familial, and communal relations.
And, as that analysis also demonstrates, the home is not always well suited for
this securing task. Whether boring and banal as in *Pleasantville* or containing disturbingly uncanny relations as in *Little Children*, homes are troubled
sites. It is this contrast between the hopes placed in homes and the difficulty
homes have in fulfilling these hopes that creates the suburban home's challenges. In this chapter, I explore the ways contemporary suburban housing
developments in the Intermountain West directly address and capitalize on
these challenges.[2] In the following exploration of these suburban domestic
landscapes, I argue that the architecture develops a topos of roots and walls

that locates residents in time and place through appeals to nostalgically limned memory and pastoralism. This topos not only situates suburbs in time and place but also, more specifically, imagines the comforts of a whole and familiar family, a family that strives for connectedness through community. All together, these appeals to past and place, family and community, create what I will call an *affective aesthetic of safety*, offering to residents both an experience of and a hope for security. My argument unfolds in four parts. First, returning to the exploration of home in chapter 1, I expand on the home as a central organizing image and institution of modernity and late modernity as well as a site of modernity's anxieties. Second, I explore the affective and social relations developed in suburban marketing materials. I then turn to critical analyses of visual and material rhetorics of a collection of actual residential neighborhoods surrounding Denver, Las Vegas, and Phoenix, indicating the ways these developments draw on pastoralism as a way to connect brand new homes to memory and place. Fourth, I draw together these analyses into a consideration of the affective aesthetics of safety offered within these middle-class suburban residences.

Finding Home in Suburbia

There is a real sense in which the home is a central structure in the new ways of thinking and being that characterized modernity. In 1970, John Lukács argued that "domesticity, privacy, comfort, the concept of the home and of the family: these are, literally, principal achievements of the Bourgeois Age."[3] In the shifting relations of modernity, the house represents and contains the commingled development of the modern individual and of the intimate family. This modern family was marked by a shrinking size, intimacy, and a new set of spatial relations.[4] It is in the middle-class families of northern Europe that homes began to develop with separate rooms for parents and older children. These separations allow and depend on a wholly new concept: the husband and wife as individuals conjoined as a couple that is separated from the rest of the family and community.[5] "Before the idea of the home as the seat of family life could enter human consciousness," Witold Rybczynski argues, "it required both privacy and intimacy, neither of which had been possible in the medieval hall."[6] Home, then, developed as a complex of spatial, emotional, and relational characteristics.

But the home also developed in the nexus of the economic and ideological transformations of industrial and consumer capitalism. The separation of public and private, male and female was connected to the industrial revolution and capitalism and supported by an ideology of the male bread-winner and patriarchy. By the late nineteenth and early twentieth century, employers and unions agreed for the need of the male family wage, which allowed men to make enough money to support the whole family, including the purchase of a home, while women were engaged in unpaid housework.[7] In this system, the father and husband escaped the home for the public sphere and women's housework was firmly rooted in the private sphere of the home.

In the twentieth century—and certainly in the immediate post–World War II era—the home became a site for the family to enact new negotiations between the public and private. In postwar suburbs residents did not simply disappear from public space. "Instead," Lynn Spigel writes, "the people secured a position of meaning in the public sphere through their new-found social identities as private landowners."[8] The family and the domestic sphere served as a site for negotiating contradictory impulses between creating "a private haven on the one hand, and community participation on the other."[9] These contradictory impulses are built into the suburban domestic landscape as homes are at once connected to each other and separated by yards, fences, and culs-de-sac.[10]

The contemporary suburban home resides in these difficult relationships between public and private as political rhetoric locates agency and responsibility for social and political justice in the family and the individual.[11] This shifting of political responsibility to the individual and family "dislocates social and political conflicts onto individuals or families, privatizes both the experience of oppression and possible modes of resistance to it, and translates political questions into psychological issues to be resolved through personal, psychological change."[12] If the family is the final stage of political action and the scene for the making of the good life, then the protection of the family and traditional family structures becomes of central importance. Suburbia becomes a refuge from the maelstrom of late modern culture that threatens not just individuals and individual identities, but the family as well. Within this political and cultural context, domestic architecture forms the center of the suburban good life.

As home and family have become the center of political discourse, home itself has been marked by nostalgia.[13] Home is nearly always rooted in history or the past.[14] Since the security home offers is partly security created through the accretion of well-worn patterns of behavior, and home is a location of ideologically compelling images of a family—images that are themselves rooted in nostalgic imaginings—then it should not surprise us that domestic landscapes strive to root themselves in time and place.[15]

In working to take root in place and time, contemporary suburbs serve as a bulwark against the threats posed by the city, by contemporary culture, and by (late) modernity.[16]

In fact, modernity, marked by a sense of the uncanny or unhomeliness, makes creating a comforting home difficult. Most famously theorized by Freud in 1919, the uncanny is a species of the frightening. The fright occurs in a moment when, because of doubling, repetition, or revelation, the familiar becomes disturbingly strange.[17] Freud begins his argument with a long discussion of the German words *heimlich* and *unheimlich*. *Heimlich* (usually translated into English as homely or homeliness) means "belonging to the house, to the family, not strange, familiar, tame, dear, and etc."[18] But heimlich is more complex than this, because even as it means the familiar and the comfortable, it can also refer "to what is concealed and kept hidden."[19] This second "very different" but not contradictory meaning of the word (indeed of or belonging to the family often implies secrets) begins to open up into the meaning of *unheimlich* as a fright caused by a disturbing return of something that was once familiar. In fact, the unheimlich refers to those moments when secrets meant be kept hidden "come into the open." Thus, though the fright of the uncanny appears to be about something new or unfamiliar, in fact "this uncanny element is actually nothing new or strange, but something that was long familiar to the psyche and was estranged from it only through being repressed."[20] And what is it that has been repressed and that returns if always askew and with fear according to Freud?[21] In a word: the original home, that is, the mother's womb.[22]

Tellingly, as Freud is explaining the ways uncanny doubling of objects expresses desires not fully walled off by the ego, he repeats a story of wandering in an unknown Italian town. As he is wandering the town, he happens into a neighborhood of "painted ladies." He quickly exits the narrow street, asks for directions and proceeds on his way. Before long he finds he has accidentally and uncannily returned to the same street of the painted ladies. Again he leaves the street but finds himself once again in the same neighborhood. Drawn by repressed desire, Freud repeats a spatial pattern taking him again and again into a place at once familiar and strange.[23]

Freud wrote this short, strange essay in the years immediately following World War I, a fact to which Freud alludes in the essay and which haunts the paper.[24] It is not all that surprising that Freud turns to the problem of homeliness and un-homeliness in postwar Vienna (though this is not the first instance of his concern with the unheimlich). Shattered by the most devastating war in the Western world, home itself seemed under attack, and the taken-for-granted grounding of daily communal life seemed torn to shreds.[25] World War I only confirmed what many had already asserted about modernity. From Karl Marx's (and Marx's and Engle's) discussion of estrangement in the mid-nineteenth century to Heidegger's assertion in the twentieth century that this estrangement has produced a sense that "homelessness is coming to be the destiny of the modern world," home, homelessness, and the uncanny were fundamental experiences of the twentieth century.[26]

The post–World War II suburban development directly engages these difficulties and opportunities surrounding the home. As Joan Faber McAlister argues, a rising sense of postwar middle-class rootlessness corresponds with the rapid growth of new suburban developments. McAlister asserts that the "widespread anxiety over rootlessness and loss of community directed attention to domestic space at the close of the twentieth century. The proclaimed need for roots provided a rationale for the new crisis to focus on a particular place as the site for both the decline and potential rebirth of community: the suburban home and neighborhood."[27]

Even as the suburban subdivision could be the cause of late modernity's rootlessness, many also hope to find suburban soil rich enough to support fledgling new communities.[28] The metaphor of roots implies connections to the earth and—by extension—to place. But roots also suggest stability over time as a tree's roots allow it to weather the storms of winter and summer. Thus the texts promoting middle-class suburbs draw on discourses of history and memory in response to the deep desire for rootedness.[29]

More, however, contemporary suburbs strive to connect memory to images, ideas, and materializations of place. Indeed, as Bachelard argues, the securing force of the house depends on its spatiality rather than its temporality. Certainly, the original securing home is lodged in memories of childhood. Nonetheless, affectively meaningful memory is secured in place.[30] In fact, memory places—whether official memory places like museums or memorials or the more banal spaces of housing developments and strip malls—powerfully trigger memory through their "presence effects."[31] Memory places, by materializing the past in the present, construct compelling past-present-presence relationships. It is possible that no space is as heavily laden with the materiality of memory as the home. Rooted in our deep past, linked to essential cultural conversations that connect the personal, familial, and national, the home brings the past into the present in fully embodied, fully material ways. The home spatializes memory, materializes bodies, and places individuals, families, and communities in time and geography. It is in this sense that home is affectively rhetorical. The home connects our present to our past, offers the hope of comfort, and places our memo-

ries of ourselves and our most intimately connected others into meaningful concrete relations.

The worry, of course, is that the home or its immediate surroundings
are unhomely and disturbingly (un)familiar. And, as McAlister persuasively
argues, few places confront this worry as directly as the spaces of the suburbs. Offering to consumers the comforts of home in completely new landscapes, connected by vast highways, and served by seemingly placeless strip
malls and megamalls, suburban residential neighborhoods raise the concern of the unhomely in disturbingly banal ways. At its best, the home
spatializes and materializes securing memories, and yet brand new homes
in brand new neighborhoods often in brand new towns cannot offer their
own history as grounding for self-securing home memories. Thus, even as
the suburban home offers a powerful memory place, the suburban home
can also be risky.

Memory is a very precise response to the discomforts of these wholly
new homes. Residential developments offer memories not just of the past
but always and necessarily of a place. In the residential neighborhoods I
studied, home is sewn into complex localities that derive their affectivity
from their geography. Situating the warmly remembered home into the se-
curities of geography through images of nature and nature's tamed cousin
the pastoral makes it possible for suburbs to create meaningful places out
of otherwise apparently empty landscapes. Residential locality roots residents in time and place through materializations of memory and geography and does so both through suburban marketing materials and their material instantiation in the built environment.

Imaging the Good Home

The advertising and marketing of contemporary suburbs helps produce
a suburban imaginary that connects particular times and places. As I will
show in this section, advertising and marketing consistently gesture toward
the past and, at the same time, offer images of particular places through
references to local cultural practices or geographic features. Take, for example, the advertising and marketing of Historic Castle Rock. Several years
ago, while wandering through Park Meadows Mall—an upscale shopping
center anchoring Denver's south suburbs—I saw a marketing display for a
suburban development in Historic Castle Rock. Made of rustic-looking
wood with a steeply canted roof, the display captured my attention. Here,
neatly encapsulated in the display and the development's slogan, was the
late modern desire for and commodification of past and place. Set in a

relatively new mall while drawing on historicized images of small towns and bedrock American values, the display proclaimed the production of a history built of whole cloth, a brand new suburban development rhetorically sutured into stabilizing relations of past and of place and the production of the past and place as commodities. This display, the suburban development it advertises, and the discourses of nostalgia on which the display relies, are central to the visual and material rhetorics of contemporary suburbia. Moreover, this display is representative of marketing's suburban imaginary, which constructs the contours of possibility in the suburbs and urges people to migrate from city, country, and old inner-ring suburbs into new and better spaces.[32]

Like Yi-Fu Tuan's mental maps, these ads work to move people.[33] Mental maps, and by extension, the spatial imaginary, urge people to reimagine their world. Similarly, the suburban spatial imaginary can move people and can help to explain the massive postwar war migrations to the great suburbs of the Sunbelt and the West. This suburban imaginary drew residents in droves, helping them imagine suburban possibilities shaping the building and experience of suburban landscapes.[34]

Of course, the marketing materials for suburban domestic landscapes draw on and revise the visual and discursive suburban themes that preoccupy the suburban films investigated in the previous chapter. Here, too, are well-kept lawns, leafy suburban parks, and a separation of residential from commercial and industrial spaces. But where banality and compensatory risk serve as the boundaries of the spatial imaginary constituted by many suburban films, safety is the central trope of these marketing materials. By drawing on images of open and natural places, producing historically grounded authenticity, and expunging diversity and any reference to the city this suburban imaginary creates an aesthetic of security.

Open to Safety

The Meadows at Historic Castle Rock dramatizes these modes of creating safety. "The Meadows," emphasizes the development's connection to nature and its location within open space. The front of the postcard features five pictures, nearly all of which emphasize wide-open spaces, vast blue skies, and homes perched on the plains with grand vistas of the Rocky Mountain foothills. The postcard urges me to visit the website, and so I log on. The home page repeats the postcard's visual themes.[35] On the left, a towering pine is green and brown against a blue sky with the foothills in the far distance. On the right, three young girls gambol on a mountaintop. They appear dressed for school, but are walking on a dirt trail, with no signs of streets, houses, or schools. In large print, the home page continues to emphasize nature, announcing that the development is located in midst of "True Colorado Open Space."

The consistent repetition of nature images has multiple rhetorical consequences and is a theme I return to throughout this chapter. As I will detail, the suburbs have consistently been imagined as a hybrid space between the human densities of the city and the empty vastness of the rural landscape.[36] Crucially, many contemporary images of suburbs in the Intermountain West downplay the built environment and human intervention of the suburbs, emphasizing instead images of nature. Among its many rhetorical inducements, these particular images of nature—especially with nature figured as open space—are crucial for developing a sense of safety. Disguised as a discourse about natural beauty,[37] the language and the pictures emphasize the absence of people, crowding, and, thus, diversity. On the postcard, for instance, of the eight pictures, only two include people. Similarly, while the website is filled with pictures, less than half include people, and when they do they are almost always individuals or familial groups, and these individuals are often white children. Further, many of the people pictured are shown within the "true Colorado open space" rather than in groups engaged in city or town living.

Other developments expand on the theme of open space as safety. The upper-middle-class development The Timbers emphasizes the beautiful setting of the development and the exclusivity of both the geography and website. The introduction to the website is composed of a forty-second slide presentation. A soothing female voice, with an accent and tonality resonant of an archetypal newscaster or an actor representing an upper-middle-class, well-educated suburbanite and thus coded as Euro-American, intones the qualities of this development, while the slides demonstrate the visual beauty of the setting. The voice-over begins by asserting that The Timbers offers "living in Colorado the way it ought to be," and ends the sales pitch by asserting that this place captures the "true spirit of Colorado." Within the context of the migration to Colorado from the cities of the West Coast and the Midwest, framing The Timbers as embodying the "true spirit of Colorado" argues not only for what Colorado is but also implies what Colorado is not.

Attending to the rest of the script clarifies Colorado's true spirit. Central to this spirit is the protection of "family privacy." Family privacy is secured by placing each home on large lots and by embedding these lots within "over three-hundred acres of open space." This open space is part of an even larger old pine forest that frames "spectacular mountain vistas." The home page emphasizes exclusivity and privacy, asserting that The Timbers at the Pinery affords "residents a sense of privacy and seclusion rarely found in today's busy world." The script clearly distinguishes The Timbers from urban settings, whether the city from which one is fleeing is Denver or Los Angeles. The rural—or, perhaps better, nonurban—setting creates privacy for the family.

This privacy implies the all-important value of safety. The seclusion and antiurban vision proffered by the script is reinforced by visual images emphasizing the beauty of the setting and the size of the homes and home lots. Of the eight images that appear in the forty-second slide show, none show more than one home at a time, several show the setting without homes or people, and only one includes images of people: two middle-aged Euro-American men golfing. This slide presentation, with its technological demands, its verbal and visual images of nature and solitude, the willful absence of images of cities or even multiple houses, combined with its only explicit clue about who belongs—white country club men—makes for a compelling if subtle image of white suburban space.

Safety through Nostalgia and Authenticity

As important as these themes are, just as crucial are the ways the builders draw on nostalgic architectural codes, codes that not only embed homeowners into warmly remembered pasts, but also play on the hopes for authentic experiences. McStain Neighborhoods, for example, offers a series of homes in "authentic" and "historically accurate" craftsman, French Normandy, and shingle architectural styles, while Village's homes come in Tudor, French, and classic.[38] These advertised architectural styles represent the two broad aesthetic forms used in nearly all developments: the houses either refer to historical US American styles like colonial, shingle, Spanish mission, or craftsman; or the architecture refers to Europe and England with Tudor, French, Normandy, and the more generic cottage style.

The popular US American styles are instructive. The craftsman homes (often designed in ways that would be unfamiliar to progenitors of craftsman architecture like Charles and Henry Greene) refer to what might more colloquially be thought of as a form of midwestern architecture familiar from US small-town residential building around the turn of the twentieth century. Mission and colonial refer directly to the colonizing of the continent by Europeans; Spanish mission draws on a Mediterranean aesthetic and is common in the US Southwest; and colonial draws on early

US American styles from the East. While there is an apparent diversity of architectural styles throughout contemporary suburbia, the aesthetic history on which these forms draw is a history that is explicitly white and nearly always middle class.

These historically US American architectures coexist with styles referencing Europe and England where we often get the mixing of middle-class with lower- and upper-class details. Tudor, French, and Normandy provide inspiration for many of the homes built in these new developments. McStain claims that their French Normandy architecture draws on "authentic details"[39] to produce architecture rooted in particular geographies and cultures. Striving to build an authentic, culturally resonant experience can extend from individual home models to the style of an entire subdivision. In Sheffield's Villa Avignon at Brookhaven Lane, French Normandy is not one choice among many; it is the overall style of the neighborhood. Because of the accuracy of the architecture and the layout, Sheffield can confidently proclaim that living in their development is "as authentic as living in the French countryside, only better."[40] What makes this housing better than living in France is that "residents will enjoy pocket parks, walking paths and lush landscaping of common areas where the sights and sounds of nature abound. With only two access points for the community, privacy and seclusion will not be compromised."[41] Authenticity of architectural style combines with privacy and seclusion to build an aesthetic of safe space.

The combination of texts and visuals draws together the central themes of safety. The sounds of nature assure potential buyers that their houses are far removed from the struggles of the city and remind them that the site will be surrounded by acres of open land. As if the separation created by both location and open space were not enough, individuals can only enter the development through two entrances, further securing individuals within their space. The combination of nature and open space with restricted access creates a powerfully reassuring paradox: that of space that is at once open and closed, free and restricted. Residents of this development, then, become embedded in the safety of paradoxically open and closed space, and can live a nostalgically construed authentic life through the architectural details of the houses around which their lives circulate.

Cultural and economic capital combines with architectural details and site planning to make a space that is secure and securely white. Sheffield Homes would resist this reading, however, for in only one click from the home page the viewer will see a white couple and a black couple toasting their happiness at choosing Villa.[42] This sort of multiculturalism does little to undermine the whiteness of the site. That this is the only image including nonwhite individuals is instructive. Indeed, rather than seeing this moment of inclusion as progressive, it is better to see the picture as the type of misdirection crucial the maintenance of what George Lipsitz calls the white spatial imaginary.[43] As a form of misdirection, this image can serve as an alibi for the images of whiteness.[44] This website works to insist that it is not racist and is not offering an image of whiteness by saying, "See, there are blacks here and they are friends with whites." Thus, rather than undermining the whiteness of the site, this image bolsters whiteness's invisibility and maintains white privilege by short-circuiting critical assessment of the site and its design.

As such, this image, this website, and nearly all the advertisements and marketing material help create a suburban white spatial imagination that "structures feelings as well as social institutions. The white spatial imaginary idealizes 'pure' and homogeneous spaces, controlled environments, and predictable patterns of design and behavior." This whiteness is bolstered not only by the visual images I have been analyzing here, but also by a series of neighborhood covenants and Home Owners' Association documents that, while apparently neutral, work hard to maintain the racial purity of the neighborhood.[45] Often these covenants are justified as a way of maintaining property values and are thus modes of economic privilege built right into the physical landscape. Indeed, the white spatial imaginary, "is inscribed in the physical contours of the places where we live, work, and play, and it is bolstered by financial rewards for whiteness."[46] This aesthetics of safety, then, is also an aesthetics of whiteness and, as an aesthetic that works as much by implication and misdirection as by direct assertion, functions more affectively than rationally, proceeding through a series of "structures of feeling" and offering a sense of comfort and security. These images are topoi that provide resources for the imagining and building of suburbs and for the affective experiencing of the spaces.

Thus the spatial imaginary produced within the marketing materials is less complex than that of the films. Where the films offer a bleak vision of suburban banality and offer risky adventures with diversity as leavening, the marketing materials repress diversity and repel risk. Audiences may acknowledge the blandness of suburbs and desire compelling, compensatory riskiness in films about suburbs. But advertising for actually existing suburbs tells a different story. Here, instead, we get an aesthetic of safety and security that responds directly and without hesitation to the spatial anxieties of modernity. The uncanniness of suburban homes is thoroughly shifted into fictional suburban scenes and carefully blocked in the marketing materials. In these materials the home is clearly set off from the spatial anxieties of modern life. Almost exclusively about privacy and intimacy and set within a bucolically imagined natural world (where, apparently, the material storms of plains and mountains are also absent), the market-er's suburban imaginary builds homely, historically rooted, and geographi-cally meaningful domestic landscapes. The affective loss, uncanny fear, and soul-deadening boredom encoded in suburban films is pushed to the side and replaced with delights of family, the beauty of nature, the security of well-lit pocket parks, and the pleasures of carefully patrolled walking paths. As I will show in the next section, this imaginary is constructed out of existing suburban landscapes. At the same time, our understanding of the suburban imaginary—both constructed in films and in marketing mate-rials—orients us to those landscapes, shaping and framing our experiences of actually built landscapes.

Building the Good Home

Because suburbs are rapidly built on land figured as empty, there is often a palpable sense of placelessness in suburban landscapes. In fact, the suburbs studied here are carved out of the inhospitable landscapes of desert or near desert terrains of Arizona, Colorado, and Nevada. As John Beck argues, "The idea of a desert . . . at least in cultures that draw upon Hebrew and Christian traditions, involves a cluster of notions including vacancy, expan-siveness, and fearful potentiality."[47] In fact, Beck argues that the desert—imagined as without form and void—is very precisely a site/sight of the unheimlich. As a void that disrupts Anglo-Saxon ways of seeing with mi-rages and unfamiliar colors, the desert can foster a sense of dread. "Unlike fear, dread has no thing or nothing as its object, and is thus much harder to make sense of. Dread is often evoked by the sense of something uncanny, or unheimlich, unhomely; something not right, felt as present but not seen or known. Unlike outright fear, there is nothing to hold on to or focus on."[48] The desert of the US American Southwest is at once the site of rapid building of homes and a site of fundamental twentieth- and twenty-first-century unhomeliness. It is into this context that suburban housing devel-opments work to create a sense of home, and they do so by striving to su-ture the home into time and place.

Location in Time

The most apparent way that residential landscapes weave themselves into time is by knitting themselves into a historical trajectory and a comfort-ing past. Residential landscapes use two main rhetorical modes of creating

Figure 3.1. The entrance to The Heritage Estates in Las Vegas. The memory implied by the name is reinforced by the textured road that announces the entrance to the subdivision. The brick or cobblestone-like roadway is a fully sensual announcement of the place's connection to the past. Driving over the textured road creates a vibration and low rumble that announces arrival in the past. Photograph by author.

a sense of historicity: names on signs and architectural references. The first and perhaps most obvious way of creating a historicity is through naming and signage. Throughout suburbs in the West, for example, subdivisions are named Heritage Estates,[49] Traditions,[50] or Reunion[51] (figure 3.1). The Reunion website proclaims, "The name Reunion was chosen to represent a deep appreciation for the past, a sense of wonder about the future, and a commitment to living every moment to the fullest."[52] Reunion and these other historically named subdivisions work in this nexus between the past and the future. The spatial metaphor ("deep") is crucial here, for it indicates the ways the past can serve a locating function for suburbs by situating the new building in a narrative arc. Reunion does not simply reside in the past. Rootedness in history, it seems, provides the necessary resources to imagine the future optimistically. Taken together, the rootedness in the past and the hope for the future offer residents an ideal setting for living the good life in the present.

A consistent set of visual references to the past powerfully augment the historical referencing of the signs. Many suburban development names do not refer directly to the past. Nonetheless, a sense of history or tradition is a crucial component of the suburban development. Take for example the signs throughout the Surprise, Arizona, subdivision of Surprise Farms. The name of the subdivision—Surprise Farms—makes an oblique reference to the past: there are clearly no farms in Surprise anymore, unless row upon row of stuccoed houses can be an agricultural product. But the obliqueness is rendered clear by the sign and the setting. Placed in a rugged stone post anchoring the stone walls that separate the neighborhood from the busier arterial roads, the metal sign uses the Surprise Farms logo of a windmill set in the middle of abstractly rendered farmland. This reference to an imagined agrarian past articulates with the creation of place-bound identity that I will engage below. For now it is simply necessary to note the ways these brand new building sites work hard to locate themselves in a past and particularly an agrarian or pastoral past.[53]

Even more important in creating a past for the suburbs are the consistent and constant use of historical forms in new residential building. The examples are endless, so let me just point to two banal and, thus, typical, examples. In Phoenix and Las Vegas vague but comforting references to "Southwest" architecture frame nearly all the housing in the suburbs. For example, the relatively humble model in the Las Vegas development of Stonebrook is adorned with old-fashioned carriage lights on either side of the garage, tan stucco walls, long windows, and light accents near the ground, all of which lend the house a sense of history. Move upscale, and the historical referencing becomes more explicit (if more muddied). Balconies, wrought iron, tile roofs, and nonfunctioning shutters mark these more expensive homes, like the Jasper at Greenwood home. Here tall windows, detailed molding, a wrought-iron balustrade, tile-roofed awning, and an entrance shaded by an arched alcove all place this house in a vague form of Mediterranean- or Mission-style architecture. Throughout Phoenix and Las Vegas and across much of the Southwest, these forms—red-tiled roofs, pastel or earth-toned stucco walls, arches—create a kind of indigenous or vernacular architecture that at once refers to southern European traditions and to Native American forms with inexpensive stucco replacing the more traditional adobe.[54]

As different as the historical references across suburbs are, what remains remarkably the same is the centrality of the historical trope. There is a sense in which the specific historical references are unimportant (thus names like Heritage Estate, Traditions, or Reunion). More important is both an aesthetic and affective sense that these new suburbs are part of a longer, larger, history. These neighborhoods, this historicity suggests, are rooted in the past and part of a familiar narrative about the good life. But it is also important to recognize the very real differences between the historical forms used to create this sense of place.

I have suggested that there are regional differences among the traditions referenced. Denver suburban architecture is blended from midwestern and northern European references with nods to the Southwest, mission, and adobe styles. Phoenix and Las Vegas look more like each other than Denver, and more fully partake of the Southwest, mission, and adobe styles. These differences are not happenstance, nor is it enough to name the differences. Instead, these differences begin to indicate the importance of geographical dimensions in creating a sense of place. Suburban architecture does not just offer images of particular pasts, but of pasts located in particular places.

Location in Place

One of the most popular ways of naming contemporary subdivisions follows this form:[55] "Reston Rockwood at Prescott Park," or "Alvarado Madera at Vista Verde," or in a slight variation "The Villages of Coyote Springs."[56] While many of these names reference the "natural" world (Coyote Springs or Rockwood[57]) what captures my attention at this point is the little "at" or "of." The preposition suggests that the particular development exists somewhere and is a part of the already existing natural and social world. The place in the name can be mapped geographically and culturally. Prescott Park or Vista Verde, apparently, existed before Reston Rockwood or Alvarado Madera, suggesting that this particular Reston Rockwood (as though there could be another) has a special place in space. Put differently, Coyote Springs is the "there" that grounds The Villages. The constant repetition of the place-based preposition suggests an anxiety about place, a constant and iterative return of a repressed hope that if repeated often enough these brand new places that could be anywhere are, instead, actually here. Oddly, the phrase that follows the preposition is never more geographically or historically certain than the phrase before the preposition. We never find, for example, a Coyote Ridge at Denver or a Sunset Lodges at Phoenix. In short, the "at" names an anxiety over a fact that the "at" embodies; there is, in fact, no there, there. Instead, we are well into a simulacrum where the place that places place is always already an image.

This infinite regress and disappearance of place is beautifully captured in the name of the wine festival in Castle Rock: "This year," enthuses the website, "we celebrate our 3rd annual event at The Grange at The Meadows at Historic Castle Rock™."[58] There are at least three important characteristics to point out in this sentence. First, the three names refer to three of the major localizing rhetorics within suburbs. "Historic Castle Rock" sews the space into time. "The Meadows" knits the site into nature. And "the Grange" sutures the site into a specific relation between time and place, namely, a remembered pastoral scene (to which I will return). Thus, even as I am analytically separating time and place (history and nature), this sentence very neatly works to combine these modes of localizing. Second, even as this sentence offers three rhetorics of locality (time, place, and the blending of the two in images of pastoral landscapes) it is unable to finalize or concretize these relations. As much as the sentence works to settle the unsettledness of a new suburb built on the empty spaces between the Rocky Mountains and the Great Plains, this sentence simply fades away. In place of the security of lived memory and concreteness of long relations to the land, the sentence offers us capital letters turning meadows into Meadows and history into History. Finally, even the shift of uninflected nouns to proper names is not enough to provide the desired security. So, when all else fails, the sentence resorts to the legal assertion that a town name can be trademarked by a private company. And so, even as suburban builders strive to locate their buildings somewhere, their effort always points to the impossibility of the task at hand.

Even as, however, the prepositions linking nearly nonsensical proper names point to the anxieties involved in locating oneself in time and place in the western desert suburb, it is also impossible to deny the realities of the environment into which these developments are built. In fact, the climate, topography, and soils resist the complete rationalization of suburban development and serve as a way of creating a visuality of the local. Indeed, one of the most obvious ways of creating a sense of place is, in some senses, out of the hands of homeowners, builders, and suburban designers. The climate, flora, and the nonbuilt landscape of the suburb necessarily connect the suburb to its particular location. Even if the exact same model of house can be found in northwest Henderson, Nevada; Surprise, Arizona; and Highlands Ranch, Colorado, the simple and material facticity of their location already begins to shift the sense of place in the suburb. All of these places, of course, are blessed with abundant sunshine, and the heat and dry air of Surprise is similar to the climate of Las Vegas, though the surrounding mountains are a bit gentler. But the red desert soil of Arizona is different from the arid, red-rock-strewn landscape of the Rocky Mountain foothills. And of course, the rising mountains of the Rockies to the west and long, downward sloping plains to the east of Highlands Ranch is a significantly different landscape than either that of Las Vegas or Phoenix.

These differences—which are seemingly outside of the control of designers and homeowners but which they can use to create a sense of place—show up in the designs of the homes and the yards and also in the ways builders market and announce subdivisions. As important as the sunshine and weather may be for selling the desert homes of Las Vegas and Phoenix, Colorado suburbs push the outdoors and natural beauty to the forefront of their image making. Highlands Ranch is a prime example of the importance of the outdoors in creating place. The entire development is laced with trails and small trailhead parks. The extensive trail system consists of nearly seventy miles of concrete, crushed gravel, and single-track trails that meander through the two thousand acres of open land, down into ravines, and along small streams.[59] The ravines are filled with native grasses, small shrubs, and, along the streambeds, cottonwood trees. Perhaps most importantly the trails offer panoramic views of the mountains to the west, with the light-colored two-story houses settling along the ridges.

The trail system through open land set aside in the midst of extensive building points to the connection between human action and natural spaces. Designed to take advantage of Colorado's relatively mild climate, year-round sunshine, and the premium placed on natural beauty, the open land serves as a site of human creation and recreation. In fact, the trails play a paradoxical role in the natural space. Clearly not natural, the trails cut through the land, offering comfortable paths for walking, running, and biking through nature. At the same time, restricting human activities to the trails helps preserve the fragile landscape and leaves the wild animals in relative peace. In fact, the most remote portions of Highlands Ranch are closed during winter to protect the elk and deer that migrate out of the mountains in search of food and warmer weather. And so, even as the housing developments remake and destroy uninhabited land, the developers set aside "open land" crisscrossed with trails and layered with rules that at once draw humans into formerly wild lands while simultaneously setting aside the land for native plants and animals.

The open, wild land knifing through the suburbs is a compensatory gesture. Even as bulldozers level ridges and fill canyons to make way for street after street of homes, a small portion of the land is preserved in the name of environmental protection and stewardship. This open land is a visual and material response to the guilt some may feel about the environmental consequences of sprawl. This concern over environmental consequences of suburban sprawl may be particularly salient in Highlands Ranch

Figure 3.2. Paved trail meandering through Highlands Ranch. Photograph by author.

and other Colorado suburbs, since Coloradoans consistently see managing growth, protecting the environment, and fostering a strong economy as their three most important political concerns.[60] Building suburbs with open land and trails is one way of responding to the concerns over growth and the environment, making the suburban growth seem more environmentally friendly and less like mindless sprawl.[61]

Just as importantly, this open space is part of the long historical connection that suburbia has had with the rural landscape. Always imagined as precisely the place between the culture of the urban landscapes and the nature of the rural landscapes, suburbs are a hybrid space. In ideal visions of suburban life, suburbs are able to offer the best of the urban and the rural blended with comforts of the warmly remembered hometown. The view from the trails of Highlands Ranch is a visual embodiment of this blending.[62] In the near ground are the plants, rocks, and wildlife of the open space (figure 3.2). If you hike down into a ravine, perhaps you will hear the burble of a brook. In the middle ground are the houses curving along the ridges. In the background rise the snow-capped Rocky Mountains, visually and culturally anchoring the landscape. The wonder of this suburb is the ability to immediately immerse oneself in nature just by stepping out the back door onto the trail while, at the same time, living only minutes from shopping malls, lifestyle centers, and the high-paying technology jobs located at the Denver Tech Center. The carefully developed and tended trails embody and enable this hybridity of city/nature.[63]

Blending Time and Place in the Suburban Pastoral

While the design of Highlands Ranch clearly brings the wild into the suburban space (and thus acknowledges and manages the suburban colonization of the wilds), just as important in the relation between the country and the city is the image of rural farmland. The name Highlands Ranch makes this explicit connection. Even as the material and visual design of the space emphasized nature, the name calls on an agricultural heritage. Indeed, the founding narrative of Highlands Ranch draws far more heavily on the Western idealization of the ranch than on the untamed wilds. "Before it was claimed as Spanish territory in the mid-1500s, our Highlands Ranch community was a prime hunting area for the Ute, Cheyenne, and Arapaho Indians."[64] Thus begins the short history of Highlands Ranch as told on the Highlands Ranch website. The narrative quickly turns to famous Europeans and Euro-Americans who visited and owned the land. As the land passed from one owner to the next the parcels grew larger, but the purpose continued to be agriculture through the late twentieth century. By the early 1980s, however, the land was owned by a real estate company. "In 1981, the Phil and Kaye Scott family led a group of 'pioneer' homeowners to the Highlands Ranch we know today, where homes were built and districts were created."[65]

The narrative of Highlands Ranch is embedded in a familiar Western narrative of settlement and land use, and relies on the affectively powerful pastoral aesthetic. In art, literature, and music the pastoral places action in the midst of idealized visions of an agricultural world in which life is simple, the earth is turned abundantly to the needs of human life; fecundity is a central trope. The pastoral offers a very particular vision of the good life marked by abundance and a simplified set of moral and social relations. Just as importantly, the pastoral connects these images of abundance and simplicity to the land itself. The pastoral is a place- and environment-based vision of abundance, one that offers to place consumer visions of plentitude within romanticized social and cultural relations. As Leo Marx, in his study of the American pastoral, argues, the pastoral expresses "something of the yearning for a simpler, more harmonious style of life, an existence 'closer to nature,' that is the psychic root of all pastoralism—genuine and spurious. That such desires are not peculiar to Americans goes without saying; but our experience as a nation unquestionably has invested them with peculiar intensity. The soft veil of nostalgia that hangs over our urbanized landscape is largely a vestige of the once dominant image of an undefiled, green republic, a quiet land of forests, villages, and farms dedicated to the pursuit of happiness."[66] As Marx argues, the pastoral is an image that combines a sense of place ("quiet land of forests") and time ("the soft veil of nostalgia"), rooting the nation into resonant aesthetic that structures social, temporal, and geographic relations.

Marx is clear that the US American pastoral is a powerfully aesthetic notion. He focuses primarily on written and visual images produced by US American (white, male) writers with references to the paintings that also constantly frame our understanding of the American pastoral. "The cardinal image of American aspirations," Marx writes, "was a rural landscape, a well-ordered green garden magnified to continental size. This is the countryside of the old Republic, a chaste, uncomplicated land of rural virtue."[67] This vision of the nation relies in part on the material land, for when compared to Europe in the eighteenth and nineteenth centuries, the US landscape appeared relatively untrammeled and immensely productive. Just as importantly, however, the land is also a "landscape—an image in the mind that represents aesthetic, moral, political, and even religious values."[68] Wrapped together in the pastoral image are a material land and a way of seeing, feeling, and thinking that expresses deeply held values.

Crucial, however, to the pastoral is the role of human agency.[69] The pastoral is quite precisely an image of the land bent by human agency offering its bounties to human living. The image of the "self-made man," the yeoman farmer, the pioneer, and the cowboy that are so crucial to the development of US American personal and national identity depends on this pastoral landscape in which human agency transforms the land into a productive home, community, and nation.[70] In fact, the image of yeoman farmer forms a cornerstone of US American national identity. "Washington and Jefferson," writes Loren Baritz, "along with many others, insisted that political intelligence, public morality, and national prosperity depended on the continued dominance of pastoral America, secure it in its republican virtue."[71]

These images of the pastoral are also deeply connected to images and imaginations of a middle-class life. By the nineteenth century "architectural manuals, literary essays, and promotional materials" clearly linked middle-class housing aspirations with the pastoral aesthetic that at once fostered a putative return to nature and a rejection of the ills of the city.[72]

At the same time, these pastorally contoured, middle-class housing aspirations were implicitly and explicitly linked to a shifting, post–Civil War national identity.[73] With both US American and middle-class identities tied to the pastoral scene, the city is always suspect even as the city becomes an engine for immense wealth and power.[74] Pastoralism, then, provides aesthetically compelling images of individual, communal, and national identity that can be made to intersect with suburban living. In fact, suburban domestic design is rife with pastoral aesthetics.

This pastoralism finds its individual literalization in the suburban lawn. By the turn of the twenty-first century, lawns are more than grassy patches, but are often productive gardens: producing identity, beauty, and even, in some cases, homegrown tomatoes. As separated as the suburban home might be today from an actual farm, the idea of the single family home on its own land has its roots in this middle-class pastoral scene. A house, sited on its own bit of property and set in the midst of a semirural scene, allows for an all-important sense of retirement. Early English and US American versions of suburbs depended on an idea of retirement, where retirement was an active withdrawal from the public world for the purpose of contemplating great ideas and considering themes of human life. The pastoral landscape was ideal for this vision of retirement because it offered open spaces and retreat from the urban conflicts but was also created by the owner's forethought and reflected the owner's sense of self.[75] The yard with its green grass, shade trees, and shrubs is important in many Colorado suburbs. But in the desert Southwest landscapes of Surprise and Las Vegas where the heat scorches grass and water is a precious resource, the yard takes on a different visual form. While grass remains in many yards, it seldom covers the whole expanse. Instead, grass provides a cool oasis set in the midst of decorative gravel. Trees are drought resistant rather than the more familiar elms, sycamores, and cottonwoods. Even with this shift away from the patch of green lawn, the yard and garden remain important in the image of the residential good life.

At the same time, these differences in lawns and gardens offer ways of locating the development in its own particular place. Because of the particularities of residential landscaping, developments in the desert Southwest cannot easily be mistaken for suburbs in the Midwest. The decorative gravel of Las Vegas and the drought-resistant trees and palms in front of Surprise homes root these suburbs in their particular climates, while the grassy lawns with red stone accents and hiking trails slicing through foothill ravines serve a similar purpose in Highlands Ranch. This shifting in lawnscapes is one of the crucial ways that suburbs make a claim for a sense of place. While one suburb may not be that different from another in the same town or region, there are very clear regional differences. These regional differences reflect the constraints placed by the natural world.

While the lawn—with its flowers, trees, grass, and occasionally in the backyard, a few vegetables—serves for the individual homes and homeowners a small bit of a larger pastoral living, the homes are also often sutured into a broader aesthetic of pastoralism. For example, The Grange at the Meadows at Historic Castle Rock is an explicit visual reference to an agrarian heritage. The grange is a postmodern hybrid of a farm building and a ski lodge. The tin-like roofs over the awnings, the brick red siding, and the steeply peaked roofs all reference barns and farm outbuildings. The generous use of stone, the visual centrality of the chimney, and the expansive use of glass all point toward a lodge or mountain conference center. Finally the name—The Grange—refers directly to an agricultural heritage. In fact the reference is quite specific. The word *grange*, coming from an archaic meaning of the word granary, can mean an association of farmers, the building in which the association meets, or the residence and outbuildings of a gentleman farmer. All three senses of this word are appropriate. The building allows residents to imagine themselves as middle-class farmers (perhaps they subscribe to *Hobby Farms*), the neighborhood's Homeowner Association (HOA) becomes an association of the farmers, and the building serves as an outbuilding of the homes dotting the landscape around the grange.[76] Regardless, the building materializes and aestheticizes the affective relations of the pastoral, offering the suburbanites a nostalgic connection to the earth.

An even clearer visual reference is that of the barn-like building housing the recreation center at Reunion in northeast Denver. Here the references to a barn are much more literal and unmixed than in the grange in Castle Rock. The building is red, long, and narrow with white-painted barn doors. The barn even has a brand on it—the Reunion "R"—and of course branding itself refers obliquely to cattle ranching in the West. The barn—like a Hereford—is branded, marked, and is also, at the same time, a branding image. Finally, Surprise Farms in Surprise, Arizona, uses agricultural references in its signage. On a major intersection in Surprise an apparently real, though nonfunctioning, windmill announces the development (figure 3.3).[77]

These agricultural and rural references largely disappear in the interstices of the suburban developments. Clearly some homeowners turn to western, ranch, or country for interior and exterior decoration, but neither the houses nor the streets point directly to farm styles.[78] Regardless, the con-

Figure 3.3. Surprise Farms windmill on North Cotton Lane and Bell Road. Photograph by author.

nection to the earth through farms, ranches, and estates is a major trope in naming and imaging suburbia. Combined, images of nature and agriculture create a suburban pastoral scene. These newly built suburbs draw on the long aesthetic, moral, and political history of the American pastoral to connect middle-class landowners with idealized visions of republican virtue, moral goods of self-reliance, and the leisurely ideals of retirement. Separated from the strains of urban living and the stresses of the work-a-day world, pastoral images offer idealized visions of social and material relations and thus materialize the suburban good life.

The suburban pastoral effectively and affectively brings together suburban references to time and place. As the windmill logo for Surprise Farms makes clear, the pastoral is linked to the past. The farms referenced are not the massive, agribusiness farms where tons of soybeans and corn are produced as commodities by giant machines and petrochemicals. Instead, these references—with the red barns and nineteenth- and early twentieth-century windmills—locate this landscape in the (imagined) pre–World War II family farm. The landscapes call forth images of farms built of a few acres of land, some head of cattle, a small kitchen garden, and perhaps a few chickens scratching in the backyard. This image is powerfully nostalgic, relying on the long history of the American pastoral Leo Marx writes about and central to imaging the nation. More, however, than placing the landscape in nostalgically thought time, the pastoral also places the landscapes in a nostalgically imagined place: the homestead farm, located a short ride from the farm town, somewhere in the rural but productive landscape. And so the pastoral suburb is nostalgic in the full sense of the word, expressing a bittersweet longing for home and hearth, family and farm, past and place.

Suturing suburbs into past and place are central to imaging safety; the nostalgically tinged, warmly remembered relations of past and place offer succor in an insecure and constantly changing world. Indeed, this nostalgic suturing of time and place to contemporary suburban landscapes is the central function of pastoralism.[79] Pastoralism offers not only a nostalgic rendering of the past but also locates this past in a particular vision of place, arguing that location in time and place are deeply connected. The bifurcation of time and place is better understood as an analytic tool than a lived experience.[80] This theoretical point is well made in the suburbs themselves. As I have shown, Highlands Ranch's narrative of itself is at once about history and the pastoral scene. Or, to be more precise, it is a narrative of continuous and progressive pastoralism in which the suburb is a natural growth from hunting grounds and potato farms.

Imaging Safety through Nostalgia (and Rent-a-Cop Signs)

In this final analytical section, I want to draw these strands together to indicate the ways residential enclaves weave a sense of safety into their design. One of the most important ways suburbs suggest their safety is by restraining access. Gated communities—the fastest growing form of more exclusive development in cities like Los Angeles, Las Vegas, and San Antonio— are the most militant about limiting access.[81] Typical gated developments limit access to the development to one, or at the most, two roads. A gate bars access to the development. The most exclusive form of gated development employs uniformed guards to observe the gates, less exclusive developments use codes or pass-cards to limit access. In all cases, however, the gates and the high walls that surround the development literally limit access to those granted permission. Just as important, of course, is the visual and cultural resonance of the gates. As Setha Low argues, "the logic of the symbolism satisfies conventional middle-class understandings of the nature of criminal activity . . . and justifies the choice to live in a gated community in terms of its moral and physical consequences."[82] The gates do not in fact keep out the criminals or hold down crime (the statistics of

Figure 3.4. A typical curving arterial street in suburban Las Vegas, with the stuccoed or cinder block walls separating residential streets from through traffic. Photograph by author.

otherwise similar neighborhoods bears this out), but the gates do provide an image of safety.[83]

But many suburbs—even brand new ones—are not gated. In place of actual gates, these suburban developments use stuccoed or cinder block walls surrounding the developments' perimeters and limit access from major thoroughfares to one or two entrances. Without the gates, the walls and the limited entrances perform a vision of safety (figure 3.4). Most obviously, the walls mark the boundaries between inside and outside of the residential space. At the same time, they are material ways of limiting the possible enunciations within the space. The walls limit the places through which residents and nonresidents can enter and leave the developments. Crucially, within the context of the vast emptiness of the West, the walls strive to create boundaries where once there was nearly limitless open space. And so, even as the walls may keep out unknown and undesirable individuals, the walls also carve out of emptiness spaces to be filled with the hope for community.

Carving out of emptiness the spaces for community is further emphasized by designs surrounding the entrances that pierce the protecting walls.

These entrances are typically more than simply breaks in the wall letting through cars and people. Instead, the entrances are like introductions to speeches or the ornate doors in Gothic cathedrals through which medieval worshippers walked. The entrances announce, in shorthand form, the values of the development. Here we see the return of memory. Where the walls suggest in barest form the difference between in and out, the entrance suggests what we will find once we enter the development. The signage at Mountain View, for example, is large, surrounded by grass, trees, and well-tended flowers. Here, in a thumbnail sketch, we can imagine we are entering into a space rooted in time and devoted to the pastoralism captured in the residents' yards.

Or, even more instructively, notice the south side of the intersection of North Cotton Lane and Bell Road in Surprise, Arizona (figure 3.3). On the southeast side, at the corner of one of Surprise Farms' shopping areas with its Albertsons grocery store and bevy of other services, we see a nonfunctioning windmill that serves as the development's logo. On the southwest corner, set back from the sidewalk, is a curving brick and stucco wall announcing the boundary of Surprise Farms. On the wall, in large metal letters, is written "Surprise Farms." Above the name is the development's logo—a windmill in the foreground against the Arizona hills in the background rendered in metal but reminiscent of a woodcut print or a printer's block. Extending this wall is a short, rustic-looking wooden fence. Taken together, the windmill, the name, and the entrance wall announce to the resident or visitor that s/he is entering into a pastorally constructed suburban development.

The walls and entrances do more than simply demarcate by limiting movement into and out of the space, more specifically, they frame the suburb. Like a picture frame, the walls indicate the inside and outside of the art, but also like the frame, the walls announce the nature and importance of the art contained with the frame. The pastoral framing of these entrances indicate that the safety promised by the walls is deeply connected to the ways the suburbs suture themselves into time and place. The walls not only keep out undesirable people but also strive to hold at bay the disconcerting placelessness of wholly new suburbs built on the vast spaces of the arid western landscape.

The comforts of neighborhood walls are echoed in the exterior design of suburban houses. Take for instance the consistent—even pathological—repeating of the hidden entrances of the suburban homes. In nearly every house in these suburbs, the front doors are recessed behind jutting two- and three-car garages.[84] It is easy to understand the prominence of the garage

Figure 3.5. Typical of Surprise, Arizona, suburban homes, this house combines the se-cluded door hidden by a decorative arch and behind a jutting garage all protected by the blue ADT sign. Photograph by author.

in the contemporary suburban home as a privileging of automobiles. As reasonable as this interpretation is, just as important but more subtle is the importance of the massive, blank garage to creating a bulwark of safety between private and public. Meanwhile, even as the garage has grown more important visually, the porch has shifted from the quasi-public space of the front of the house into the deck on the back of the house hidden by a privacy fence. The doors are often further hidden by decorative arches, well-established trees or palms, or, in some cases, by locking, wrought-iron gates. The final crucial maneuvers involve the ubiquitous ADT and West-corp signs promising swift, armed response to potential threats (figure 3.5).

What I hope is clear is that safety is a visual and material rhetoric that relies in part on visually cordoning off individual developments from the larger suburban and urban scene. Safety and security is as dependent on the ways the suburbs are sutured into time and place as it is reliant on the restrictions and constraints of movement created by the walls, entrances, curving streets, and hidden doors. Safety becomes a vision and a perfor-mance reliant not only on crime statistics or on shifting social relations, but rather on an assertion of secured space—space that is secured through walls and rent-a-cops, through nature and memory, and through the powerfully resonant imagining of suburbs as agrarian and pastoral.

The Affective Aesthetics of Safety

The aesthetic of safety, then, is a complex weaving of material and symbolic gestures to locality produced by appeals to memory, nature and the pastoral, and a literal and figural walling off of the house and the neighborhood from the larger world. Locality as formulated in the housing development can be thought through the spatial and natural metaphor of roots. As Joan Faber McAlister argues and as my analysis of both marketing materials and architectural practices indicates, this rooting situates homes in memory. Appeals to idealized visions of past homes and connections to historical US American and European architecture work to situate homes in a warmly remembered past. Connecting home building to memory is a literalization of nostalgia or the longing for home. Nostalgia expresses the disease and discomfort of being uprooted from home. At the same time, the appeals to memory in the new homes strive to take on vestiges of memory that can express and cover the longings.

Nostalgia, at least in its formulations in the eighteenth and nineteenth centuries, was a deeply place-based longing. Soldiers, hundreds of miles from home, longed not just for their childhood but for their childhood homes.[85] Likewise the attempted rooting of the suburbs also depends on a set of place-based appeals. There are at least two to consider carefully. First, as I have argued, many suburbs make appeals to nature. In advertisements and marketing, many developments are imagined in the center of forests or in the midst of meadows with pine trees surrounding the neighborhoods and rising mountains in the background. In other developments, natural areas and open spaces honeycomb the space, bringing nature closer to home. Second, by itself, nature cannot fully express and respond to nostalgic longings. In fact, the vast open spaces of the West can raise the sense of the uncanny and nostalgia to new heights. In the place of wild nature and untamed open space, suburbs bend nature to human need through the pastoral. Windmills, granges, barns, and the constant repetition of agriculturally based place names (Highlands Ranch, Surprise Farms) sew the houses into a pastorally imagined landscape. This pastoralism is literalized in the yards, trees, picket fences, and home gardens central to the suburban spatial imagination and landscape. This pastoral not only remakes nature in the image of humans but is also a remembered image, for the pastoral offered in these landscapes is that of the middle-class farmer, of Jeffersonian republicanism, and of a polity and community situated in the eighteenth and nineteenth centuries.[86]

Crucially, however, this pastoralism also serves as a doubled barricading of suburban developments from immediate, regional, and global neighbors. First, there is a walling off of the present by situating the suburban developments securely in the past. The memories offered and engaged in these spaces are not designed to open residents to new possibilities or imagine new ways of making homes, but rather to create spaces in which there is a hope of return to a simpler and clearer past. In this sense suburbs are, at least in their built form and imaginary, literalizations of contemporary neoconservativism.[87] But suburban pastoralism is also a barring in a second way, for it depends on separating each house from the next through (often very small) yards and each grouping of yards separated from other developments, nearby cities, and the larger world by fences, walls, and gates. The aesthetics of safety depend on this blockading of the world. From the hidden doorways fronted with iron gates and Westcorp rent-a-cop signs to the ten-feet-tall stucco walls surrounding many developments, these suburbs imagine themselves as safe from danger because they are separated from the excruciatingly scary world outside. Setha Low, in her study of gated communities in the United States and Latin America, notes that residents' fear of crime drove them to the gated communities. For many residents discussions of crime quickly transformed into discussions of class and race. "Desire for safety, security, community, and 'niceness,'" Low writes, "as well as wanting to live near people like themselves because of a fear of 'others' and of crime," is a central concern for the residents of gated communities.[88] The dialectic of crime and safety serves as an alibi and justification for suburbanites' living choices, as many residents recognize that their decisions indicate a fear of diversity even as they desire to see themselves as open to "others."[89] In a similar way, the public messages of these suburbs encoded in their marketing materials as well as produced through the European and middle-American architecture all emphasize homogeneity of aesthetics and of the kinds of people invited to pass through the suburban walls.[90] Fears of the challenging world figured as fear of crime motivate the material rhetoric of the suburban development.

Together, roots and walls serve as powerful topoi for imagining, performing, and materializing a very particular suburban good life. This is a suburban good life that constitutes and is constituted by the home's interiority:[91] the interior of the home guarded by hidden doors and private security signs; the interior of the development guarded by culs-de-sac, limited entrances, and walls; and the interior of the past separated from the concerns of the present or the future by constant appeals to heritage and to the pastoral. This fetishization of the interior (and of a very particular exterior environment) turns not only on the valuing of the inside but also on the expulsion of the outside. The walls keep out and keep in, the iron gates repel and attract. Instead of the permeability Bachelard imagined, there is a rigidification of the difference between in and out, a rigidification that is literalized by limiting the numbers of roads or sidewalks that can pierce the walls of the development.

The constant separating of the inner from the outer home begins to help us see the rhetoric of the good life these suburbs offer. Rather than offering permeability, accessibility, and reciprocity of the sustaining outwardly directed home, many suburban developments are filled with houses that are inaccessible, isolated, and fragmented.[92] Imagined as comforting and safe, these homes offer a public message of separation and disengagement. As such, they literalize the suburb as a site of individual and familial continuity at the expense of connectedness, openness, and porosity. If the good house is a site that can protect from the ravages of the world's storms so that the residents can engage the world beyond, these houses offer a limited, thin, and denuded vision of this ideal home. Here roots support single trees and small gardens, and the walls are penetrated by few doors and breached by few entrances.

This limiting vision of the relation between inside and out is justified by and depends on a cultural attraction to the idea and instantiation of home. This longing for home is directly connected to the opportunities and challenges of finding ourselves. "Our love of home," Alain de Botton writes, is "an acknowledgment of the degree to which our identity is not self-determined. We need a home in the psychological sense as much as we need one in the physical: to compensate for a vulnerability. We need a refuge to shore up our states of mind, because so much of the world is opposed to our allegiances. We need our rooms to align us to desirable versions of ourselves and to keep alive the important, evanescent sides of us."[93]

For de Botton, home—and architecture more broadly—enunciates and enables our best selves and our vision for an ideal life. At the same time, the home provides sanctuary for the self.[94] Confronted by the realization that our selves are multiple and often fragmented, we seek in our houses and homes space that can comfort and contain us, that can "align us to desirable versions of ourselves." The desirable version of selves enunciated in the housing developments studied here are selves that are deeply wary of the world, worried about the world's storms, and afraid of the consequences of engaging with and living next to others who may be illegible and unknown.

Roots and walls imagined within aesthetics of the pastoral and nostalgia are very particular ways of locating the self in place and time, ways that shut out, close off, and reject difference. They are also powerful responses to the anxieties of the contemporary age. In the face of the unrootedness that leads to the dis-ease of nostalgia are offered nostalgically limned pasts. In the milieu of the unhomeliness of the modern city and modern world, houses are walled from other houses, subdivisions from other subdivisions, new suburbs from older suburbs, and both of those from the city. In the context of modern agoraphobia linked to the vast spaces of the urban plaza and the modern interstate, the suburb offers culs-de-sac, curving roads, and carefully maintained trails and pocket parks.

This then is the affective aesthetics of safety. As suburban topoi, these aesthetics address fear of crime most apparently but also the anxieties expressed in uncanniness, nostalgia, and agoraphobia. But these aesthetics resonate in an affective as much as a cognitive or symbolic register. Certainly the windmill on the corner to the entrance of Surprise Farms functions symbolically, standing in for an older western landscape and the pastoral vision. But it can also register in a split second without referring outside of itself as the symbol would do.[95] The windmill can, in an instant, evoke the security and comfort of the pastoral. It can literalize the sense of roots proposing in one quick gesture the possibilities of fecundity and the (re)production of a comforting sense of place.[96] The windmill does not gesture beyond itself; it does not have a meaningful or symbolic telos other than its immediate, instantaneous weaving together of suburban landscape, space, subject, and body. Likewise, the walls, gates, hidden doors, green lawns, and culs-de-sac constitutive of contemporary suburbs do not only argue for safety and they do not primarily symbolize security. Instead they write on the retina and the skin the moral worth of the landscape. They materialize with intensity the safety, security, and locality they also symbolize.[97]

In fact, it is extraordinarily crucial that this aesthetic of safety symbolizes and materializes safety. Symbols always gesture outside of themselves and always differ from and defer the thing for which they stand. The topoi of walls and roots are more powerful if they are not only symbolic, if they do not only gesture beyond themselves. The suburban material rhetoric is profoundly interior to both space and time, offering safety and security in this moment, not later, and in this place, not some other.[98] As such, these design elements and the suburban residents function something in a way that is reminiscent of Jane Bennett's partial collapse between subject and object. This collapse recognizes that humans and other objects in the world are assemblages of materials. The walls, yards, gates, garages, windmills, and suburban residents "are various materialities constantly engaged in a network of relations."[99] It is in this network of material and agent-full relations that humans and the suburban landscape intertwine. And for the human, at least, this intertwining touches the soul at an almost autonomic and affective level.[100] And so, suburban developments create an affective aesthetic of safety responsive to material and psychological opportunities and threats by turning inward, downward, and backward; by building walls and growing roots.

Of course this turning in, down, and back has consequences. As McAlister argues, the post-9/11 vision of the US American home "excludes other times and other places" and "foreclose[s] opportunities to critically examine the when and where of democratic deliberation."[101] Foreclosed and forgotten is violence against women located within the suburban house; the cruelty of poverty often located in the city, the countryside, and the suburbs; the violence meted out on men, women, and children in the name of the global war on terror. A sight and a site of security, these homes and neighborhoods also embody troubling relations between inside and outside, between locality and globality, between homogeneity and heterogeneity.

But there is also a recognition in the suburbs that this particular version of walling and rooting is not sufficient for a good life. While it provides protection from the world's storms, it does not offer the richness necessary to feed the suburban soul. The suburbs also express and embody the need to reach out to the world, a desire to connect with identities other than and spaces different from their own. The desire to extend out from the home into the world is expressed and materialized in the suburban chain restaurant. Serving as the suburbs' kitchens, these restaurants often offer the "world on a plate" and serve as a second way that suburbs strive to locate suburbanites in the world.[102] I turn next to these restaurants.

4
Eating the Good Life
Authenticity, Exoticism, and Rhetoric's Embodied Materiality
in the Italian-Themed Suburban Restaurant

> Every alimentary custom makes up a minuscule crossroads of histo-
> ries. In the "invisible everyday," under the silent and repetitive system
> of everyday servitudes that one carries out by habit, the mind elsewhere,
> in a series of mechanically executed operations whose sequence follows
> a traditional design dissimulated under the mask of the obvious, there
> piles up a subtle montage of gestures, rites, and codes, of rhythms and
> choices, of received usage and practiced customs.
>
> —Luce Giard

> There is something very soothing about sharing a meal. Just think about
> the phrase "having a place at the table." I think if you have a place at the
> table—which can be extrapolated as a metaphor for your place in the
> world—it helps you feel a little more grounded. . . . I worry about kids
> who are eating standing up or next to the microwave—where are they
> finding out how to fit into the world?
>
> —Marialisa Calta

The contemporary suburban home is devoted to roots and walls. And yet,
as I suggested in the previous chapter, this particular inward, downward,
and backward vision of community is unsatisfactory. As Gaston Bachelard and Alain de Botton argue, the beautiful and securing home is a retreat and a sanctuary, but it should also be the foundation from which its
residents can stretch out into the broader world. For polemicist and cookbook author Marialisa Calta, this securing and extending is modeled and
taught during family dinner. Family dinners where parents and children
have "a place at the table," help each family member to feel "a little more
grounded."[1] Calta is worried about how children are going to imagine their
place in a difficult and challenging world, and she offers the family dinner
and the family dinner table as one solution to these difficulties. Calta's assertion of the importance of the family dinner articulates with the culturally held ideal of families, dinners, and homes. In this vision—much like
the vision I explored in the previous chapter—the home and the home's

table provides the secure grounding that makes possible careful engagement with the broader world. As I will explore in this chapter, suburban
chain restaurants work hard to link into this well-worn narrative structure.

In fact, the family dinner table is an idealized vision of both home and
family, and many families share evening meals at home one or more times
a week. Although the family dinner has a strong hold on the middle-class
imagination, the number of family dinners shared per week has been slowly
dropping over the last fifteen years, while the number of meals eaten away
from the house has increased.[2] Meanwhile, family members, including adults
and children, express a desire to eat meals together more often, seeing family
meals as central performances of family life, a time when children and
adults share their days.[3]

Contemporary suburban chain restaurants are at the nexus of these coun-
tervailing trends and desires. To the desire for more time to eat together
as a family, suburban restaurants offer a dining room away from home. To
the increasing demands on family life, the suburban restaurant presents the
convenience of dining out. Appealing directly to families and family life,
postwar chain restaurants inserted themselves into suburban culture and
have become distinctly suburban spaces. By intersecting with family life
and growing consumer culture, the chain restaurant is a prototypically suburban space, depending on and partially constituting the suburban landscape. Suburban restaurants are important because they serve as a crucial
material and affective node in suburban family life. They offer relational
and caloric sustenance. But chain restaurants are also important to the suburban landscape and the suburban good life because they are compelling
spaces through which suburbs acknowledge and negotiate globalization.[4]
The restaurants I am investigating here offer to suburbanites a circumscribed but affectively powerful mode for experiencing the world beyond
the suburbs' gates. For Calta the family dinner helps children "figure out
their place in the world," presumably by sewing children into the fabric
of the family. From the family and the home, she suggests, individuals can
move into the world around them with a better understanding of themselves and their place. If the domestic landscapes' response to the pres-
sures of globalization is through roots and walls and, in Calta's vision, dinner tables, chain restaurants offer a differently imagined relationship to the
forces of globalization. Restaurants stretch from the interior of the home
into globalized flows, a stretching that is at once obvious and hidden in the
food itself. The food appears on plates and the wine in glasses from across
the globe, a fact the restaurants will frequently produce as a material or
symbolic provenance for the food. Indeed, as Ian Cook and Philip Crang

argue, contemporary food practices offer "the world on a plate."[5] This material metaphor is resonant, for it indicates the powerful ways restaurants extend and bound their offered experiences.

Investigating these restaurants as global institutions inserted into local spaces, I begin to understand how "globally extensive networks and flows of foods, people, and culinary knowledge are being locally articulated," and, further, how these material, rhetorical, and performative articulations matter in suburbs.[6] In fact, the restaurants under investigation here imagine extension into the world through consistent material and symbolic referencing of global cuisines with particular emphasis on Italy. At the same time, much of the costs and consequences of these global flows are hidden behind walls and are bound by the edges of the dinner plates. Exploring these restaurants will provide me with an opportunity to more carefully and concretely investigate the ways the suburban landscape embeds suburbanites in carefully imagined and materialized global networks.

By offering an image and materialization of home and the world and by doing so through food, suburban restaurants stage the opportunity for diners to fully engage all of their senses in the negotiation of a suburban identity. Suburban restaurants make possible the incorporation (literally, taking into the body, the corpus) of suburban identity. In restaurants, eyes read the menu and gaze on the decorations; noses sniff the wine and smell the melting cheese; ears hear the carefully selected background music and listen to the dinner conversation; hands reach for the garlic bread and feel the texture of the cloth napkins; mouths take in the food, tasting its flavors, examining its textures, experiencing its warmth.[7] All the senses are engaged, and the entire body is part of the performances offered and structured by the restaurant. While these restaurants depend on globalized networks of food procurement and production and use globalized financial and labor flows for material support, at the moment of the meal all of these practices are radically localized, drilling all the way down to the individual's body. If the residential neighborhood can offer powerful rhetorics of locality that suture individuals into warmly remembered time and place, how much more powerful might be the opportunity to eat this locality? Indeed, the chain restaurants I investigate here are deeply rhetorical performances that work hard to bring body, self, home, suburb, and globe into alignment. This alignment is performed though an abundant presentation of food, the creation of already familiar pastoral images of home, and spectacular enactments of ethnicity, which provide a compelling and apparently rich mode by which to experience globality.[8]

In the first section of this chapter I will argue that food and food practices are particularly resonant ways of locating the body in reference to an idea of home and also in the context of globalization. Because of the intimacy of food and because of the ways we imagine food and home together, food practices are often laden with the kinds of nostalgia constitutive of the contemporary suburb. In the second section of the chapter, I will turn to Italian themed, suburban restaurants to explore the ways restaurants and their food practices offer a compellingly embodied rhetoric of locality that depends on visions of an ethnic other to ground their images of comforting locality.[9] I will intersect this analysis of Italian food with an analysis of American-themed suburban restaurants as a way of exploring the importance of nostalgia and home in creating embodied rhetorics that align the self, the suburb, and the globe. In the final section of the chapter, I broaden my critical lens to explore the suburban topoi offered in the restaurants and how these topoi enliven and reinforce the embodied experience offered in residential developments.

Food, Home, and Nostalgia

Perhaps there is no single human activity that brings together everyday practices, consumption, materiality, and embodiment more completely than does eating.[10] It is not surprising that volume two of Michel de Certeau's path-clearing *Practices of Everyday Life* focuses particular attention on food shopping and cooking.[11] Nor is it surprising that, in Pierre Bourdieu's influential *Distinction*, everyday food practices serve as deeply embedded structures that mark and shape class distinctions.[12] For Claude Lévi-Strauss, myths of cooking serve as hinges on which kinship swings.[13] Mary Douglas argues that food and eating are crucial ways of thinking about the pure and impure, the safe and the dangerous.[14] In one of the epigraphs that start this chapter, Luce Giard poetically invokes the deeply quotidian nature of familial food preparation. "Dissimulated under the mask of the obvious," she writes, "there piles up a subtle montage of gestures, rites, and codes, of rhythms and choices, of received usage and practiced customs."[15] These gestures, rites, codes, rhythms, and choices are the warp and woof of the city, of familial life, and of an embodied culture of acquiescence and resistance.[16] Food, then, becomes yet another way of making, constructing, and consuming the good life.

Food and food practices are profoundly intimate and are first learned and made sense of in the home. The earliest requests we make and the earliest desires we express involve food. Starting with nursing and slowly moving toward more social food practice, eating is connected to care, care giving, and the intimacy of familial relations. In the contemporary United States, food and food practices are deeply intertwined with family and all the powerful social connections family implies. The most important US family holidays—Christmas and Thanksgiving—are imagined around the home's table laden with rich food.[17] Similarly, many, though certainly not all, of the shows on the popular cable channel the Food Network place food in the home and the preparation of food as a primary way for (women) to take care of their families.[18] Throughout this popular discourse on connecting food to home and family runs the idea that dinner time with the family holds a very special place in socialization.[19] Calta sums up this attitude in an interview with Catholic Online, "There is something very soothing about sharing a meal. Just think about the phrase 'having a place at the table.' I think if you have a place at the table—which can be extrapolated as a metaphor for your place in the world—it helps you feel a little more grounded. . . . I worry about kids who are eating standing up or next to the microwave—where are they finding out how to fit into the world?"[20] Calta moves fluidly and quickly from dinner table to home to world. In the home and at the dinner table we generate a powerful sense of how to fit into the world, and we learn to be at home in globalized space.

While Calta places the family dinner table at the center of feeling at home in the world, food takes on even broader functions for negotiating our relationship to the world and to others. Whether thinking about food within the context of the environment and sustainability, health and obesity, globalization and localization, food has become a nexus of crucial conversations about our most intimate and embodied selves and our most social and abstract identities.[21] As Elspeth Probyn writes, "In eating, we grapple with concerns about the animate and the inanimate, about authenticity and sincerity, about changing familial patterns, about the local rendered global."[22] Probyn captures many of the impulses that seem to drive contemporary discussions of food. Images of and concerns about authenticity, family, local, global are all wound together in the everyday and banal practices of feeding ourselves.

Of course we have seen these same concerns in residential neighborhoods. But, while residential neighborhoods offer images of home, place, or history, meals can offer materializations and embodiments of home, place, and history. In a glass of wine, cup of tea, or a mug of coffee, drinkers can taste the terroir of the drink.[23] Cookbooks that focus on traditional southern, Creole, or soul cooking provide cooks and their families with the promise of connecting to time and geography.[24] High-end grocery stores like Whole Foods rely on rhetorics of authenticity and locality to help make more concrete the global networks that move food from across the world into the pantries and refrigerators of individual homes.[25] Food, in its concrete materiality and in its corporeal consumability, necessarily offers embodied social structures and, more importantly for my purposes, can connect us to home as a geographic, social, and interpersonal space.[26] This connecting to home is also offered as a way of connecting to the world, of bringing the world into our bodies and of extending our bodies into the world. Thus food's potential as an expression of locality and nostalgia is rich. Already and almost inherently connected to home, to childhood, and to tradition food and food practices can evoke connections to place, family, and history.

At the same time, food is increasingly produced as a commodity and traded in global markets. Many of us are abstracted from and ignorant about the ways food actually moves from farm to table.[27] This ignorance is not purely accidental or simply a by-product of globalization. Instead, both our ignorance and knowledge about food are socially produced. As Ian Cook and Philip Crang argue, knowledge about food is "bound up with a 'double' commodity fetishism: that on the one hand limits consumers' knowledge about the spatially distanciated systems of provision through which food commodities come to us; but, on the other, and at the same time, also puts an increased emphasis on geographical knowledges about those widely sourced food commodities."[28] By the time grain is made into cereal, packaged in boxes, shipped to the local supermarket, and poured into a bowl with milk whose journey onto the table is equally mysterious, food can lose its ability to evoke home and suture individuals into their place in the world. More importantly, this commodification of food turns food into an object that raises the anxieties of late modernity. Rampant food scares—E. coli in peanut butter, spinach, sprouts, and hamburgers, for example—consistently remind us that our food travels in unknown circuits and can pick up deadly pathogens along the way.

Discourses of food nostalgia make perfect sense within this context where food evokes home and at the same time raises the problems of globalization. Food nostalgia serves to "'re-enchant' (food) commodities and to differentiate them from the devalued functionality and homogeneity of standardized products, tastes and places."[29] This re-enchantment depends on what Cook and Crang call "geographic knowledges"; that is, knowledge of the places, spaces, and environments of the production of food.[30] Recognizing that food has never been pure or exclusively local, we can see food "not only as placed cultural artefacts, but also as dis-placed, inhabiting many times and spaces which, far from being neatly bounded bleed into and indeed mutually constitute each other."[31] The nostalgia offered in much food discourse recognizes, utilizes, and responds to this displacement across time and place. In particular, food nostalgia seeks to locate food and its consumer through major themes of ethnicity and family, both of which can offer comforting images of time and place.

Of course, this food nostalgia responds to particular kinds of concerns. The successes of modern capitalism, argues Diane Negra, seem to tear at the fabric of traditional familial life. With its bigger houses, unending consumer goods, and easy mobility across space and time, modern capitalism has stripped many of familiar social relationships. Responding to the sense that current culture abstracts white US Americans from place and time, recent interest in ethnic food exhibits a desire for more concrete roots. Negra argues that popular culture food texts like films and restaurant ads "exaggerate ethnic food as a sensual, reproducible sign of a mode of ethnic kinship that is simultaneously mourned, romanticized, and nostalgically reenacted in popular culture. Food stands in for a way of life our contemporary culture has largely left behind and that we now identify with an American immigrant past and with cultures other than our own. . . . Food . . . is a conduit through which we invent, claim, and perform a sense of heritage from which we have become alienated in other ways."[32] While dinners at home may provide children with a sense of their place in the world, images of otherness in prepared food and restaurants can also serve as a way of restitching (white) US Americans into more concrete social relations.

Indeed, from the Budweiser "wassup" ads to recent food films like *Chocolat*, *Like Water for Chocolate*, and *Woman on Top*, images of nonwhite, non–US American others serves to reimagine and solidify white privilege.[33] For example, by utilizing and universalizing a presumed authentic expression of black masculinity, Budweiser's wassup beer commercial, "Constitutes and administers cultural 'authenticity' as a market value. . . . The intensity of the pleasure of consuming the other is directly (and paradoxically) related to the replication and magnification of 'authentic' difference."[34] In a similar way, food films "use food to engage and assuage anxieties attendant to contemporary cultural ambiguities and permeabilities, especially around race/ethnicity and gender." The films, Helene Shugart continues, "Offer food as a rhetorical device through which discourses of privilege are reconciled with and reestablished against contemporary practices of desire and consumption, especially (and increasingly) for and of the 'Other.'"[35] Food, images of food, and practices surrounding the growing and preparing of food present the possibility of authenticity drawn from images of and imaginations about more authentic Others stripped of disturbing and confounding difference and turned into a sign of authenticity.[36]

Contemporary scholarship on food suggests that food and food practices are powerfully embodied topoi for thinking and performing contemporary culture. Linked in material, social, and interpersonal ways to the home, food at once raises and assuages desires for home. Connected to region and geography, food can help people imagine their place in the world. Arising out of the embodied and historical practices of food communities, food can suture individuals into comforting ethnic relationships. Finally, as a form of incorporation, food offers the possibility of taking into the body the visual and tactile rhetorics of locality offered in residential neighborhoods. In the face, then, of the abstractions of globalization outlined in chapter 1, food and food practices offer fully embodied and performative rhetorics of locality.

The Suburban Dinner Table

In suburbia these embodied food performances often occur in the homes themselves. For more middle-class suburban families, the family meal is taken in the suburban restaurant rather than around the family dining table.[37] The "gestures, rites, and codes . . . rhythms and choices of received usage and practiced customs"[38] of suburban eating are often performed within the rituals of going out to eat. Indeed, over the last five decades the proportion of food dollars spent on *away from home* to *in home* food has nearly doubled. In 1950, about 25 percent of US families' food dollars were spent away from home. By 2005, nearly 50 percent of US food dollars were spent away from home.[39] On average, nearly 4 percent of individuals' annual income will be spent in full-service restaurants, and families eat nearly six meals a week away from home.[40] In short, eating out has become a crucial part of US American lives.

Suburban chain restaurants are not only important because of the amount of money and time suburbanites spend in them, but because chain restaurants are a constitutive suburban landscape and thus are central to thinking carefully about suburban living. Just as the mall and the suburb constitute each other so too do chain restaurants and suburbia. While the first chain restaurants like Howard Johnson's appeared well before World War II, their growth became exponential after the 1950s. The growth of the chain restaurant coincides with the growth of consumer culture more generally and the growth of increasingly self-reliant suburbs. By the 1950s, suburbs began to offer improved opportunities for work and built more complex and complete communal infrastructures, including more places to eat.[41]

Perhaps the most important of 1950s suburban restaurant was the mass-produced, though individually owned, diner. Before World War II, the prefabricated diners successfully offered meals to workers in inner-city, ethnic neighborhoods. Offering quick, relatively inexpensive, and ethnically specific meals served over the counter, these early diners fed men as they traveled between home and work. In the postwar world, diners repositioned themselves as more generically American and appealing to suburban family appetites through menu, architectural, and marketing shifts, all of which deemphasized ethnic specificity and appealed to returning Victorian familial values.[42] Meanwhile, nearly 40 percent of women worked outside of the home, and so diners were able to make themselves places that could provide traditional family meals without women cooking in the home. These diners, with their shifts to more homogenized aesthetics and menus, presaged the rise of chain restaurants that applied the lessons learned in the remarketing of the diner to create branded and, in many ways, generic eating spaces.[43] But the diners and the growing chain restaurants and the welter of other suburban consumer spaces served crucial links between modern and late modern modes of living. As Andrew Hurley argues, "In the supermarkets, automobile showrooms, drive-in movie theaters, and fast food franchises of the commercial strip, American consumers encountered the products and services that redefined mainstream consumer culture. And there retailers and manufacturers forged a new consumer culture that both finessed and exploited emerging and eroding social distinctions."[44] Thus, even as the mall was remaking shopping, in the postwar suburban restaurants, diners and fast food franchises were remaking US American ways of eating.

The Return of Ethnicity and the Embodiment of Suburban Restaurants

While the immediate postwar suburban restaurant strove to empty its food and space of the localizing aesthetics of ethnicity, by the end of the twentieth century mass-produced chain restaurant food returned to ethnicity with a vengeance. "In place of the 'traditional'" US American diet, there "emerged a strong emphasis on culinary multiculturalism and the ability to pleasurably claim ethnicity through food consumption. The relative decline of a monolithic U.S. cuisine in the 1990s suggested a fracturing of

consensus about the meanings of positive Americanism."[45] Suburban restaurants were not simply replacing the home dinner table. Instead, by the
1990s these restaurants were also offering an embodied experience of multiculturalism, or at least multiculturalism as imagined by global capital.

The aestheticized ethnicity of the suburban restaurants responds directly
to the problems of locating ourselves in time and place. Just as in late modernity it is difficult to locate ourselves in time and place so to it is difficult to locate a natural body behind the technologies and cultures of the
extended corpus. Our bodies are reshaped by plastic surgery; made stronger
by hormones; made (to) fit through detailed exercise regimens; and enabled
to reproduce or not reproduce with pills, implants, and test tubes. Our
moods are altered by licit and illicit drugs, while our imaginations about
the good body are formed and reformed by a constant production of discourses about our bodies.[46] Increasingly, the body we experience is extended through "institutional, semantic, and technological structures that
produce the body in culturally significant relations of power and meaning."[47] The body is shaped by technology, refracted through images, and
(re)produced in networks of power. But this does not mean the body dis-
appears in late modernity. Instead, rather than functioning as an ontological grounding for identity it is a site through and with which subjectivity is
enacted and enunciated.[48] And this enactment is always an enactment that
depends on and produces space.[49] The subject is both embodied and emplaced, for the subject goes nowhere without its body and the body must
always be a space of its appearance.

The domestic landscapes explored in the previous chapter protect suburban bodies with walls and roots. Cafés, bars, and restaurants can be even
more powerful in this process of sewing the body into time and place. In
these places of eating and drinking, we most clearly and directly address
our bodies. In restaurants we talk about, read about, and consume food.
For example, we might say an especially rich dessert is to die for. We mean
this, of course, metaphorically (here is food that is so good I might have it
as my last meal). But we also reference our embodied sexuality (this food
is like the "small death" of an orgasm). And we are also if indirectly, referencing what we fear is a fact (the fatty, salty, abundant food passing my
lips leads to my obesity, to my lack of fitness, to my approaching mortality).
Here lies a fundamental paradox of the chain restaurant (and, perhaps, of
suburbia). Even as we recognize that our ever-growing girth is detrimental
to our health, we return again and again to restaurants that offer the embodied comforts of fat, salt, sweet, and abundance.[50]

But, as Cook and Crang point out, we want "the world on a plate."[51] The world is a big place, awesome in its distances and abstract when imagined as "the world." But when we enmesh our embodied desires and fears in the sensual aesthetics of ethnicity, we raise the possibility of the ethnic, raced, and historic body. Here might be a body bound by the traditions and genetics of a people, place, and time. Here are images of families rooted in communities, ingrained in geographies, and embedded in histories. As we will see, the plentifully flowing pasta makes concretely abundant our embodied suburban identities. The differences that can enliven suburbia and sketch our place in the world are served to us in wine glasses and salad bowls. We can take the world into us through our mouths, ears, and noses.

Spectacular Places

Within this context of placeless suburbs, embodied subjectivity, and the hope that we can find our place in the world around the family dinner table, Olive Garden, Macaroni Grill, and other suburban restaurants make sense. Olive Garden and Macaroni Grill materialize ethnicities and families in ways that directly respond to suburban familial concerns and, at the same time, oppose the trends of late modernity to produce the generic spaces that can smooth the flow of globalization. Generic spaces are thin and stretched out as they make little reference to the specific time and place of their creation and enactment. They are extended—almost infinitely— through geography and history.[52] Generic spaces also rely on simple aesthetic forms (a color or two, a word or two) that can be easily recognized and reproduced over time and space and which, because of their simplicity and thinness, appeal to wider-ranging audiences. Even as these generic spaces make sense in the context of globalizing marketing, they do not make for particularly appealing places to eat or live. What is more, this aesthetic thinness runs the opposite direction from the need to find places for bodies.

In contrast to thin, generic space, the imagination of the good life offered by the Olive Garden and Macaroni Grill is of abundance and place. Many chain and local restaurants could serve as the sites for this investigation, since in fact, the purely generic spaces of the late twentieth century seem to be losing their appeal.[53] Olive Garden and Macaroni Grill will serve as representative anecdotes of the twined cultural impulses to serve the world on a plate and to suture diners into warmly remembered and geographically rooted social relations. In short, Olive Garden and Macaroni Grill embody and perform the central topoi of contemporary sub-

urban restaurants—namely, abundance and a fully embodied form of nostalgia striving the give home a place—and thus are good places to start an
argument about suburban dining.

Abundance

One marker of many middle-class restaurants is the emphasis on quantity
of food offered for the price paid. For example, the urban and then suburban diner offered to its working-class and then middle-class customers
large simple meals for a small price. Indeed, to pry families from their
homes for meals, the restaurants had to assert their value. The most obvious
way the restaurants here signify abundance is through the abundance of
food itself. Olive Garden famously offers endless bowls of mixed green
salad and basket after basket of hot garlicky bread. Endless salad is occasionally joined at the Olive Garden by the "never ending pasta bowl." This
endless-food form of abundance emphasizes value through quantity, sat-
ing bodily desire through eating to capacity. The abundance implied by
the never-ending salad and pasta is reinforced by an abundance of choice,
as the menu is large and varied and, to make even more choices available,
offers customers the chance to design their own repast.

Compare this endless abundance to Macaroni Grill's abundance. Macaroni Grill does not offer endless bowls of salad or pasta. Instead, customers
can design their own pasta and choose from a large menu of salads, soups,
pastas, pizza, meat, seafood, dessert, and drinks. And then there are the giant
bottles of wine. If ordered, house Chianti is brought to the diners' table in
a large bottle along with small, simple glasses. The diners pour the wine for
themselves and, at the end of meal, tell the waiter how many glasses were
consumed. The wine is cheap and nearly endless. While this not an "all
you can drink" form of abundance since each glass must be paid for, there
is a signal of abundance through the size of the bottle and the fact that the
diners neither have to pay for the whole bottle (as they would if they ordered a bottle of wine from the wine list), nor do they have to order additional glasses from the wait staff.

Like the never-ending pasta bowl, this is a semiotics of abundance; however, it is an abundance that appeals to different values. Macaroni Grill's
abundance of wine rather than pasta is an adult indulgence and less appropriate for children. Even more important, this abundance appeals to consumers who pair wine and food, a pairing that, in the United States, anyway,
specifies the audience even more clearly. Wine consumption in the United
States is connected to particular structures of cultural capital. Where in

France, Spain, or Italy wine accompanies meals of families from all classes, wine as part of the meal is far less frequent in the United States. Thus, this abundance also serves to call forth a particular audience that identifies with continental dining, thereby connecting rhetorics of abundance with that of time and place.

While Italian themed restaurants offer an abundance of wine and pasta, American themed restaurants offer their own versions of gustatory abundance. At the sit-down hamburger restaurant Red Robin, the never-ending salad bowl is replaced by bottomless French fries, and build your own pasta is replaced by a build your own burger menu.[54] On the Red Robin website, the burger menu asserts, "Our gourmet burgers and sandwiches go on and on and on."[55] The restaurants also often advertise specials that increase the amount of food you might eat. In early 2010, for example, TGI Friday's offered a starter, main course, and dessert for $12.99. Not only could customers purchase "three full courses" for a set price, but they could also choose from "over 300 combinations."[56] Restaurant after restaurant offers these kinds of mix-and-match deals that offer the double abundance of food and choice.

But abundance in these restaurants goes beyond the amount of food or drink one can consume in the space. This gustatory copiousness is located within large, often meandering buildings that are imposing and colorful from the outside and minutely detailed on the inside. The exteriors of Olive Gardens and Macaroni Grills are rustic and relatively complex. Olive Garden entrances are often set in the midst of carefully designed landscaping, fronted on each side by large terra-cotta planters and wrought-iron benches and chairs (figure 4.1). The entrance itself is set into heavy, large stone walls and shaded by an overhanging tile roof. Beside and just above the front doors are old-styled lamps that match the lighting of many of the lifestyle centers and strip malls in which the restaurants are located. Indeed, these restaurants integrate with the design of the larger landscape of many lifestyle centers even as the restaurant exteriors are often far more detailed and specific in their references. Where a lifestyle center may incorporate some stone in strategically located settings, the restaurants make much heavier use of the stone and tile than their surroundings. What is more, the footprint of the restaurant is often more complex than the gussied-up boxes surrounding them in the local strips and lifestyle centers. Restaurants are, in short, more copious in their styling.

While I will return to the ways in which these exteriors gesture to place and time, for now it is enough to note how the exteriors announce a copiousness to be found within the restaurants' walls. Perhaps nothing makes

Figure 4.1. Olive Garden in Northglenn, Colorado. Heavy stone walls, tile roofs, and the three-dimensional grapes spilling toward the door announce the restaurant's copiousness. Photograph by author.

this relationship between the design of the exterior and the quantity of food to be found inside as clearly as Olive Garden's signs over the main entrance. In the sign, large purple grapes spill down the right side of the logo, looking like a vintner's version of the Thanksgiving horn of plenty. The abundance implied by suburban restaurant exteriors is not limited to the two Italian-themed restaurants under consideration here. The oversized horses in front of every P. F. Chang's, the whimsical Beaux-Arts cupola and florid script over the entrance of the Cheesecake Factory, and the candy-striped awnings of TGI Fridays all announce from the outside the abundance found inside.

Stepping inside the doors of one of these restaurants reinforces the richness of design. The restaurants are often large, sprawling buildings with upscale bars just inside the doors, while numerous rooms filled with tables and booths stretch out beside and behind the front doors. In Macaroni Grill, booths are slightly raised from the floor and separated from each other by faux stone arches supported by rustic, heavy wood beams and posts. On mantles separating the booths, tall candles with wax drippings down their sides stand in rough-hewn candleholders. Behind the booths in one Macaroni Grill, opaque, warm-colored pendant lamps hanging from a high, dark ceiling cast low light over a dark distressed bar. Some Macaroni Grills have semiprivate rooms separated from the rest of the restaurant with richly textured, heavy tapestry-like curtains. When the room is not in use, the curtains are held back by large, soft-looking cords tied to wrought-iron stays. Throughout the restaurants, arches, stone, wrought iron, and dried flower arrangements in bucolic vases fill otherwise empty spaces. Recent Olive Garden redesigns use multicolored tile on the floor, striped awnings, unfinished wood chairs, strings of bare lights across open spaces, and two- and three-story spaces made to look like a small piazza in the middle of a Tuscan village.[57] The attention to design detail does not stop at the tile on the floor or the paintings on the wall, as the apparently hand-painted plates in many restaurants coordinate with the colors, patterns, and textures of the rest of the space. The copiousness of the visual design elements—the lighting for each table, the trompe l'oeil effects, the rough-textured walls— in their quantity and variety assert a visual context for the abundance of food served in the space.

Placing the Suburban Dinner Table

What is more, this abundance of visual style within the restaurants is a rhetorical intervention into a late modern moment in which style is central to the production and performance of self. More than simply cosseting the pasta and salad in stylized spaces and in painted bowls, the restaurants embed the visitors in these copious images. With lifestyle at the center of identity construction and performance, individuals not only need to take style onto the body through clothing, accessories, and bodily performance, they also need stages on which to perform their identities. Places like Olive Garden and Macaroni Grill offer nearly ideal spaces for the enactment of (suburban) identities. Take, for instance, the language of the designers of recent Olive Garden interiors: "The restaurant became a Tuscan Village; each dining room had a unique character, but all patrons in every location were to be treated to a festive, warm, inviting atmosphere; a celebration of food, family and friends."[58] The restaurant was not like a Tuscan village, nor did it simply conjure the emotions or the visions of the village but was, itself, the village. While the restaurants (located in Altamonte, Florida, and Denver, Colorado) are Italian villages, each room has a "unique character." Having distinctive character, the rooms are partners in, as well as stages for, the enactment of festive family life.

It is precisely in these intersections of rooms with character and the gestures toward comforting (and distinctly European) ethnicity that these restaurants assert their very particular rhetorics of locality. Specifically they work to stitch together the suburban homes with concrete aestheticized images of ethnicity. This sewing together of visual identities depends on the ways the restaurants aesthetically gesture to the surrounding homes and to imagined relations to the home country. The restaurants incorporate a number of aesthetic moves central to residential suburban design while also gesturing out to Italian villages. In so doing the restaurants provide suburban dinner tables that connect to and reinforce the lifestyle choices of the suburban homeowners, while embedding these choices in a nostalgic narrative of village life.

The aesthetic and emotional connection to the suburban home is crucial for the success of these restaurants. The wealth represented within the restaurants is not meant to be opposed to dearth within the home. Rather, the restaurant becomes a home away from home, a semipublic site in which to experience and perform a much desired plenty. The restaurants consistently emphasize that the food is homemade, carefully crafted, and made to order. Olive Garden, for example, asserts that while in the restaurant, the customer is partly "family." The open kitchens of Macaroni Grill invite the customer to see the food preparation much as they would were they in their own home, while the restaurant's honor system wine drunk out of small, octagonal glasses works to create a home-like setting. Abundance and home cooking come together in these sites, working to suture the customers into familiar and familial settings.

Beyond offering the spatial imaginary of fresh, home-cooked meals, the restaurants also connect to suburban homes through their architectural style. The stone facades, tile roofs, and complicated footprints all intertwine with surrounding domestic architectural styles. Like many neighboring homes that draw on vaguely imagined Mediterranean visual cues, these restaurants use tile, stucco, and rustic details to articulate together the homes, the lifestyle centers, the restaurants, and the fantasy of southern Europe. In addition to the tile and stone of the designs, the restaurants also often include cathedral ceilings in their entrances, welcoming visitors into the restaurants just as these same ceilings welcome families into their suburban homes. Importantly, as tall as these ceilings are and as large as the restaurants may be, dining occurs in more human sized rooms that seem more like a home's dining room or, if it is near the open kitchen, can feel like eating in the home's kitchen.

Finally, the restaurants are designed in styles that work to reference villas and large homes rather than, say, civic or industrial buildings. Like the

Figure 4.2. Entrance to Macaroni Grill in suburban Las Vegas. The stone entrance, simple columns, chimneys, and tile roofs point more closely to the surrounding residential architecture than to civic or commercial building. Photograph by Donovan Conley.

homes of some upscale suburban developments, these buildings appear to be manses imported stone by stone from some Tuscan or Provençal hill. Take for instance, a run-of-the-mill Macaroni Grill in suburban Las Vegas (figure 4.2). The entrance of this restaurant with its peaked and tiled roof framed by chimneys in the near background, the stone entrance with porthole window, the "M" on either side of the doors, and simplified columns all reference forms of residential architecture. The architecture points to some of the nicer houses in the more exclusive neighborhoods of Las Vegas and around the West or can be read as an improved version of more basic models. In both the residential architecture and the restaurant, tiled and peaked roofs, tan stucco walls, rounded windows or doors, and traditional architectural details suggest that both kinds of buildings are enunciating an underlying design aesthetic. The restaurant partakes of an aesthetic that, in these neighborhoods at least, speaks the language of home. Perhaps this restaurant is a grander, better-kept home, but it is like home nonetheless.

But the restaurants are like home in a second way. In the previous chapter, I argued that housing developments in suburban Denver, Las Vegas, and

Phoenix all used images of the Mediterranean and Europe more broadly to assert a sense of place or as a mode of the suburbs' rhetoric of locality. These restaurants make the same gesture. Like the homes surrounding them, they gesture to an idealized version of northern Italian building practices as a way of stitching themselves into an authenticating aesthetic. Crucially, however, the restaurants borrow from very particular northern Italian models. Rather than reproducing, for example, the urban architecture of Renaissance Florence, the restaurants turn to images of rural (if grand) farmhouses. Although located on busy thoroughfares in the middle of massive suburban developments and surrounded by the macadam of nearly endless parking lots, the buildings themselves assert a position on rural farmland.

Situating themselves as Italian farmhouses has at least a triple rhetorical purpose. First, it places the restaurants squarely into a version of ethnicity that can connect the food to both history and time. Like the connection between food and ethnicity found in recent food films and advertisements, of course, this ethnicity is one that depends on aestheticized and mass-produced differences.[59] In a gesture to authenticity, the image of an other is produced (even as potentially disturbing differences are scrubbed from the image) and offered for consumption. In the case of Macaroni Grill and Olive Garden the ethnic image is that of rural Italy and Italians. This is an image offered to us in powerfully idealized ways in other texts (in the book and subsequent film *Under the Tuscan Sun*, for example).[60] What is more, Italy and Italian food have increasingly come to stand for excellence in taste produced through fresh ingredients and cooking that relies on ancient traditions and earthy products.[61] Italian food (or the Mediterranean diet) is also offered as a healthier way to eat compared to more traditional US American cooking. Olive oil replaces Crisco, fresh produce and fruits replace canned peas and mashed potatoes, lightly prepared fish replaces chicken-fried steak, red wine replaces Coke. As a spectacularized image of Italy, the restaurants offer the possibilities of eating authenticity that not only helps locate consumers in the world but also does so in a heart-healthy way.

Second, the restaurants as imagined farmhouses reproduce in precise form the pastoralism that is foundational to the suburban developments' rhetorics of locality. In the restaurants, however, the connection to the land is more thoroughly perfected. Beyond the references of a name (Surprise Farms) and image (the nonfunctioning windmill) or the farm-like common building (the Grange at Historic Castle Rock) that serve as markers of pastoralism in residential developments, these restaurants serve food that, presumably, comes from the land referenced in the architecture. While the food is clearly sourced from globalized and industrialized food systems, the restaurants continually strive to maintain the fiction of their localness and locatedness. Macaroni Grill's wine comes from their own estates. The Olive Garden grates Romano cheese imported from Italy. The chefs of the Olive Garden train at the Culinary Institute in Tuscany, which, the picture on the web page asserts, is housed in the rambling farmhouse that the restaurants themselves seem to reference.[62]

Here then is an opportunity to eat in a pastoral way, to situate the body in the localizing rhetorics of planting, harvesting, preparing, aging, and eating. Much as Starbucks involves the customer in coffee production (naming the places from which the coffee comes but also revealing the bean grinding, milk steaming, and the personalization of each cup), so these restaurants offer to place the visitors into older, simple moments in food production and consumption.[63] Meanwhile, as the restaurants offer to connect visitors directly to the preparation of the food and the land where the food is grown, the restaurants also hide the industrialization of their food. Hidden behind stucco and tile are the impoverished farm laborers who grow the food and the semi trucks that deliver the products to the restaurant.[64] Brought to the forefront are our fantasized concrete relations with farmfresh foods. And so, like the developments of which they are a part, the restaurants enunciate a vision of pastoral possibilities.

The restaurants offer images of geographic locatedness of foods and wines that seem linked to specific landscapes. But these images, even as they offer rhetorics of locality, displace consumers' understanding of the ways food actually arrives at the dinner table. Cook and Crang argue that this is a doubled form of food fetishism—the food fetish that at once limits knowledge about food's spatial journeys from farm to table while at the same time emphasizes "geographical knowledges about those widely sourced food commodities. These geographical knowledges—based in the cultural meanings of places and spaces—are then deployed in order to 're-enchant' (food) commodities and to differentiate them from the devalued functionality and homogeneity of standardized products, tastes and places."[65] This re-enchantment not only transforms homogenized food into Italian food, it also magically turns the patron into a Tuscan villager and, because the restaurant is also a farmhouse, magically turns the restaurant table into the (farm) family's dinner table.[66]

The third and final rhetorical function of this attention to ancient Italian foodways is to produce a particular vision of family. That family is central to the restaurants' rhetoric can be seen in Olive Garden's motto "When You're Here, You're Family." Olive Garden's all you can eat, family-style salad bowl and Macaroni Grill's shared bottle of wine and white paper tablecloths with crayons for children (of all ages) materializes the family-ness of these restaurants. It is within this intersection between imagining high-quality food and easily approachable tastes and ingredients that the Olive Garden inserts the marketing of the training kitchen located in Italy. Run by Romana Neri, Olive Garden's executive chef is imagined as the personification of the Italian grandmother.[67] The images of the training kitchen and the description of Neri's pedagogy strenuously assert this deep connection between family cooking and excellent flavors. Family, within this context, is rooted in a geographic space—Tuscany—and in a time that is present but still deeply embedded in traditional folk and foodways.

It is not a mistake that these Italian styled restaurants link themselves to family. As Davide Girardelli argues in his critical analysis of Fazoli's, Italy, Italians, and Italian food are closely associated with family. Fazoli's, Girardelli argues, consistently returns to stereotypical visions of family in its use of photographs of families and weddings, its family friendly atmosphere, its evocation of a family or bistro kitchen.[68] This link among family, Italianness, and food is reinforced in Marialisa Calta's introduction to her book *Barbarians at the Plate: Taming and Feeding the American Family.* "The family dinner," she writes, "has fallen on hard times. Among its enemies: jobs, school, sports, music lessons, any kind of lessons, the telephone, after-school clubs, homework, exercise schedules, television, special diets, computer games, night classes, community meetings, and instant messaging."[69] Ruing the ways contemporary culture has undermined the family meal (and, she argues later, the family itself) Calta nostalgically recalls her own childhood: "I come from an Italian family with a long tradition of great family meals,"[70] where her grandmothers, aunts, mother, and very occasionally her father made family feasts. Like her own mother, Calta has devoted large parts of her time to feeding her husband and children. Calta's narrative—a narrative that is implied in the restaurants—is clearly structured on tradition-ally organized heteronormativity and organized with mothers cooking and the rest of the family eating.

These (imagined) families serve as a critique of contemporary society in which the technologies and demands of the late modern world seem to be tearing at the fabric of familial life. As Diane Negra argues, recent television and cinematic food images unconsciously "propose . . . a more radical critique of present-day social structures, suggesting that moderni-zation and prosperity have wrought dubious achievements. An imagined return to the ethnic family and community bonds of the past, while intensely desired, must also be disavowed to some degree, for it is fundamentally at odds with our national narrative and its imperatives of constant dynamic transformation forward momentum."[71] It is precisely into this discursive nexus of familial anxiety and nostalgia that Olive Garden and Macaroni Grill build their farmhouses. Looking like home, partaking of suburbia's fascination with pastoral settings, drawing on spectacular images of ethnicity, and offering family friendly environments, suburban restaurants provide dinner tables that are at once stretched out to meet the world and located squarely within comforting traditions.

Performing and Embodying the Family

And so, the rhetoric of locality offered in these restaurants drills all the way down to the dinner table and the dining body. Made possible by the abstractions of globalization that can cause the uncanniness and nostalgia characteristic of late modernity, these restaurants offer fully embodied and performative rhetorics of food and family. This performance of locality, it first appears, is produced through the geographic knowledges the restaurants offer. As Macaroni Grill used to assert, "This is all the Italian you need to know." But even more powerfully—that is to say, more affectively—the restaurants locate food, food practices, and eating in the intimacy of the family. The family dinner table is at once a metaphor and an embodied performance. The dinner table offers an image of families together, talking about their day; of parents teaching children the manners of civility and helping them find their place in the world. The site for consuming the family's food and doing the family's business, the dinner table can be the suburban home's locus. The table is a nexus where the discourses of a particular family and of family and home more generally are articulated. In suburban restaurants—an odd hybrid between the public space of civic discourse and the private space of the suburban home's interior—families congregate to enact themselves, to perform their suburban selves.

Or at least this is the restaurants' rhetoric. Pastoral manses, built into fields of macadam and adjacent to often humbler homes, the restaurants offer the possibilities of enunciating—of articulating in word and deed—a place in the world. Certainly, these restaurants offer geographic knowledges placing both consumer and food in well-worn paths. The (re)constituted family becomes authenticated through globalized food practices. But the enunciation of this geographic knowledge is more than a cognitive knowing. It is also an affective knowing.[72] These restaurants are nodes and points on affective maps as they draw together otherwise disconnected cultural contexts, including the desire for secure and securing family relations, the longing for home expressed both as nostalgia and a sense of the uncanny, and the growing hunger for food that can serve the world on a plate and offer material instantiations of authenticity.

To sit down with family and friends around the table at the Olive Garden is to situate ourselves into profoundly complicated relationships. The acts of choosing the restaurant, ordering the food, lifting fork to mouth, and conversing with table partners are all complex articulations of our place within the world. Inside these walls painted with the colors of Tuscany, on these plates covered with food that imagines Italy, and with these friends and family, we enact our love of food and fellowship. Points on the maps of our daily lives, articulated within the circulation of globalized images and food, and sewn into the material landscapes of suburbia, these restaurants offer embodied and enacted nostalgia. Even as the home seems to fall apart, even as the purity of national identity seems shattered into fragments, even as the borders that once offered security are repeatedly breeched in banal and spectacular fashion, entering into these farmhouses and eating this located and locatable food within (the hope for and image of) a family offers the possibility of eating, enacting, performing, and embodying the nostalgia offered as image in suburban movies and as buildings in suburban houses.

And these embodied longings for and articulations of home and family are abundantly affective relations. Loving the food, loving the community, loving the family are all wrapped up in one place, served with endless salad (at Olive Garden), endless wine (at Macaroni Grill), and endless French fries (at Red Robin). Finally, then, the spectacularly banal abundance of these places is not so much a copiousness of food but an outpouring of the emotional and relational life of the suburbs. Families may not be big, but the houses, restaurants, and portions are. In the boring world of late modernity—boring because the world is so overwhelmingly scary, so abstracted, so inscrutable—suburban restaurants and their articulation of family offer the possibility of powerful emotional lives: the size of the serving stands in for, represents, and elicits the size of the emotional life proffered.[73] If, as Sarah Ahmed argues, happiness is less an emotion in itself but is the association with what we associate with happiness, then the nostalgically rendered happiness of the restaurants is the instantiation of happy relationships.[74] This big, powerful, familial emotional life is secured in these restaurants by memory and food (or, perhaps better, memories of family meals we may never have actually had). Memory offers the family a place in time, food offers the family a place in geography; together the memory and food suture the familial body into a comforting locality.

As is evident by now, restaurants and eating are not exclusively discursive; we cannot eat our words (though we often wish we could). And so the restaurants create spaces that do not simply gesture out toward the possibilities of the good life, of an ethos. Instead, these gestures out to the good life are themselves the material and embodied enactment of this ethos. In Olive Garden and Macaroni Grill, customers imagine and enact, consider and perform suburban ethos. What makes restaurants particularly powerful sites of suburban dwelling is that they provide an opportunity to, in very literal ways, consume and incorporate the values desired. The restaurants' abundance functions materially as the large portions, spicy sauces, big bottles of wine, and endless bowls of salad proffer the body an opportunity to bring these public visions—these images and imaginings—into the body itself, to materialize and incorporate the abundance imaged in other spaces. But this embodying of abundance is also an emplacing of abundance, for in the end the food enters the individual body; the tongue tastes, the teeth chew, the throat swallows, the food becomes part of this body, and this body only. This is symbolic consumption, to be sure, but it is also consumption materialized. This is social consumption, but it is consumption radically individualized as well. While Macaroni Grill may be a generic space and Olive Gardens may grow in every suburb of the nation, the mouth that eats and the body that consumes is always, only, here. Its ethos and dwelling place, while imagistically extended through the networks of the late modern world, is also so very here, and so very material. The images of place and abundance come home to the (late modern suburban) body. This is a body that is at once profoundly alone and absolutely social, a body that is deeply individual and extended into the globalized spaces of the current condition. Tossed on a sea of late modern possibilities, this body seeks comfort of authenticity, of place, of abundance. It seeks to finally be settled and to be full, and this body may find (temporarily) what it seeks in these banal and transcendent spaces.

Taken together, chapters 3 and 4 have offered an analysis of the ways suburban architecture materializes the home and the family, suggesting that the family serves as suburbia's central bulwark. What this analysis has offered, however, is a concretization of this more general claim. In houses and restaurants, the family is materially and symbolically rooted into time and place—what I have been calling locality—primarily through memory and appeals to place. In fact, I have been taking nostalgia's longing for home seriously as both a longing for a past and a place, as well as a fully embodied longing. The compelling topoi of contemporary suburban housing developments and recent chain restaurants combines past and place as a way of materializing and concretizing the family and of locating an otherwise abstract and abstracted family into warmly remembered social and geographic imaginaries.

At the same time, houses and restaurants offer different versions of these nostalgic memories. The domestic landscape almost obsessively turns into itself, offering an aesthetic of security that looks inward and backward and consistently works to reject and wall off the outer world. Restaurants, on the other hand, work to extend suburbia into the world and bring the world into the suburbs. In response to the inwardness of the domestic landscapes and the thinness of modernity's generic spaces, Italian themed restaurants offer a compelling and apparently rich experience of globality. The restaurants use nostalgic renderings of ethnicity, European pastoralism, and gustatory and architectural abundance as topoi that specify, extend, and enrich suburban relations to the world. And yet, as I have argued, these extensions and enrichments—while certainly a critique of the abstractions of modernity—are thinned out and reduced to conform to the needs of global capitalism. In fact, these restaurants' versions of globalization work hard to create a sense of place in time even as they maintain the smoothnesses offered by global capitalism. Writing specifically about food, Cook and Crang argue that this effort to create narratives of place and time about food is a "re-enchantment" of food whose purpose is to create geographic and historic authenticity and in so doing hide the abstractions of global food chains.[75] Even as the restaurants extend suburbanites into the world, they do so in ways that well articulate with the aesthetics of safety developed in the domestic landscape. Although an extension into the world, the restaurants secure this extension through embodied gestures that hide more than they reveal and strip from the diversity they offer anything threatening or troubling about the suburbs' relations with global others.

The restaurants considered here connect home and globe, familial kitchen and transnational corporations through materializations of abundance and pastorally framed memories of ethnicity. Restaurants rely on fecund memories—on pasts and repasts—to weave families into comforting narratives. As fully embodied, completely spatialized, entirely materialized topoi, restaurants and the housing developments they serve locate patrons in place and do so affectively in the moment of their performance. Topos must, then, be thought as not merely an argumentative turn, a discursively built line of reasoning, but as a touchable and tasteable rhetorical enactment. The plate of food—with its tastes, smells, textures; and its emplacement in space and time—can root us into the kinds of relations of which the good life can be built and in which the good life is (already) enacted. But what happens to this vision and performance of the good life as visitors move from home and table into the more public spaces of church and the lifestyle center? I turn next to these more public spaces to explore the suburban good life as constructed in sacred and civic space.

III. Consuming Suburbs: Building Sacred and Civic Space

5

Worshipping the Good Life

Megachurches and the Making of the Suburban Moral Landscape

Churches connect the divine with the human, values with social forms, and aspiration with present reality. At once messengers and agents, mirrors and actors, they enable people to think through their ideas about religiosity and convey them to the rest of the world while, in turn, influencing ideas and shaping religion and society.

—Jeanne Halgren Kilde

March 4, 2007, dawned bright and warm, as early March days often do in the desert Southwest. Three colleagues and I were headed to the Central Christian Church in Henderson, Nevada, a large suburb to the southeast of Las Vegas. We walked over the gravel parking lot through the crowds toward the building. Near the front entrance church workers shaded by a tent were selling large shrink-wrapped boxes proclaiming the month's theme: "Freedom: The Pathway to Recovery from Habits, Hurts, and Hang-Ups." We entered the church, made our way into the sanctuary, listened to and swayed with the Christian rock band, watched two videos announcing the week's programming and introducing the day's message, and, finally, Jud Wilhite—the church's head pastor—began his sermon. We are in church for the first Sunday sermon of the month-long series on freedom.

To understand this early twenty-first-century sermon, it is helpful to go back forty-two years, to the first Sunday of 1965. On March 7, six hundred civil rights activists left Selma, Alabama, marching toward Montgomery. Their march was designed to draw attention to the lack of voting rights for African Americans across the south. Six blocks after setting out, as the activists were crossing the Edmund Pettus bridge, state and local law enforcement officers met the peaceful progression with violence. They attacked the demonstrators with truncheons and tear gas, driving the marchers back to Selma. Two days later, Martin Luther King Jr. led a symbolic march to the bridge while the protestors petitioned for court protection for their march. Finally, after receiving the federal court protection, marchers again left Selma. The intervening weeks swelled the number of marchers. Over 3,200 people left Selma on Sunday, March 21, and by the time they arrived at the capital on the twenty-sixth, they numbered 25,000. The march marked a high point of the civil rights movement. Five months after the marches, on August 15, 1965, Lyndon Johnson signed the Voting Rights Act into law.

Bloody Sunday had become particularly important in the first days of March 2007. Both Hillary Rodham Clinton and Barack Obama had just begun the official phases of their presidential campaigns. Both were assiduously working for the African American vote. And both were at the remembrances of this conflict in Selma, a fact that was the talk of the weekend's news. Anyone watching CNN or listening (as I was) to NPR would have been aware of the political machinations of the two leading Democrat candidates, and they would have had at least a passing understanding of Bloody Sunday and its importance in US American political life.

But had you joined me at the March 4 service about freedom in suburban Las Vegas, this history of social struggle would have been completely absent. As the service began, I was struck by the incongruity of the celebrations of freedom in Selma and those in Henderson. I waited for Wilhite to at least mention the connection between the day's sermon and this larger history. Wilhite, after a few jokes (involving throwing bananas into the audience), settled into the sermon and, as is always the case in Evangelical megachurches, introduced the biblical text that would serve as the foundation for his teaching. He turned to the book of Exodus. As he explained, Exodus means "the way out." And he further acknowledges that, in Exodus at least, the way out is for an oppressed people.

Of course, Exodus was and is a crucial text for the civil rights movement. The narrative of Exodus tells the story of God calling Moses to lead the Israelites—enslaved by the Egyptians—out of the oppressor's country to the Promised Land. The book tells of the miracles God worked to protect the Israelites as they wandered in the desert for forty years and of Moses's sins that kept him from getting into Canaan with the people he had led. This story of a long and tortured journey from oppression to freedom resonated with African Americans and others struggling for freedom in the United States. Indeed, Martin Luther King Jr.'s speeches were laced with references to the Exodus story. The conclusion of King's speech given the night before his assassination calls directly on the Exodus story: "Like anybody, I would like to live a long life. Longevity has its place. But I'm not concerned about that now. I just want to do God's will. And He's allowed me to go up to the mountain. And I've looked over. And I've seen the Promised Land. I may not get there with you. But I want you to know tonight, that we, as a people, will get to the Promised Land!"[1] In spite of all of these resonances of date, topic, and text not once did Wilhite suggest that the struggle for freedom may be a struggle against social, political, or economic oppression. Instead, in the church of 2007, the struggle for freedom is a struggle against drug addiction, childhood wounds, and bad habits. Even as Wilhite tells the story of God calling Moses, the story's social message is left behind, replaced by an image of freedom that focuses exclusively on individuals and families, and offers escape from painful hangups and destructive habits. The social and the political have disappeared behind the vale of the personal and the familial. The good life and the freedoms this life offers are located in the nexus of the individual, the family, and the church community. Finally, this good life is devoted to the present and the future and nearly devoid of any historical understanding beyond the individual's own story of loss and redemption.

I begin with this extended narrative of one Sunday's service in a megachurch in suburban Las Vegas because it condenses many of the crucial issues I will engage in this analysis of suburban megachurches. The narrative, at least as I experienced it, is one about remembering and forgetting. Even as the pastor and congregants remember popular culture references to freedom and enslavement—from the biblical Exodus story to images of gorillas on our backs and references to familiar familial hurts—their memory practices almost obsessively ignore social and structural struggles for freedom. This dual relationship between remembering and forgetting—or at minimum, ignoring—is central to understanding the megachurch's rhetoric of the suburban good life. Just as this particular service remembered narratives that emphasized individual and familial freedoms and enslavements, the megachurch as architecture, institution, and performance connects to popular culture's therapeutic obsession with individuals and families while compulsively ignoring social and structural possibilities and difficulties.[2]

But memory and forgetting are not simply the polar ends of a bimodal spectrum. While asserting that memory and forgetting are linked or are dialectically related is a common topos in memory studies, the relationship between memory and forgetting is extraordinarily complicated.[3] This relationship is complex for at least three reasons. First, to assert that memory also involves forgetting tells us very little about the particular pasts that are forgotten or denied or, for that matter, the memories proffered and preserved. At the very least, there cannot be a one-to-one relationship between memory and forgetting, for the number of past events, experiences, and affects forgotten are nearly infinite, where the number of past events, experiences, and affects that are remembered—especially when compared to all that is forgotten—is remarkably finite. Second, this partiality of memory is particularly striking when we investigate memory places, for the effort, time, and money necessary to etch specific memories into stone and build them of brick and mortar dramatically limits the proliferation of memory places.[4] While it is simply impossible as well as impractical to remember everything, this is not the same thing as saying the remembering of one thing necessarily leads to the forgetting of the remembered object's opposite. This nonnecessary relationship between remembering and forgetting leads to a further complication. Even as remembering one thing does not imply forgetting memory's opposite, it is also the case that competing public memories can be very alive, and, what is more, competing public memories may animate one another. For example, remembering Exodus as a narrative useful in imagining and inspiring personal freedom does not depend on forgetting the uses of Exodus for social and systematic change and, in fact as King demonstrates in his mountaintop speech, a powerful message can be created by intersecting the personal and the social. Asserting that memory demands forgetting makes it difficult to think carefully how various memories vie for attention and may be more or less present in a mnemonic performance.[5]

Third, while competing memories do not necessarily force one memory into abeyance, there are moments when publics can actively strive to forget. This active process of forgetting is, as Bradford Vivian suggests, itself an act of memory. Rhetoric as persuasive enactment can call forth memories and then argue that these memories should be forgotten, rejected, or replaced. Public appeals to forgetting, "Function rhetorically by calling on the public to question whether communal affairs would be improved by radically altering the normative form and content of collective memories that have hitherto defined its past, and hence its current identity."[6] It is possible that a community's public memories restrain, hold back, or undermine the possibility of community renewal or progress. In response to this sense that current memory structures are damaging, public forgetting offers persuasive arguments to forget or lay aside these debilitating memories. Public forgetting urges communities to reformulate their pasts in ways that, the rhetoric suggests, better match present conditions and help imagine an improved future. What should be clear at this point is that forgetting and remembering are linked, intertwined, and interanimating in complex ways that demand more than the simple assertion that remembering one thing causes or relies on forgetting some other possible memory.

For rhetorical criticism, forgetting becomes an important analytical possibility when the critic can argue that that which is forgotten has rhetorical meaning.[7] Identifying what is forgotten or discovering what is actively and consequentially left out is unusually difficult. Since nearly every possible memory is necessarily absent from any memory context, how does the analyst discover that which is missing, absent, or forgotten with rhetorical consequence?

In some ways, the acts of public forgetting Vivian discusses are the easiest forms of forgetting to identify for they may name themselves as acts of forgetting. Lincoln in the Gettysburg Address and the second inaugural, for example, urges his listeners to actively forget the atrocities of the war in hopes of building a more humane future.[8] There are in megachurch services similarly explicit calls to forgetting. Pastors frequently urge members to pray but to not be confined by the forms of prayer of their past. As one pastor said as he described his conversion experience: "I prayed, but it wasn't a prayer like my parents would pray." In this consistently repeated call to nontraditional prayer, the pastor at once remembers the "thees" and "thous" of older churches and at the same time suggests that these traditional forms—and the religious experiences they recall—constrain conversion and confession.

There are, however, other ways of finding rhetorical, significant acts of forgetting. Carefully attending to memory texts and contexts can afford critics clues about the specific memories that are pushed aside, are actively made absent, or are repressed.[9] To investigate the entanglement of remembering and forgetting, I need to carefully attend to what memory texts and contexts tell us about the relationship between remembering and forgetting in particular, concrete settings. One way of identifying consequential absences is by attending to the experiential landscape of the memory place.[10] The concept of the experiential landscape offers a way of thinking about how a concrete memory text is entwined with surrounding landscapes, including a range of other physical landscapes, the cognitive landscapes of the memory text's audiences, and the ways the experiential landscapes literally and figuratively position audiences. Experiential landscapes suggests that "spaces of memory are better thought of as constitutive elements of landscapes than as discrete texts, that landscapes entail both physical and cognitive dimensions, and that such landscapes offer fully embodied subject positions, which literally shape visitors' practices of looking."[11] Analysis of what is remembered and forgotten in the megachurch depends on this understanding of experiential landscapes and memory spaces. As distinctly suburban structures, megachurches co-constitute the suburban built environment and so must be understood in relation to the surrounding landscapes. At the same time, as sacred spaces the experiential landscape of megachurches includes past church forms. As part of the experiential landscapes of suburbia and (primarily) evangelical Christianity, the megachurch draws on and remakes the values of suburban life and of Christianity.

It is within these intersecting experiential landscapes that I can begin to identify rhetorically meaningful remembrances and forgetting. In the story with which I began this chapter, I began to explore the possibility of analyzing meaningful forgetting. While the preacher could have connected Exodus to innumerable past narratives, that he did not link his narrative to an immediately and obviously available story in the cognitive landscapes of the parishioners—the remembrance of Bloody Sunday by two prominent candidates for the presidency—is meaningfully glaring. Likewise, the near total absence of references to church architecture traditions in megachurch designs is also meaningful. Meaningful as well are the consistent, constant, repetitive remembrances of usually banal secular popular culture architectural and other media forms.

The service on the first Sunday of March, 2004 is, then, an interpretive hook into the rhetorically meaningful remembrances and forgettings of the suburban megachurch. If public forgetting is a way of clearing out obsolete memories for the purpose of building new communal forms on newly invigorated memories, then exploring the structures of memory and forgetting in the megachurch will delineate the hopes and fears of the suburban good life. Through twined rhetorical acts of remembering and forgetting, many suburban megachurches studied here urge a performance of the good life that is ahistorical and presentist; devoted to popular culture expressed in music, consumption, media technologies, and branding; focused on the traditional family; and offering respite from the late modern world through appeals to therapeutic cultural norms. Several of these elements should no longer come as a surprise: consumption and family have been central to the foregoing analysis of the suburban good life.

And yet there are surprises here. For some Christians and historically for many Protestants the church has been a site of resistance to or even rejection of surrounding cultural norms. Megachurches offer the exact opposite. Rather than rejecting popular culture, megachurches embrace that culture as a starting point from which to evangelize. Equally surprising is the rejection of historical forms of Christian worship and Christian building. Rather than drawing on a deep history of worship practices and architectural forms, megachurches explicitly reject these forms as off-putting and even detrimental to living the Christian good life. As we will see, this rejection of history and memory—this active forgetting—opens material and symbolic space for accepting and celebrating larger cultural norms. What does all of this portend of the good life as imagined by the megachurch? The megachurch offers comfort within a troubling world by embedding its celebration of popular culture and extant suburban values of the consuming individual and family within a larger Christian narrative offering a sacralization of these suburban norms.

I make this argument in five stages. First, I briefly describe the churches I investigated. I then turn to analysis of the ways megachurch architecture responds to earlier forms of Christian sacred architecture to investigate the ways current churches actively reject traditions with the sacred experiential landscape while they invigorate more recent secular aesthetic elements of the suburban experiential landscape. Third, I shift to a longer analysis of the uses of popular, consumer culture within the churches. Fourth, I engage the ways these presentist images from popular culture are embedded in securing images and performances of the family. Finally, I connect this analysis of megachurch architecture and religious performance to discussion of therapeutic discourse in contemporary US popular culture, a therapeutic discourse that depends on interwoven acts of remembering and forgetting.

The Texts

As in the previous two chapters, my argument draws on detailed analysis of particular megachurches placed within their larger cultural and spatial contexts—that is, within their experiential landscapes. Central to this analysis is my study of Radiant Church in Surprise, Arizona, which is triangulated with detailed analyses of Timberline Church in Fort Collins, Colorado, and Central Community Church in Henderson, Nevada. What makes Radiant a nearly ideal place to study the rhetoric of megachurches is the fact that it is not particularly exceptional; it is not the largest, wealthiest, or best known of the megachurches. Those honors would have to go to churches like Saddleback Community Church in Southern California, Lakewood Church in Houston, or the Willow Creek Community Church in suburban Chicago. Further, unlike pastors Joel Osteen or Richard Warren, Radiant's pastor, Lee McFarland, has not published a best-selling religiously themed self-help book.

This is not to say that Radiant is unimportant. Indeed, major local and national media outlets have noticed Radiant. The local ABC television station dubbed the church the blue jeans church, and the church was featured in a *New York Times Magazine* article on megachurches.[12] With an attendance of nearly six thousand among the four services each weekend, Radiant is in the middle of megachurches in terms of size and attendance. Megachurches are typically defined as churches with a weekend attendance or a membership of at least two thousand people. Many megachurches have far larger crowds, and the biggest churches draw tens of thousands of people each weekend.[13] Radiant, then, is neither the smallest nor the largest of megachurches. It is, in short, typical.

Being a typical megachurch, Radiant is an outstanding example of what is arguably the most important form of Christian sacred spaces and practices today. Megachurches attract a plurality of all Christian church attendees in the United States. The largest 1 percent of Protestant churches are the church homes of 15 percent of all "people, money, and full-time staff. The biggest 20 percent of churches have between 60 and 65 percent of all the people, money, and full-time staff."[14] Churches are getting bigger and big churches are getting bigger at an even faster rate. Since overall church attendance has been flat for years, big-church growth skews church size from smaller to larger churches.[15]

Radiant Church, located in the northern Phoenix suburb of Surprise, is, like most other megachurches, part of the suburban landscape. Megachurch placement in the suburbs is no accident. Suburban landscapes are fertile sites for structures like the megachurch. Easy access to freeways, large tracts of open land at relatively reasonable prices, surrounding residential growth, and the relative economic wealth of many of these suburbs all provide the material and cultural resources to drive and house church growth.[16] Located in the heart of suburbs, these megachurches condense and respond to suburban anxieties and hopes. Since megachurches are sacred spaces, they lay particular claim to imagine and materialize the suburban good life. It is no mistake that Jonathan Mahler's *New York Times Magazine* article on megachurches is titled "The Soul of the New Exurb." What are the contours and the contents of this soul? And what might understanding this soul teach us about the suburban good life?

This Is Not Your Parents' Church

Radiant Church sits on twenty acres of land between two of Surprise's east–west major thoroughfares, just west of the town's civic center and large spring training baseball stadium. If you are driving north or south on Reems Road past the church it would be easy to mistake the building for a regional bank, a professional office complex, or a small mall. Driving north on Reems, if you are paying attention, you see a fairly large building set

Figure 5.1. Radiant Church from the east. On the southeast corner is the four-story prayer tower, the tallest part of the building. Hardly towering (and with almost no connotation to prayer), this highest point only reinforces the low-lying horizontality of the building. Photograph by the author.

in the middle of an expansive parking lot, and fronted by a low sign reading Radiant Church fixed to a low, earth-toned stucco wall (figure 5.1).

The building is low-lying and linear. There is nothing about the building that announces to passing motorists that this is a church; there is no cross, stained glass window, or steeple to beckon drivers. The peaked roofs over the entrances are the architectural elements closest to traditional church architecture. And yet even this potential gesture to traditional sacred form is more easily read as a reference to nearby shopping plazas and office buildings. For example, the popular and busy lifestyle center Desert Ridge Marketplace near Radiant Church (and to which I will return in the next chapter) offers similar forms to invite visitors to stop and shop (figure 5.2). Radiant church encourages us to see the connection of these peaks to the shopping mall not simply through reference. Indeed, under the southeast peak is the Seattle's Best Coffee drive through (figure 5.3), while under the much larger porte cochere on the northwest corner of the building, which shields the church's main entrance, are scattered café tables where congregants can

Figure 5.2. South entrance (picture taken from the north) to the Desert Ridge Market Place. Like one of the entrances in Radiant Church, here is the peaked roof inviting visitors into the pedestrian mall and offering respite from the Arizona sun. Photograph by the author.

sip the coffee drinks they bought in the Radiant Café in the "narthex" of the building (figure 5.4).

What should be clear by now is that Radiant Church eschews more traditional church architectural forms for forms familiar to visitors from contemporary business architecture, including the mall and the office building. In referencing surrounding suburban architecture rather than traditional US American or European church form, Radiant's architecture and design are very much part of contemporary megachurch architecture. As James Twitchell argues, "The mall and the megachurch look alike for a reason: they are institutionalized communities, growing outward, not upward."[17] Bill Hybels, founder of Willow Creek Community Church on the outskirts of Chicago, explicitly models his new church on commercial architecture. Hybels points to secular buildings folks are comfortable in—hotels, amusement parks, and corporate headquarters—as models for the new churches. "What I want him [unchurched Harry] to do is just say, 'I was just at corporate headquarters for IBM in Atlanta Wednesday, and now I come to church and it's basically the same.' Neutrality, comfort, contemporary, clean: Those

Figure 5.3. Seattle's Best Coffee drive-thru on the south side. Photograph by the author.

Figure 5.4. Radiant Church's main, northwest entrance. Through the doors, a café is to the left and the bookstore is to the right. Photograph by the author.

are the kinds of values that we want to communicate."[18] Hybels indicates a crucial component to the success of these buildings: they are familiar buildings referencing their late modern, secular, consumerist, and implicitly suburban landscapes.

The History of Ahistorical Church Architecture

These megachurches, while clearly the Christian sacred spaces of the postwar suburb, are not completely new. In fact, megachurches are part of an ongoing debate about the nature of sacred space and religious practice. In the sixteenth century, Protestant dissenters, in particular Calvinists, consistently critiqued the use of icons and images in church architecture as Catholic and standing in between worshippers and God. During the European Renaissance it was not at all unusual for groups of fervent Protestants stirred by powerfully persuasive preachers to attack and destroy the paintings, sculptures, and stained glass windows that marked many churches and cathedrals.[19] This suspiciousness of overly ornate spaces was accompanied by deep concerns over traditional liturgical forms of worship. As with the iconographic decorations, Calvinist thinkers argued that the liturgy was not strictly biblical and stood in place of a personal commitment to God. Puritan worship moved away from liturgy to the sermon as central to the worship service.[20] This shift demanded architectural changes, in particular the creation of a central speaking area. This newly designed pulpit replaced the altar as the focus of the building and the service.[21]

These Protestant concerns about architecture, design, and church practice found outlet in the early New England meetinghouse. The meetinghouse was not considered sacred and offered few architectural clues to its status as church. Most important was the development of a functionalist architecture. The Puritans as dissenters from the Church of England rejected the beliefs of the church as well the liturgical mode of worship and architecture. For the dissenters, church indicated a body of believers who gathered to worship, not a building. The church building or place of worship was not, itself, sacred as it is in the Anglican and Catholic traditions. The neutrality of the name "meetinghouse" neatly encapsulates this belief about sacred spaces and community.[22]

The functionalist architecture of the meetinghouse, along with the new focus on the pulpit and the minister, met the evangelical revival of the nineteenth century in the theater. In fact, one of the earliest evangelical churches of the Great Revival was housed in a former theater; the Chatham Theater became Charles Grandison Finney's Chatham Street Chapel on

May 2, 1832.[23] Moving church into a theater—site of the worldly pleasures revivalists often inveighed against—was controversial. Given, however, the Protestant history of investing sacredness in the people rather than the building of the church and the Protestant focus on the preacher rather than the liturgy, a theater makes some sense. A theater is well designed for large audiences to hear and see a compelling speaker on stage. What is more, the revival focused on the unchurched poor. The theater, with its connection to popular culture, reduced potential attendees' anxiety about fitting in. Further, evangelical services, whether held in a permanent space or a tent, were far more emotive, expressive, and more closely aligned with popular culture than more traditional Protestant worship. The theater was a nearly ideal house for this new form of worship.[24]

Three crucial elements of the megachurch are now in place: church space need not be radically different from secular space, in fact secular spaces can make ideal models for evangelical congregations; church space need not be ornate or filled with icons and images from the Christian past, in fact plainer, simpler buildings may be more welcoming to visitors; and finally, evangelical churches focus attention on the stage and the activities on the stage, searching for an emotive, theatrical worship service. These are clear predecessors to the contemporary megachurches, which, as we have seen, draw on the secular architecture for their models, eschew most religious connotations in the architecture and design, and focus attention of the worshippers on the stage and the musicians and pastor.

But one last line of influence needs exploration: nineteenth-century churches, far from rejecting the burgeoning capitalism around them, incorporated, even praised, capitalism. Nineteenth-century churches became increasingly showy, architecturally interesting, decorated with stained glass, while the front of the sanctuary was often a huge bank of organ pipes. These showier, more expensive, bigger churches indicated an integration of evangelical Christianity with capitalism even as they referenced earlier, more formal sacred spaces. This created a tension between the tradition of evangelical Christianity in rejecting the world and more contemporary and more accepting forms of evangelical worship and architecture. Kilde argues that the churches were not so much co-opted by capitalism but were instead examples of "evangelicals' struggle to create something sacred within the expanding capitalist milieu."[25] The churches were at once sites of capitalistic apologia and an honest effort to create religious meaning in a new world. These churches—many of them in relatively wealthy first-ring suburbs—blended older traditions like stained glass windows, large pipe organs, and tall steeples, with more modern sensibilities as congregants worked to think about the relationship between Christianity and the rapidly changing modern world. Unlike the megachurch, these churches attempted to combine sacred mnemonics with modernity—the past with the present.

It is into this historical context that megachurches assert themselves. Like their nineteenth- and early twentieth-century predecessors, megachurches "help to spread the evangelical message by offering an attractive religious haven within a turbulent world."[26] Most importantly, the megachurch responds very specifically to suburban concerns, locating "itself precisely at the junction between everyday life and religion."[27] The new megachurch needed to be relevant to the suburban middle-class experience. It is precisely through an appeal to and a use of popular culture forms that these churches draw in their largely middle-class audiences.

What makes these ahistorical, amnemonic megachurches odd in the suburban landscape is that the surrounding environment is flooded with memory images. As I have already argued, domestic landscape and restaurants explicitly reject the ahistoricism of the immediate post–World War II suburb. In place of the placeless ranch home, developers build historically rendered houses. In place of the generic dinner, restaurateurs offer ethnicized suburban restaurant food. And, as I will argue in the next chapter, lifestyle centers work hard to invoke memories of traditional small towns and cities in place of the aesthetically numbing mall of the 1960s, 1970s, and 1980s. Why, when all of the other quintessential suburban landscapes make a hard turn to memory, does the megachurch so thoroughly reject the historical references that had been typical of the suburban church of the late nineteenth and twentieth centuries? Why does the megachurch shout and whisper that this is not your parents' church?

Investigating megachurches in between secular landscapes' return to memory and churches' rejection of memory suggests that megachurches are engaging in rhetorically consequential forgetting. The megachurch's exterior form, at least, rejects both the mnemonics of the surrounding suburban landscapes and the mnemonic potential within sacred architecture. Such an explicit and visible double forgetting has rhetorical consequences. The building, reminding the parishioner more of malls and transnational corporate headquarters, clears room in cognitive and material landscape to produce a religious experience that need not be fettered by sacred traditions. At the same time, as a sacred space—or at least a space in which sacred performances are enacted—the megachurch can make sacred the secular enactments to which the building refers. This is, in fact, what occurs in the megachurch. By actively rejecting and forgetting sacred traditions and offering the tokens of contemporary secular culture in their place, the sacred and the secular are, potentially, remade. This remaking sews the discomfiting practices of late modernity into a sacralizing narrative.

Rock Bands, Hawaiian Shirts, and the Blue Jeans Church

When nineteenth-century evangelical church designers looked to secular architecture for inspiration they found the theater and the auditorium. There were important cultural and technological reasons these buildings were so compelling. The theater was a crucial institution in the popular culture of the nineteenth century. Further, it offered the acoustics and sight lines designers of larger churches needed. Like popular entertainers, pastors strove to engage large audiences. To do so they needed everyone in the audience to be able to see the stage and to hear the message and the music.

While the megachurch retains an emphasis on performance spaces (here seen as the concert venue or the athletic complex), the megachurch also draws its inspiration from different popular forms: the mall and the business office. Looking to the mall for inspiration should not surprise us, since consumer culture is such a significant part of everyday life in the United States. Perhaps even more importantly the mall is the quintessential suburban space. One of the first spaces to arise as a direct result of suburbanization, the mall encapsulates the secular suburban good life. What is more, in most of its iterations the shopping complex has claimed for itself the mantle of civic and public space. As Lizabeth Cohen argues, the mall and shopping center of the 1950s were "the 'new city' of the postwar era, a vision of how community space should be constructed in an economy and society built on mass consumption."[28] And so the mall and the shopping center become the archetypal spaces of suburbia.

Coffee in Church

It is precisely within this suburban experiential landscape that the megachurch is built. The churches not only look like shopping spaces, they also incorporate important specific aspects of the shopping center, or, even better, the lifestyle center. Nearly every megachurch incorporates a coffee shop into its interior. Radiant Church is different only in the sense that it has two coffee shops—a drive-through coffee shop on the south side of the building (see figure 5.3) and a sit-down, Starbucks-inspired café on the northwest.

The Radiant Café in Radiant Church is sheltered along the north wall, just east of the main entrance. Tables are scattered through the entranceway and spill outside under the porte cochere that serves as the church's architecturally grandest space. The café—which "proudly serves Starbucks coffee"—is inspired by the raft of coffee chains that have spread through suburban developments like wildfire. In Surprise itself, every supermarket has a Starbucks inside. East from the church on Bell Road where the major shopping strips are located, Starbucks and the Barnes & Noble Café sit across from each other. The Radiant Café draws on this corporate form of coffee shop. While the name clearly locates the shop in the church, the look is not derived from the host of local coffee shops that surround, say, a university district or are typical of a gentrifying urban neighborhood. The local coffee shops (which often post signs like "friends don't let friends drink Starbucks"), strive for uniqueness and a connection to the local community.

Starbucks and other chain coffee shops like Coffee Bean and Tea Leaf and Seattle's Best Coffee, while not immune to the desire for locality, offer instead the comfort of uniformity across place. An upscale version of McDonald's, Starbucks and other coffee shops certainly strive for an authenticity and appeals to cultural capital but do so without the off-putting aesthetics of particularity. And so it is with the Radiant Café (and cafés in other megachurches). The curving, natural forms of the café's sign are strongly reminiscent of the signs in Starbucks, as are the colors of the walls and the materials in the countertop. In short, this café offers the pleasures of the chain coffee shop within the safe confines of the church.

Not surprisingly, the coffee shop is nearly always across the way from the bookstore. The church bookstore offers religious titles and selections of Bibles. Books on parenting, sexuality, worship, relationships, financial stability as well as religiously themed novels for young people and adults fill the shelves. They also stock CDs of contemporary Christian music and cassettes, CDs, and DVDs of the pastor's messages. Finally, the store is filled with gifts, T-shirts, other apparel, and jewelry. Like any other store, there is a soundtrack for the shopping experience, in this case contemporary Christian rock. Taken together, the bookstore, the café, and the informal seating in the lobby and on the patio create a comfortable and familiar consumer culture space. It is just like any other late modern, suburban public space, devoted to buying and selling but also, in this case, sutured into the commitments of evangelical Christianity.

Much as the gothic cathedral with its intricately carved entranceways taught parishioners the nature of the religious performance to be gained inside, these early introductions to the megachurch play an embodied pedagogical role for audience members. The gothic cathedral reminded visitors of the virtuous lives of saints and indicated to the audience the greatness of God and the lowliness of the individual. In the megachurches' coffee shop and bookstore virtue remains at stake, but the contours and embodied experience of virtue are very different. Rather than a space set aside from the everyday world, these contemporary spaces assert to the visitor that the megachurch wants to be an integral and familiar part of their everyday lives. Congregants can and should bring their everyday hopes and fears to this space and community. Decidedly not distinct or different from its surrounding landscape, the megachurch inserts itself into the interstices of this everyday world; into the friendships, family relationships, and activities that constitute daily life.

This everydayness of religion is reinforced by the invitation to both church workers and congregants to attend church in their everyday clothes. It is no mistake, for example, that the bookstore sells T-shirts, not dress shirts. Radiant's leader, Pastor Lee, is known for his Hawaiian print shirt worn over a T-shirt and jeans.[29] The website clearly indicates that this casualness is crucial to the church. Pastor Lee is in the center of the home page, dressed in a dark T-shirts, arms folded across his chest, a comfortable smile on his face. Behind him is artwork announcing October's messages emblazoned on what looks like a PowerBar wrapper. Just below the logo, running down the left side of the home page are five menu options, each explaining the characteristics of the church. The very first asserts that the church has "casual atmosphere." What are the characteristics of this casual atmosphere? "Wear jeans, hangout in the bookstore and the coffeeshop—be comfortable."[30] A picture of legs in jeans accompanies the description. Radiant Church, then, imagines casualness as located among the coffee shop, the bookstore, the jeans.

So where are we so far? Radiant Church and many other megachurches work hard to reduce the psychological, sociological, and spiritual barriers to entering church. Rather than creating a church set apart from the world, these are churches that are resolutely, even dogmatically, of the world. They are absolutely connected to the popular culture that surrounds them. They do not just speak to or about popular consumer culture; instead, they speak with and through popular consumer culture. Everything about the buildings embodies comfort and security, nothing speaks to sacrifice or change or distinctiveness. In short, here is a place that offers all the familiarity of surrounding suburban spaces and practices. But this familiarity adds a crucial difference: all of this popular culture is embedded in Christianity.

Rocking for Jesus

No single practice within these churches more clearly speaks to this use of popular culture to impart a religious message than the praise music that marks each of the Saturday evening and Sunday morning services. Making up more than half of the service, this music as form and performance is absolutely central to the megachurches' successes. A typical service begins with twenty to thirty minutes of contemporary Christian praise music sung by the audience led by a live band on stage. At Radiant a nine-person band plays mostly up-tempo pop- and rock-inspired songs. Keyboards, drums, bass, rhythm and acoustic guitar, and several vocalists make up the band. They are all dressed casually in jeans, cargo pants, and T-shirts. The words to the songs are projected on the jumbotrons, as are images of the band members playing and singing. The band is a well-knit, driving unit, and the volume is turned high. The lyrics flashing on the screen are simple. No one sings harmony; in fact, it is not possible to hear the audience singing over the volume of the amplified band.

The music performed at Radiant and in most megachurches is part of the larger and commercially viable contemporary Christian music (CCM). CCM is part of a centuries-long Christian tradition of drawing on popular secular music transformed with religious lyrics. Using secular music was particularly compelling for revivalists, since their effort was to attract the unchurched and convert them. While traditionalists would often critique the use of these secular forms, the forms became accepted within the church until this new form became old and a new round of musical transformations took place. In the early 1970s, evangelical Christians began to look to rock as a possible form for reaching unconverted young people. Of course, using rock forms—the devil's music many preachers asserted—stirred controversy. But by the turn of the twenty-first century, Christian rock, pop, and to a lesser extent hip-hop dominated megachurch services.

Jay Howard and John Streck suggest that most contemporary Christian music fits into one of three broad genres: (1) separational, in which the artists imagine Christ and the world as radically separated and the lyrics are the most clearly evangelical; (2) integrational, in which Christian music can help transform culture, and the music is the least distinguishable from secular contemporary music, and; (3) transformational, in which both the church and the world come under critique from Christian musicians.[31] Not surprisingly, the first two genres are the typical music of the megachurch, with an emphasis on integrational music that highlights individual relationships with Jesus. Integrational music gives Christian messages a positive pop slant. "The message is usually simple: Resist temptation, life gets tough but God is only a prayer away, love your spouse, get religion involved in your everyday life, forgive yourself, and have good time."[32] Regardless of the particular form, CCM emphasizes emotionality, individual experience, and a personal relationship with God. "Rather than being written about God," Anne Loveland and Otis Wheeler write, CCM songs, "were addressed to him, using second-person instead of third-person pronouns. They encouraged worshipers to seek a personal, intimate relationship with God."[33]

At Radiant separational and integrational CCM dominate the church service, offering the directly evangelical message of salvation with the positive messages of God helping the singer/listener through the difficulties of the day. The lyrics of the music focus on the relationship between the singer and Jesus or God. These songs are the lyrical equivalent of the jeans and the coffee shop. Rather than a formal relationship with a distant but all-powerful God, these songs offer comfortable friendship with God. God, in these songs, is not a mighty fortress or a rock of ages, but rather is a mature, strong, and wise friend. You can almost imagine sitting down to an ice-blended mocha in the lobby coffee shop with this God. You could share your daily troubles or tell a joke or two (the pastor certainly does) with the megachurch's God. In fact, you might not recognize this God since he rode up to the church on his Harley Davidson rather than arriving on a borrowed donkey.[34]

Jesus on the Screen

This commitment to consumption and CCM as a way of updating and relaxing the church service is mirrored in the church's commitment to contemporary communication technologies like jumbotrons, intricate web pages, electronic music, and instantly available recordings of the day's message. The deployment of the jumbotron may be the most striking use of technology in the megachurch. Radiant Church's auditorium features four large screens, three in the front and one in the back. The middle screen in the front nearly always projects a live image from the stage—a close-up of Pastor Lee, a musician, or a long shot of the stage. More diverse images are projected on the side screens. Song lyrics flash on the side screens during the music, allowing audiences to sing along (though there is no indication of the melody as there would be in a more traditional hymn book). During the sermon, the side screens either show the preacher or project the biblical verse under consideration. At times, the pastor will ask the audience to read the scripture with him; at other times, he simply reads what is on the screen. Regardless, the important verses are also printed on the follow-along guide handed to congregants as they enter the auditorium.

These huge screens respond to the major difficulty facing the megachurch: a loss of intimacy. Since the nineteenth century, evangelical church designers and architects have been preoccupied with creating large worship spaces that also connect audiences to the stage. The Chatham Street Church offered the theater with its raised stage and balcony as one way of accommodating large audiences while giving audience members adequate sight lines and acoustical clarity. For many designers, the auditorium church, with its raised platform and sloping main floor and balcony offered the best solution to the problem.[35] But nothing beats the jumbotron combined with tiny, wireless mics to create a sense of intimacy in an otherwise huge space. In a very real sense, there are no bad seats in the new megachurch. Huge images of the action on stage are easily visible anywhere in the auditorium, while state-of-the-art sound systems make the music and the sermon easily heard across the space. I nearly always watched the action on the screen, ignoring the actual singer or the pastor; they were so much more present on the screen than if I watched them on the stage. On the screen, I could see every facial expression and every gesture, while the person on the stage was a distant image.

The giant screen, along with the high-tech sound system, eliminates the need for expensive sloped floors or carefully designed acoustics in the buildings. In fact, the auditoriums are nearly always a simple square or rectangle shape with an open ceiling. The floors are flat, and the chairs are usually well-padded, movable seats. The flat floor and movable seats make the space more flexible. Move the chairs and you have a vast, open space available for a range of different activities.[36] More importantly, this form of projecting the service to the auditorium over jumbotrons and through multiple speakers connects the service to other popular culture forms of entertainment—the concert, the sporting event, and the motivational speech. The technology aurally and visually shrinks the space, connecting audience members with the stage. At the same time, these technologies shrink the cultural distance between church and other forms of commodified popular culture. Like the coffee shop, the T-shirts, and the Christian rock band, the jumbotron communicates that this space is not like your parents' church. Gone are the pipe organ, the formal choir loft, and the pews. Come as you are, the auditorium says, and participate in an experience that is familiar from rock concerts, comedy shows, and hockey games.

In fact, this connection of technology to the popularity of concerts is an explicit part of the church's marketing, especially to young people. The church is segmented into numerous age-specific groups. These groups are not Sunday school services, but instead are alternatives to the main service. The main service is reserved for adults, while children go to "age appropriate" services, leaving parents free to fully enjoy their own worship.

Two crucial elements combine in defining services for grade school and high school worshippers: contemporary music and technology. The Radiant website describes Elevate, the worship service for third through sixth grade, as a "high-tech multimedia experience that uses all the latest technology to teach kids about God's Word! After just one visit, we promise they'll want to come back week after week."[37] Octane, "is a rockin' service for junior and senior high school students where kids can hang out with their friends, experience some of the hottest technology around, and hear a message that will make a difference in their life!"[38] Music and technology combine to create a worship service compelling for adults, teenagers, and grade-school children. These popular forms and technologies, because they are deeply embedded in the everyday lives of the suburbanites, become the ideal modes by which to communicate a message that "can make a difference in their life."

Radiantly Branded

But it is not simply the case that the music and the technology are communication media for transmitting messages; these characteristics are key components in the branding of the churches. James Twitchell argues that a key characteristic of the megachurch is that it uses popular culture modes of branding to draw in churchgoers. "What we are seeing," Twitchell writes, "is the selling of bottled water. There is little if any product differentiation because Protestantism has become a commodity. The suppliers are redundant, and church space is oversupplied. That's why denominations need separation via branding. When you have an interchangeable product, the story becomes a necessary fiction. How you tell it becomes crucial. And the telling of it is progressively coming from the marketplace, from the supermarket, from the shelves of machine-made goods."[39] In fact, this product differentiation is crucial to the growth of megachurches. Megachurches—though they are growing by leaps and bounds—are not creating more total church members or attendees. Megachurches have made compelling claims to potential church members for their allegiance and have done so, in part, through branding.

Radiant Church is part of this move toward branding. The web page not only demonstrates technological savvy, but it is also congruent with the ways other organizations communicate themselves, creating a narrative about their relative merits. In fact, the web page, the building, and the service—as I have already argued—work hard to distinguish this church from other churches. The branding draws on all the resources other post-

Figure 5.5. RadiantChurch.com bumper sticker on a Chrysler in the Radiant Church parking lot. The three stickers on this PT Cruiser bring together the branding of the church with the use of stickers to name personal and social identifications. The driver of this vehicle asserts patriotism and evangelical Christianity in a way that makes sense in a post-9/11 world. Photograph by author.

modern organizations use—carefully designed logos, snappy advertising language, well-placed billboards along major thoroughfares, and ubiquitous bumper stickers pointing to the Radiant website (figure 5.5).

Within this branding discourse, Radiant Church serves as a department store or large institution that is itself made up of separate brands. Like Mossimo brand clothing at Target, Radiant's departments and activities have their own brand identities. It is not enough to call the teenagers' service a service for teens; it needs a name (Octane), a logo, and a narrative about technology, music, and everyday life. But youth are not the only ones branded in the church, the variety of adult options also relies on brands. Young adults are invited to Velocity, "the hottest night club in Arizona,"[40] while members struggling with addictions and other habitual sins (including homosexuality) can join Celebrate Recovery.[41]

Taken together, the appeals to consumption and consumer discourses, the performance of popular music forms, the use of entertainment technologies, and the brand narratives all indicate a deep attachment to postmodern consumer culture. Here I take consumer culture to not simply be the practices and discourses of retailing but instead an overarching way of understanding contemporary culture and society. As an economic, cultural, and social condition, consumption is, as I argued in the introduction to the book, a fundamental characteristic of the present moment. Not only do we consume material goods; more importantly, we consume images, texts, performances.

My argument began with the most obvious forms of consumption offered in the megachurch; namely, the references to malls and the material goods for sale in the coffee shop and bookstore. But I have also demonstrated that the integration of the church into popular, consumer culture is more thorough than simply selling cups of coffee and DVDs. Instead, the very form of the church service itself pays homage not to just current culture but also to popular culture as framed through a mass media founded on selling. The music of the service drawing on popular and imminently sellable forms of musical expression coalesce this connection between consumer culture and worship practices. These musical performances are absolutely intertwined with entertainment technology. The technology is offered as a means of communication, but, I have argued, is also part of the communication. The service is exciting because it is high tech. Put most bluntly, the megachurch's communication technology communicates. Finally, all of these elements—comforting spaces of consumption, entertaining performances, and technologically fascinating services and activities—become part of the church's brand. With flat overall church attendance, megachurch growth depends on differentiating self from other. This is the job of megachurch branding.

And so, I return to where I started. "This is not your parents'" church may be the simplest form of the brand. This message is explicitly offered in sermons and on websites. Just as important however are the implicit and copious assertions of newness and of separation from old forms of church. Branding not only offers this message, the process of branding already distinguishes the megachurch from its forebearers. But so do the technology, the entertaining new music, the bookstore, and coffee shop.

Kids Welcome

Clearly, integration into consumer culture is vital to megachurches' claim to the good life. Perhaps as important is the centrality of the family. Megachurches offer a wide range of richly conceived, carefully planned, enter-taining services and events for children. Radiant Church offers five separate "age appropriate" church services for children along with a family room where parents can stay with their children and watch the service on "gi-ant screens."[42] Just as importantly, the introductory video played at each adult service clearly distinguishes the adult service from the children and youth services, urging parents not to bring the children to the adult ser-vice, but to take them to their own services.

The careful attention to family recognizes and validates the importance of family within suburbia. While urban spaces may be appealing to young professionals or singles, suburbia is imagined as the ideal place to raise chil-dren, as the analysis so far in this book attests. Fascinatingly, the megachurch is an ideal place for children as a set of segmented audiences with different tastes and needs from those of adults. One of the crucial achievements of consumer culture has been to create segmented audiences to which goods, services, and entertainment products can be sold. The megachurch abso-lutely accepts this differentiation. They positively do not want the chil-dren and adults intermingling in the services. As the Radiant website ar-gues, "the best place for your children is in their age specific group."[43] For parents, of course, this offers a valued service. They can let professionals take care of their children while they attend the adult service comfort-able that their children will have a pleasant and morally uplifting couple of hours in their own services.

Megachurches' privileging of the family draws on a long tradition in protestant church building. Nineteenth-century evangelical churches in-creasingly created and relied on a connection between the family and the church by incorporating domestic architecture and design into the church. This domestication is most evident in the rooms incorporated into the church as churches began to include "kitchens, dining rooms, lounges, toi-lets, nurseries, and libraries."[44] This domestication of the church intersected with the sacralization of the family in late nineteenth-century US culture. Nineteenth-century culture often located moral training in the domestic sphere and imagined women as distinctly moral creatures as opposed to the amorality men exhibited. One way women responded to this moralization of the home and their position as the moral bulwark of society was by go-ing to church. Women were—and are—far more active than men in evan-gelical congregations. This domestication and feminization of morality of-fered architectural and cultural resources for evangelical churches, even as the domestication of the church "helped expand the conceptualization of just what constituted women's 'proper' behavior."[45] Women's cooking, for example, was sanctified both in the home and in the church.[46]

Even as society was passing to women the responsibility for the moral upbringing of children, churches began to incorporate children's moral training in Sunday schools. Sunday school as both space and practice was a controversial development. Much of the controversy stemmed from the belief that parents had responsibility for moral training. Sunday schools, some thought, would remove this responsibility for moral training. At the same time, building and staffing Sunday school spaces shifted resources from the main sanctuary and the main services. In spite of these criticisms, Sunday schools proliferated throughout the nineteenth and early twentieth centuries, becoming an accepted and central part of evangelical churches. Importantly, however, Sunday school was not designed to replace the main church service. Here lies a crucial innovation of the megachurch: rather than Sunday school coming before the main church service where families would reconnect, children and adults are now segregated during the main service, with "Sunday school" (though, as we have seen it is no longer called that—school is boring and old fashioned; "Octane" is rockin' and cool) becoming a youthful version of the main service. This shift is crucial. Parents no longer need to care for children as they listen to the pastor and sing the music. The service—a haven from the difficulties of secular life—also becomes a haven from family life even as the church asserts its care and concern for families. As Jeanne Kilde argues, compared to the domestic church of the nineteenth and early twentieth centuries, the megachurch locates itself outside of the stresses of family life, turning child care over to the church.[47]

But megachurches incorporate family not just on the weekend. Many, like Radiant, run weekday preschools. Many megachurches are also involved in grade schools and high schools. Lee McFarland, for example, is CEO of a charter school in Surprise. The school is across the street from the church. The development of the charter school connects the megachurch to the suburb in very specific ways. Suburban growth in places like Surprise has outstripped the abilities of these towns to meet their residents' needs for basic services such as schools. Since suburbs are, as I have argued, profoundly about families, adequate schools are crucial to the success of the suburb. At the same time, the megachurch is also focused on family. It has to be since its goal is to appeal to the new residents of the suburb. Involvement in providing schooling for suburban children is a natural outgrowth of the church's mission. Add to these needs a conservative suspicion of traditional public schools and a preference for charter schools and megachurch involvement in these efforts becomes a perfect way to crystallize their commitments to family, education, and suburbia.

Consuming Religion, Sacralizing Consumption, Living in Families

Crucial to the megachurch, then, is the ability to address, respond to, draw on, and transcend the paradoxes of suburban familial capitalism. As David Chaney argues, suburbanites confront a difficult paradox between the suburban ideal of a public and commonly held sociality on the one hand and a framing and understanding of the good life as created in and by the profound individualism of consumer culture.[48] The megachurch works at this precise location: a space devoted to values and community whose message is transmitted through and transmuted by consumer culture writ large.

This transmission/transmutation is announced by the architecture itself. Ahistorical and devoid of references to previous church forms, the megachurch's architecture is a blank slate on which church communities can write their late modern, high technology, consumerist identities. The architecture is marked by a dialectic between absence and presence, forgetting and remembering. While different megachurches negotiate this dialectic in different ways—some are more "churchy" than others—nearly all are marked by a relative secularization of the architecture. In the place of this absent sacred architecture, there are references to dominant post-Fordist suburban architectural forms: shopping malls, technology business parks, and professional office buildings. The public forgetting of the church makes possible the (re)membering of the mall. But more importantly, forgetting/remembering makes possible a form of evangelicalism that rejects the rejections of popular culture so crucial to earlier versions of the sacred experience in the United States. While megachurches share much with fundamentalist and Pentecostal forms of evangelism—in particular a theology of biblical inherency from fundamentalism and a Christian practice focused on experience and revelation from Pentecostalism—the megachurch is far more welcoming because of its appeal to popular culture. Far from rejecting surrounding, secular, or nonevangelical culture as the work of the devil, megachurches welcome and celebrate popular culture. As Mark Shibley argues, contemporary "evangelicals are in the world and, strategically or unwittingly, have absorbed many of the core values of contemporary American culture."[49] If we are to take the architecture of the megachurch as a sign of these absorptions, we must recognize that to absorb core contemporary values is to also reject—to forget even as you remember—at least some core values of older forms of evangelicalism.

In no performance is this remembered forgetting clearer than in the ways pastors consistently talk about their prayers. Pastor after pastor, in service after service as he begins to pray, or when he describes the prayers he offered as he converted, or when he urges the audience to take their troubles to the Lord will say something like, "this won't sound like your parents' prayers," or, "I didn't pray like my father prayed," or "you don't need to say thee or thou, just talk to Jesus like he is your friend." At once remembering these older prayers offered in traditional churches and so often offered, the pastor will say, out of a sense of guilt, these phrases also urge a forgetting of these traditions. Let go of the guilt that accompanies your memories of church, the pastor is urging, release yourself from your parents' strictures, and imagine instead a new religious life, fully devoted to the popular, consumer-culture-inflected life you are already leading. Thus more than simply absorbing core US American values, megachurch evangelicalism celebrates these values. Megachurch evangelicalism does not simply accept the values as a necessary evil, nor use the values as neutral tools to convert the unchurched. Instead, the megachurch's overwhelming reliance on contemporary consumer culture for its architecture and design, its worship practices, and its organizational structure indicates that the good life resides very precisely in these contemporary values.

And what, according to the megachurch, are these values? First, contemporary moral life ought not be constrained by tradition (or at least not by the traditions that separate congregants from popular culture). In this sense, megachurch morality is very much of a piece with modernism's deep suspicion of tradition. The active forgetting of the megachurch's architecture and performance consistently and constantly reminds congregants that memory itself is troubling, overly constraining, and stands in the way of a rich and comforting good life. Contemporary moral life ought not to lead Christians to make too many sacrifices. Most importantly, evangelicals need not sacrifice their desire for material goods and their love of rock and roll, dancing, and coffee.

Second, heteronormative forms of family serve as the foundation of the church. The family is the smallest unit of community and serves as both the material and metaphoric boundaries on action. In this new world sex is good, but only within the context of committed heterosexual relationships.[50] In fact, in this new world, women are given increasing responsibilities and opportunities. Shibley argues, for example, that many contemporary evangelicals accept basic equality for men and women, figuring

the family in newer, distinctly contemporary ways.[51] In spite of openness to revised forms of marriage, women and men are still best seen as
conjoined within traditional, heterosexual marriage. But the heterosexual
family serves also as the metaphor for the megachurch community. New
members are immature, like children in their spiritual lives. The church
guides new members, who have been "born again" into Christian adult-
hood. Not surprisingly, many of these guides are men who, like compas-
sionate fathers, guide God's children to maturity. This all-encompassing
rhetoric of family values offers a powerful counterweight to the apparent
liberalization of attitudes toward secular culture. As Dana Cloud argues,
family values foster a deeply conservative vision of the world in which social responsibility is privatized even as social ills are scapegoated onto dysfunctional families.[52]

The privatization of social responsibility implied by the rhetoric of
family values is directly tied to the third, and perhaps most important,
megachurch value: the importance of personal, individual happiness. The
church's message of acceptance of consumer culture and its privileging of
the family are all, in the end, justified as modes for greater personal happiness. It is no mistake the Joel Osteen's and Rick Warren's best-selling books
are, in the first instance, self-help guides for personal improvement.[53] Certainly, these books—and megachurches more broadly—include service to
the world as part of the mission, but this service is emphatically not justified as good in itself nor is it the focus or purpose of life; instead, personal
development is fundamental to the Christian life and the Christian message in these churches. These are, in short, powerful sites of contemporary
therapeutic culture.[54] The megachurch offers a haven that protects the attendees from the vagaries and difficulties of the late modern world.[55] This
need to offer a haven is part of the reason why the church makes so few
demands on its members. It is also the rhetorical force of family values,
as these values serve as individualized bulwarks against ever-encroaching
late modernity.

As he drew on the Exodus story to narrativize the 1960s civil rights
struggles, Martin Luther King Jr. was not particularly concerned with the
hurts, habits, and hang-ups of the audience's personal lives. He does not
draw on popular culture references to reinforce, justify, and sacralize the
present. Instead, he draws on deep wells of memory to imagine a world
radically different from that in which he lived. For King, along with gen-
erations of Jews and Christians, Exodus has offered the hope for a profoundly reformed life. But in the megachurch of the early twenty-first century, the freedom offered by the Bible is personal and familial. This makes

perfect sense in a church devoted to selling coffee and clothes, where the mall and the office complex offer more affective and aesthetic inspiration than does the great sacred architecture of the past. Religious architecture, Alain de Botton asserts, can recall us to our truest, best selves.[56] The best and truest selves offered in the megachurch are no different from the selves available at Crate and Barrel, at Starbucks, or at Olive Garden.

Megachurches, then, are a crucial part of the suburban good life. Perhaps, better than any of the other landscapes, megachurches are able to bridge the contradictions of suburban life. By sacralizing contemporary consumer culture, placing this culture in the family and as part of God's plan, megachurches can authenticate and justify the very performances that many find so troubling about suburbia. Where residential architecture and consumer architecture draw on nostalgia and commodified visions of difference, the megachurch rejects an aesthetic of the past. It can do so because it offers a performative narrative that embeds the suburban good life in a meaningful story—the greatest story ever told.

6

Buying the Good Life

How the Lifestyle Center Became Suburbia's Civic Square

Megan Beam and Greg Dickinson

> The proclaimed dissolution of public and private on the botanized as-
> phalt of shoppingtown makes possible, not a flâneuse, since that term is
> anachronistic, but an experience of "modernity" for women in which
> it is vital to not begin by identifying heroines and victims (even of con-
> flicts with male paranoia), but rather a profound ambivalence about shift-
> ing roles.
>
> —Meaghan Morris

As essential as all of the foregoing suburban spaces are to the suburban
landscape, few are more important than the shopping mall. In the postwar
era, suburbs became increasingly independent from cities, an independence
materialized and made possible in part by the ever-growing shopping mall.
Indeed, by the 1980s and 1990s, the massive regional mall was a centerpiece
of the suburban landscape. By the early twenty-first century, however, their
time had come and gone. In the place of enormous indoor malls, developers began building smaller, outdoor "lifestyle centers." No longer anchored
by large department stores like Macy's or Sears, lifestyle centers focus attention on smaller lifestyle retailers like J. Crew, Coldwater Creek, Pottery
Barn, Pier 1, and Barnes & Noble and include a wide range of chain restaurants and coffee shops. In these new malls, parking often fronts individual
stores and pedestrians wander carefully designed streets and sidewalks. Even
though the regional mall of the previous century strove to be the suburb's
civic center, the new lifestyle centers work hard to recapture the aesthetic,
affective, and spatial conditions of urban and rural downtown America.

The eclipsing of the regional mall by the lifestyle center, however, was
not a harbinger of the end of consumer culture or of the intertwining of
shopping and suburbs. In fact, in the days of the early twenty-first century,
consumerism reached a zenith. Never before had such a large portion of
the national economy depended on consumption. And never before had
so many people gone so far into debt to access the goods of consumer culture.[1] Suburbanites were going into debt to buy big homes in the walled

and gated communities of the far-flung suburbs I investigated in chapter 3. As people bought these bigger houses, they also bought consumer goods to outfit the dens and dining rooms, decorate the walls and landings, and fill the closets and garages. A large portion of individual incomes and personal wealth were bound in the new homes suburbanites were buying. As home prices increased, homeowners realized dramatic growth in personal wealth. Many accessed this wealth through increasingly obscure mortgages used not only to buy bigger and more prestigious homes but also to create cash for additional cars, clothes, furniture, electronics, appliances, and all the other accoutrements of the suburban lifestyle. This ever-growing home equity bubble enabled individuals to buy more and more goods.[2] In short, the homes investigated in chapter 3 also enabled other forms of abundant consumption, consumption performed primarily in malls, commercial strips, and big box discount outlets.

Oddly, however, even as the big box stores were getting bigger, the large indoor regional and mega-malls were losing ground to newer, smaller, specialized retail districts known as lifestyle centers. In fact, by 2006 no new regional malls were on the drawing boards, while lifestyle centers—smaller-scaled, open-air shopping centers—were being planned in communities across the country.[3] Many factors account for this shift in retailing. Lifestyle centers are smaller and thus less expensive to build. Using less land, they can be sited more closely to the suburbanites who are their main audience. The economics of the regional mall is dependent on large department stores as anchors, and these department stores are losing ground to big box discount stores like Target, Wal-Mart, and Kohl's and to smaller, lifestyle retailers like Banana Republic and The Gap. As important as these factors are, the lifestyle center's nostalgically rendered mnemonic references to urban and small town landscapes situate the lifestyle center as the suburb's town square, create a late modern image and enactment of civic space, place otherwise placeless suburbs, and, because the lifestyle center is devoted to family experiences, locate the consuming family at the center of the suburb's public values.

This argument proceeds in four stages. First, we trace shifting post–World War II suburban spaces of consumption from the large regional mall to the contemporary lifestyle center. Second, we place the rise of the lifestyle center into discourses of gentrification and New Urbanism, both of which, like the lifestyle center, use memories of the city to create meaningful place within late modernity. Third, we turn to a close analysis of lifestyle centers, in particular Centerra Promenade in Loveland, Colorado, to demonstrate the material and symbolic construction of a civic space that produces civic subjectivity whose primary affiliation is structured within the family and whose chief mode of civic choice is within systems of consumption. Finally, we use our analysis to reflect on the consequences of this materialization of these suburban civic spaces.

Suburbs and Consumer Culture

It is hard to imagine the postwar suburb outside of the contexts of consumer culture and of brand-new consumer landscapes. Although the mall as consumer landscape stretches back to at least the early 1920s in the United States, this consumer landscape became prominent in the 1950s. Before World War II, those living in the suburbs had to drive or take public transportation to urban retail areas to do their major shopping.[4] As suburbs dramatically expanded after World War II, suburban developers, who were also often owners of downtown department stores, began to realize that the suburbs were ripe for commercial development. As we have already seen, these new postwar suburbs were increasingly built for the car, were situated farther from the urban center, and housed a growing concentration of the US American wealth.[5] With suburbia's growing population and increasing disposable income, developers began building what became the quintessential consumer landscape of the twentieth century: the regional mall.

If the domestic landscape of suburbia was not completely new in the postwar era—indeed, the postwar suburb simply perfected the kinds of suburban housing developments started in the 1920s and 1930s—the mall was a new building form. And it was fitting that the mall would appear in the heart of new suburban towns. First, the mall was appropriate because it was in the postwar period that the US economy took a hard turn from a production or industrial economy to a consumer economy. Over the course the five decades from the 1950s to the early 2000s, consumer spending increased dramatically and became the driving force of the economy. In what some have called the shift from Fordist to post-Fordist economics, the US economy increasingly depended on selling goods and on the growth of a whole host of information and service sector industries.[6] This shift away from an industrial economy to information and service economies enabled the development of the growth of suburbs while deeply damaging cities. As place-based industries lost workers, the urban landscapes that depended on the factories and industrial workers began to wither. The withering industrial urban core only sped the growth of suburbs, as white, middle-class urbanites moved to the suburbs searching for a life framed by homogeneity. In this context, people were not only moving to the suburbs, they were also fleeing a city increasingly imagined as a dangerous and fearsome place.[7] White flight from the cities made returning to the urban retail districts for shopping trips unappealing for many suburbanites.

Second, as the suburbs continued to get bigger and a larger portion of the population moved from the city to the suburbs, suburban designers and residents began to feel the need for a central space that could replicate at least some of the social and civic roles downtowns performed for cities. Initially, suburbs, which had been built almost exclusively as residential landscapes, were oriented toward the city for culture, shopping, and civic engagement. But in the 1950s suburbs began to look away from the city, turning instead to new suburban forms as a replacement for the services and opportunities downtowns had once offered. As Lizabeth Cohen argues, the postwar mall and shopping center "was the 'new city' of the postwar era," creating "a vision of how community space should be constructed in an economy and society built on mass consumption."[8] The mall was more than just a space of consumption, it began to serve as suburbia's new downtown.

Third, transportation changes embedded into suburbia—the government-funded road system and the increased number of families with cars—not only made living farther from the city possible, it also made building consumer spaces designed for the car more viable, even necessary.[9] One of the crucial innovations of the malls was to build them in the middle of large parking lots.[10] Where urban retail districts were embedded in densely settled commercial and residential landscapes with limited parking spots, shopping malls offered shoppers plentiful parking. The regional mall, anchored by familiar department stores and filled with smaller shops, replicated many of the services of downtown shopping, but with the convenience of a large parking lot and the comfort of climate-controlled indoor shopping.

What the mall embodies, then, is not just a new kind of retail space, but rather a whole set of new spatial and social relations that created new ways of thinking about citizenship and everyday practices. In its initial incarnation, it concretized the ways suburbia was deeply and completely embedded in the new economies of consumerism. While the mall owners quickly reversed their initial framing of the mall as a new civic space (for example, mall owners moved to squelch speech rights, arguing that the mall was private rather than public property[11]), the presence and development of the mall clearly signaled the centrality of consumerism to the ways suburban designers and residences imagined the suburban good life.

From Malls to Lifestyles

While the regional mall seemed a nearly ideal solution to the rising desire for efficient and compelling shopping located in the suburbs, it also articulated with the spatial anxieties of the postwar suburb, in particular with agoraphobia. As suggested in chapter 1, modernity and postmodernity are marked by spatialized anxieties, many of which are mobilized around the concept of home. Agoraphobia drives people into the home, for it is often triggered by the vast open spaces of the modern city. Crossing boulevards that offer no shelter can halt agoraphobics in their tracks, overwhelming them with anxiety. But if the boulevards of the nineteenth century are overwhelming, how much more so are the giant structures of the postwar United States, and in particular the structures that make suburbia possible? Take the interstate freeway as an example. Not only did the freeway open urban hinterlands to suburban development (just as did the interurban trams of the late nineteenth and early twentieth centuries), but the interstate also created a whole new landscape. Indeed, Reyner Banham writes that Los Angeles was the postwar model of suburban development and postmodern placemaking, whose characteristic landscape was the freeway.[12] Like the mall, the freeway is a nearly new architectural form. Clearly, the freeway is about the car. The car and the freeway coproduce each other. Increasing car ownership produced the need for freeways even as the new freeways enabled the growth of car culture.[13] The freeway connects suburbs to other suburbs and cities, and connects all of these to the regional mall. At the same time, freeways, and the malls they link together, are the central landscapes of twentieth-century agoraphobia.[14] The mall and the freeway—though extraordinarily efficient in moving individuals from place to place and goods from manufactures into suburbanites' homes—are also profoundly placeless. Indeed, their efficiencies depend on placelessness, on the sense that this landscape could be anywhere. But anywhere and nowhere are nearly the same thing, as malls are at once omnitopias—spaces that contain all possible spaces—and a-topias—places without any identifiable place.[15]

This placelessness is of two orders: the spatial and the temporal. The regional urban mall is relentlessly separated from its local geography. In the first instance, it is separated from its local geography by the immense parking lots that surround the mall. These parking lots, connected directly to the major arterial roads and those roads connected to the (a-geographical) freeways, all strive to disconnect the mall from the material conditions of site. What is more, once you enter the mall you arrive in a neatly and hermetically sealed interior space unyieldingly separated from the vagaries of the mall's immediate surroundings. As Margaret Morse argues, "malls are completely separated from the outside world."[16] In fact, malls and freeways (and for Morse, television) together create a new, postmodern ontology that is marked by "distraction," contoured through fluidity, and more committed to the "exchange of values" than to restrictions implied by local space.[17]

In the second instance, while nearly rabid in its separation from the local landscape, the mall is also persistently ahistoric. The ontology of distraction is a mode of temporality that collapses past, present, and future.[18] Always being updated, referring primarily to the present of retail design, the regional mall may be the most prevalent—if also the most banal—version of the ground zero building imagined by modernity's great social theorists and architects. From the French revolution through Le Corbusier's work, modernity expresses a desire to remake the world from ground zero outside the bounds of tradition or history and without the constraints of old material forms.[19] "This zero," Kathryn Milun argues, "is related to the pervasive, unrepresentable, 'central vacuity' of modern urban space" and is nowhere better expressed than in the vastness of suburban tracts, regional malls, and freeways.[20] The mall, then, can be thought of as a paradoxical place. It is deeply and purposefully placeless and is also a place that perhaps most clearly localizes the kinds of anxiety placelessness triggers. It is against this paradoxical abstraction that the lifestyle center inserts itself. Where the mall's placelessness is both spatial and temporal, the lifestyle center offers spatial and temporal concreteness.

Of course, the transition from indoor, regional malls to lifestyle centers is influenced by a range of economic as well as aesthetic and affective factors. The economics of lifestyle centers can be compelling. Where the regional mall demands large, undeveloped or underdeveloped plots of land, the lifestyle center takes up a relatively smaller footprint.[21] This smaller footprint reduces the cost of the land and allows developers to site the malls closer to desired shoppers. Regional malls depend on successful department stores like Macy's and Nordstrom to draw shoppers to the mall. The smaller, lifestyle retail stores like Restoration Hardware, Williams-Sonoma, and Banana Republic rely on the foot traffic generated by the department store anchors. However, department stores have lost sway with customers, often losing those customers to the smaller lifestyle retailers who had once depended on the department stores.[22] New lifestyle centers allow these smaller stores to develop their own identity and, increasingly, these stores are themselves shopping destinations. And so the lifestyle center offers to these retailers a number of economic advantages.

Most importantly, however, as an open air, humanly scaled shopping mall, the lifestyle center replicates important aspects of older forms of shopping in cities and towns while repudiating the temporal and geographical abstractions of the twentieth-century mall. As one developer notes, "Baby boomers will respond ideally to something that recalls their pasts."[23] What they desire is the shopping and the experience of small town Main Street and urban centers. Lifestyle centers, with their in-front-of-store parking, sidewalks, parks, fountains, gazebos, and museums offer "mini-cities" for shopping.[24] Different from the mall, the lifestyle center returns shoppers to a premall time and place. The lifestyle center looks to leapfrog over the mall back (geographically and temporally) to the urban centers and small towns that malls were instrumental in destroying.

If the new lifestyle centers offer a shopping experience to middle- and upper-middle-class suburbanites that, in some form, replicates the older, pre–World War II downtowns, it is worth exploring what this new, old town looks like. In replacing the public spaces of old downtowns as well as those of the more recent mall, lifestyle centers offer the most recent vision of what public space in suburbia ought to look like. In the lifestyle center, the late twentieth- and twenty-first-century suburb strives to return the urban scene suburbanites so studiously fled a generation earlier. But even as it might express a return of a repressed desire for the complexities of the urban life it is, at best, a glancing return, a "looking awry" at the city that strives, by gesturing to the city (and, to a lesser extent, the small town) to produce an entertaining and comforting retail district without the complexities and difficulties suburbanites associate with actually existing cities.[25] By excavating the visual and material rhetoric of lifestyle centers, we can begin to limn the outlines of suburbia's downtown. Crucially, this examination can help us understand the publicly held values of suburbia.

Gentrification, New Urbanism, and Dreams of the City

The lifestyle center is built of material and visual topoi already available in the practices of urban gentrification and the planning language of New Urbanism. At least since the mid-1980s, cities have embarked on aggressive gentrification efforts, striving to move downtowns and older neighborhoods up-market. These renewals have focused on older parts of cities, often remaking neighborhoods of the urban poor and working class. With significant support from the city, artists, young professionals, and then a broader range of middle-class and upper-middle-class people begin to move into the neighborhoods, restoring the homes and populating the retail and commercial landscapes with the institutions of late modern consumer culture like Starbucks, The Gap, Banana Republic, and Il Fornio.[26] Old Pasadena is a typical example of this gentrification. Built out of what was once a small segment of Route 66 and what had become Pasadena's skid row, Old Pasadena drew on the heritage of the site's aesthetics to offer comforts to visitors caught up in postmodernity's maelstrom.[27] By the late 1990s, what was once a street filled with dive bars, pawn shops, and adult bookstores had become a comfortable home of lifestyle retailers like Victoria's Secret and chain restaurants like Cheesecake Factory. Gentrified urbanity offers images of the past (re)built into the chaos of the city, offering to urbanites and visitors experiences of authenticity. That industrial production is replaced by chain retailers, or locally owned bars are exchanged for Starbucks, does not undermine the sense of rootedness these gentrified neighborhoods offered.

At almost the exact same time and in many ways responding to the same cultural, economic, and social conditions, New Urbanism offered its own vision of the city. Like gentrified neighborhoods, New Urbanism drew on (imagined) aesthetics of cities and was inspired by the work of architectural critics and activists like Jane Jacobs. Emphasizing narrow streets, historic building forms, multiuse neighborhoods, and pedestrian friendly residential and retail landscapes, New Urbanism offers a postmodern take on the city. Where gentrification remakes actually existing city neighborhoods, New Urbanism—for all of its talk about the urban—is an almost exclusively suburban form.[28] Perfected in such places like Disney's Celebration, Florida, and in Seaside, Florida (the set for *The Truman Show*), and replicated in developments like Centerra and Prospect New Town in suburban northern Colorado, these places combine images of a small town Main Street and the energy of a city downtown into wholly new suburban developments.[29] Rather than the semirural pastoral nostalgia offered in chain restaurants and the domestic landscapes investigated in chapters 3 and 4, New Urbanism creates place out of memories of cities. As a deeply nostalgic style, New Urbanism offers the images of cleanly scrubbed urbanity (read: whiter and more middle-class) as a comforting place to ward off the anxieties of placelessness. Drawing on the topoi of New Urbanism and gentrification, which themselves draw on (imaginatively created) topoi of small town and city Main Streets, lifestyle centers materialize these privately owned, retail sites as the contemporary suburbs' civic space. We can turn now to actual lifestyle centers to investigate the ways these lifestyle centers use memory and appeals to civicness as rhetorical topoi that suture the suburbs into an imagined urban past.

Remembering the City in the Suburban Landscape

How do lifestyle centers place shoppers within placeless suburbia? More specifically, what are the aesthetic and material rhetorical strategies lifestyle centers use to locate themselves in time and place? How, using these strategies, does the lifestyle center differentiate itself from the regional mall? As already suggested, lifestyle centers are places of memory working to suture users into nostalgically limned images of the city. They offer these memories by removing the roof; changing the relationship of the car to the space; building in outdoor nonretail spaces like bandstands, fire pits, and play areas; and by using consistent architectural references to cities and small town Main Street.

Outdoors in the Suburb

One of the innovations of the post–World War II regional shopping mall was to place all the shopping under a roof. In so doing, the mall was able to create a climate-controlled environment allowing visitors to avoid inclement weather. The roof and the climate control it afforded also allowed the mall to offer a more or less unified visual and social landscape. Control was a crucial rhetorical gambit of the suburban mall, for as suburbanites fled the city, they were, in part, fleeing the perceived increasing chaos of downtown. The mall's roof was a powerful rhetorical statement that could soothe the new suburbanite and was a compelling assertion about the city and the suburb. In contrast, every lifestyle center—and thus every major retail development built in the twenty-first century—is built as an outdoor shopping center. The brutal summer heat of the desert Southwest or the bone-chilling winter cold of the high plains of Colorado seem to argue that outdoor shopping makes little sense. Nonetheless, roofs have no place in the new lifestyle center. Building the lifestyle center without the roof obviously disconnects the lifestyle center from the regional mall even as it makes possible references to the city.

Removing the mall's roof not only differentiates the lifestyle center from the mall, it does so in a gesture that opens the lifestyle center to more persuasively speak the language of the city. Unlike the mall, cities don't have roofs; instead, they have buildings built across time, in differing styles; each with individual owners and offering city residents multiple services. The city is a site of aesthetic and material difference. Drawing on this urban difference, the lifestyle center's removed roof not only produces difference between itself and the mall, it also allows the lifestyle center to produce differences within the retail district that mimic urban aesthetic diversity. By refusing the unification implied by the roof, the lifestyle center promises at least the possibility of some of the intriguing differences often housed in the city.

At the same time, in refusing to control the weather the lifestyle center locates itself in its geography. If the regional mall sometimes felt like it could be located anywhere, wandering the sidewalks of The District under the Las Vegas sun or surveying the stores in the Promenade Shops at Centerra with the snow-capped Rockies in the background consistently situates the visitor in the vagaries of a region's weather and in the visual landscape of the lifestyle center. For example, the Rocky Mountains are archetypal of Colorado; they are to Colorado's Front Range what the Empire State Building or the Statue of Liberty are to New York. Being able to see the mountains to the west reminds shoppers they are in Colorado. But Phoenix and Las Vegas are also surrounded by mountains, though each set of mountains has its own geography and aesthetic. So here too the vision of the mountains helps locate lifestyle centers. Going roofless also situates the lifestyle center in time, as the moving sun and shifting weather patterns will constantly remind visitors of the time of day and the season in which they are shopping. Going roofless has at least three rhetorical effects, then. First, it makes possible the more specific references to the city that will locate the lifestyle center in urbanity. Second, it helps locate the lifestyle center in geography and weather patterns or, more generally, in place and time. Taken together, these two rhetorical effects lead to a third: rooflessness offers the hope that the lifestyle center will not be an overwhelming and universalizing space analogous to the huge civic square of the nineteenth century and the endless miles of the twentieth-century's freeways. This rooflessness is central to the rhetorics of locality so important to the lifestyle center.

Parking in the Lifestyle Center

In removing the roof, lifestyle centers can reorient themselves in relation to automobiles. Many (though not all) lifestyle centers provide parking for cars along the front of the stores. While Desert Ridge Marketplace in Phoenix and MonteLago outside of Las Vegas are purely pedestrian shop-

Figure 6.1. Diagonal and center of the street parking in Centerra Promenade. Photograph by the author.

ping districts, the typical lifestyle center incorporates the car into the shopping district itself. The heart of the Promenade Shops at Centerra consists of a two-block-long street that functions much as a street would in an older, nonsuburban commercial district of a city or town. On both sides of the street are many of the shopping center's stores. In front of the stores are diagonal parking spots. More diagonal parking spots line the middle of the street (figure 6.1). On both the north and south ends of the development are larger parking lots to handle overflow and to offer spaces sufficient for the multiplex and Macy's on the north and a large Barnes & Noble and several large, chain restaurants on the south.

It may seem odd for lifestyle centers to reincorporate cars into their centers at the exact time more and more cities are creating pedestrian-friendly, car-free shopping districts. However, inviting cars onto the shopping center's main street, Centerra and other lifestyle centers are explicitly referencing actual and imagined Main Streets. For example, twelve miles north of Centerra, Old Town Fort Collins offers a powerful example of a shopping district rooted in history and dependent on nostalgia. Founded in the late nineteenth century, and built over the early twentieth century, downtown Fort Collins was a prototypical business district with build-

ings in varying styles and offering a range of stores, restaurants, and services.[30] Named Old Town in the 1980s, the business district is the sort of
place that "revitalized" urban shopping districts are modeled on. More importantly, Main Street in Disneyland is modeled on Old Town Fort Collins. And, of course, Main Street in Disneyland is a representation the ideal
US American Main Street.[31] Centerra's parking spaces directly reference
a real downtown in an effort to create a new downtown and, at the same
time, through obliquely pointing to Disneyland's Main Street, reference an
ideal vision of downtown. In Centerra, and in other lifestyle centers, then,
parking is not simply a problem of transportation but rather a chance to
reference older, traditional, and idealized visions of US American towns
and cities. This formal referencing of Main Street and urban shopping also
helps create a more humanly scaled architectural form. Where the regional
shopping mall confronts the visitor with seemingly endless parking lots and
faceless expanses of stuccoed walls, visitors to the lifestyle center see man-
ageable parking spaces, narrow streets, and the entrances and facades of the
individual stores. If agoraphobia is triggered by vast expanses and placeless
spaces, parking directly in front of the desired stores, being able to place
the store in direct relation to other stores, and seeing a limited number of
cars directly addresses these anxieties. In short, parking in the middle of
the lifestyle center is a formal and aesthetic reference to urban and small
town shopping and serves to stitch the lifestyle center into an older mode
of shopping and of making cities.

Walking and Gathering in the Lifestyle Center

Removing the roof and parking cars in the middle of the center announces
to visitors that this site is leaping over the regional mall back to the older
city center. But such rhetorical references do not stop when the visitor gets
out of the car. Many lifestyle centers incorporate noncommercial, public
spaces for shoppers to gather. At Desert Ridge Marketplace, for example, a
large outdoor fireplace frames one side of a public gathering place. Centerra also uses fire in its central civic space. The Main Plaza is central-
ized along the east side of Main Street, between two separate buildings of
shops function as a gathering place like a town square or central park (figure 6.2). James J. Farrell alludes to a comparison to Central Park and other
nineteenth-century landscaping designs of parks that suggest "a counter-
point of nature and culture and a space for recreation and (perhaps) contemplation."[32] Parks such as Central Park use nature to engineer culture,
with nature serving as a sign that makes a private enterprise like shopping

Figure 6.2. The fire pit in the town square/central park is located in the middle of Centerra's layout. Not pictured is the fountain just to the left of the fire pit. Photograph by Megan Beam.

feel like public practice in a public space.[33] Likewise, the park's purpose in Centerra is to be the town square where contemplation is a shared experience and public activity.

The change in level between the buildings and the ground level of this area makes it stand out. It is a mostly grassy area surrounded by landscaping of trees, shrubs, and large slates of rock that create an easily traversable path around the place. Edward Relph calls spaces like this "quaintspace," where provisions for theater, concerts, or displays, although sanctioned, appear to invite spontaneous activities in this particular place.[34] In the middle are a large fountain and a fire pit. Although the fountain is turned off during the cold winter months, the fire pit is large, with faux logs, and resembles an invitingly cozy fireplace in the home or a mountain campfire where people gather around for warmth and to tell stories under the stars. There are ample places to rest in this space, on park benches or on the wide rock ledge that encircles the fire pit. Posts hold up strands of lights strung across the lawn. When turned on at night, the strings of light appear to bring the stars closer to earth, simulating the way stars seem much closer and clearer from high up in the mountains. This quaintspace invites people to come together. Perhaps they have been shopping separately and reconvene here to discuss their shopping experience and thus continuing the conversation of the American consumer ideal and prompting further participation. The ice cream shop adjacent to the small park invites a perfect opportunity to continue consuming with the purchase of ice cream and a place to tell more stories of the past, present, and future, linking people to those strangers around them who are doing comparable things in this space.

The Build-a-Bear shop also bordering this central plaza is in a prime location for attracting business. Children who have already built a bear can bring their finished product out to this area to play with. Other children whose parents have brought them here to play may see these bears and demand that they have one too. The Build-a-Bear contributes to the dream-making or memory-making characteristics of Centerra. Once the animal is stuffed, the builder is told to then make a wish and place a heart inside before completely sewing it up. The builder's wish becomes the most important organ to living physically and emotionally. The animal becomes a part of living memory as it can be taken home, played with, or set on a shelf as a constant reminder of the wish that was made.

More however than simply a toy, the teddy bear is a US American emblem. The Build-a-Bear Workshop company mission is, "to bring the Teddy Bear to life. An American icon, the Teddy Bear brings to mind warm thoughts about our childhood, about friendship, about trust and comfort, and also about love."[35] In the wake of the bombings in Oklahoma City and the attacks of 9/11, the teddy bear has become even more important. Responsive to what Marita Sturken names a culture of fear, the teddy bear is central to contemporary comfort culture. This culture, Sturken asserts, is depoliticizing, replacing political choice with consumer choice and makes emotional comfort the end goal of political culture. The teddy bear crystallizes this culture of comfort, for "the teddy bear doesn't promise to make things better; it promises to make us feel better about the way things are."[36] From children's stuffed animals to adult collector's items, parents and other adults can be just as affected by what Build-a-Bear nostalgically communicates to customers, which coordinates directly with Centerra's community-building strategies and invitations to memory and authenticity. Just as the teddy bear adjusts us to present conditions, the lifestyle center's town square helps us feel and imagine that we are part of civic space. Built in the shadow (and image of) the Build-a-Bear store, this town square symbolizes and invites people to be a part of a localized commu-

Figure 6.3. Sign on grassy roundabout in the middle of The District in Henderson, Nevada. Photograph by author.

nity and, at the same time, to inhabit a national consumer identity, indeed to inhabit a national identity defined primarily through the images and material practices of consumption.

This sense of the lifestyle center as equivalent to traditional, public spaces is reinforced by the dog-friendly policies of many lifestyle centers. The home page for Centerra Promenade, for example, advertises "dog friendly shopping" and includes a picture of a dog with a shopper on its carousel of images. Beyond simply inviting dogs and owners into the spaces, many lifestyle centers make other provisions for dogs, including signs urging visitors to pick up after their dogs and dog waste pick-up bags (figure 6.3). Just as removing the roof from the shopping center can change the center's relationship to cars, so to it can change the relationship to pets. As an outdoor space with parks, grassy areas, civic squares, it seems only natural to invite in dogs. Of course, actual downtowns do not need signs indicating that dogs are welcome; walking your dog on a public street is seldom prohibited. The signs in these spaces at once work to replicate the public space of downtown and Main Street while reminding visitors that they are, in fact, on private land and subject to the rules made by corporations and CEOs rather than by cities and citizens. Nonetheless, by inviting dogs into the shopping area and the shopping center's stores, lifestyle centers offer the amenities of a downtown. Taken together, then, the pedestrian-friendly streets and sidewalks along with the apparently noncommercial spaces like civic squares, pocket parks, outdoor fire places, and small amphitheaters all strive to situate the lifestyle center in the remembered relations of downtowns and Old Towns.

Remembering in the Lifestyle Center

And so the lifestyle center works to insert individuals back into downtown and onto Main Street by removing the roof, reorganizing parking and walking, and making pet-friendly spaces. Equally important to these spatial and cultural shifts are visual references. Lifestyle centers are prime examples of late modern consumer landscapes of memory. The mnemonics within lifestyle centers depend on a series of aesthetic moves, in particular the use of stone and brick in the facades, historical reference in the architectural details, and diversity in architectural forms across the storefronts.

Brick and Mortar Stores

At the height of the dot-com boom, cultural commentators wondered openly about the continued relevance of the brick and mortar store. Functioning like the metaphor *snail mail*, *brick and mortar* is a synecdoche for an old-fashioned way of doing business. Place based and rooted in community, brick and mortar stores seem slow to respond to contemporary consumer needs and desires and are unable to match the economies of scale a retailer like Amazon can achieve. Internet retailers, the argument goes, embody the smooth flows of the global economy, are acutely attuned to shifting consumer desires, and are well able to match a globalized consumer audience to globally produced goods. In short, online merchandising materializes the efficiencies of late modernity's destruction of place. But, not surprisingly, the synecdoche of brick and mortar expresses a desire as well as a reality. Latent in the figure is a nostalgia for brick and mortar retailing— and the communities and places they represent and house. More intriguingly, online retailers were not actually the harbinger of brick and mortar difficulties. Instead, the regional mall and the suburban strip had already participated in the apparent demise of the city and the town. Amazon did not so much threaten downtown department stores—which might actually be built of brick, stone, and mortar—as the steel and stucco stores of the suburbs. The synecdoche's material references recalled an even older form

Figure 6.4. Stone and mortar columns in the food court area of Desert Ridge. Photograph by author.

of retailing built in US downtowns and on Main Streets. In reaching behind the suburban mall of the postwar years to the department stores of the cities and the locally owned shops of the towns, Internet shopping is not so much imagined as killing off suburban shopping as undermining the possibilities of cities, towns, and perhaps behind that of remaking civic society itself—a revision well underway before bookselling went online.

It is precisely at the moment that brick and mortar becomes the synecdoche for the soon-to-be-destroyed place-based retailing that we see a resurgence of brick and mortar retail architecture. The most obvious architectural response is the gentrification of urban centers and the redeveloping of Old Towns. But these Old Towns, situated as they are in older, already existing spaces, are not suburban responses to the place-destroying logics of the Internet and the regional mall. For the suburbs, lifestyle centers offer literal bricks (or stone) and mortar in an attempt to reconnect suburban shoppers with place. Take, for example, the stone columns that appear to be holding up the shade-giving overhang in Desert Ridge Marketplace in suburban Phoenix (figure 6.4). Or notice the paving stones used in Monte-Lago outside of Las Vegas, replacing the cement sidewalks of downtown and the tiles of regional malls.

These stones built into the columns and laid in the ground seem to connect these spaces to historical time. They are reminiscent of the architectural details of older buildings, built before World War II certainly or even earlier, perhaps, as with MonteLago, in the Renaissance. In both cases the stones offer more than the image of the past, but are material enactments of the past. The stone-faced columns in Desert Ridge Marketplace invite visitors to touch their roughness, to, in a late evening, lean up against the stone as it is still giving up the day's warmth. While the stones or their consequentiality may never rise to the level of consciousness—in fact they are likely perceived more through the proprioceptive bodily senses that are often processed at a nearly preconscious level—they constantly and concretely enact their mnemonics and their assertion that Desert Ridge and MonteLago are not malls.

But the stone also links the sites to the earth. Quarried directly from the soil, stone has a groundedness that paint and stucco cannot duplicate. What is more, the colors and textures of the stone often reference the surrounding geography because they are sourced from nearby quarries. But the stone is more than a visual referencing to the earth, it is a material instantiaion of the earth. It has a roughness and warmth that can be felt by hand or underfoot. The paving stones in MonteLago are just slightly uneven, they are bumpy and beveled. Walking on them is a material and embodied experience that reinforces the visual references to place and time. Thus, just as removing the roof makes possible vistas of the surrounding mountains and open spaces, the stone on the facades, the columns, and the sidewalks can also place shoppers into their local geography.[37]

Lamps, Signs, and Awnings

The memory work performed by the rough-hewn stone and historic-looking cobblestones intersects with other architectural details like lamps, signs, and awnings. Take, for instance, the more or less banal architectural details on a Barnes & Noble in a small lifestyle center in suburban Las Vegas. Here a rectangular, Craftsman light is attached to a southwestern-colored stuccoed wall. Above the lamp are curved windows with frames and shapes that vaguely recall Italian Renaissance forms. Just down the sidewalk of the same strip, the lights outside Pier 1 shift from the linearity of twentieth-century Craftsman to something more reminiscent of nineteenth-century gas or very early electric lamps.[38] Where the Craftsman light references a more residential (and because of the importance of Craftsman architecture throughout the West, Western) memory, these nineteenth-century fixtures

place the buildings into a more urban, East Coast or even European tradition. Taken together, these lamps nicely express the dialectical tensions
lifestyle centers materialize.

This proliferation of stylistic references also speaks quite clearly to the
late modernity of lifestyle centers. The intersection of a wide variety of
styles—on one building the Craftsman style, on the next late nineteenth-
century urban lighting, each within colors and architectural forms that
reference the Southwest and the Mediterranean Renaissance—produces a
rhetorical amplification. This copiousness of mnemonics asserts, over and
over again, that this new place is old. More accurately, these places remember what it was like to be rooted in time and place. They recall the possibilities of being situated in a moment before the abstractions of modernity unmoored us. Since the rhetorical purpose of these designs is less to
create an authentic space than a place that recalls authenticity, there is no
constraint on the kinds of mnemonic forms use. Instead, there is a drive
to proliferate mnemonic forms. This proliferation is on view across the
street from the Crossroads Commons, the home of the Barnes & Noble and
Pier 1 we have been exploring. Here, Fort Apache Commons is announced
by a combined campanile and gatehouse built of stone, topped by a brass
rotunda, and covered with signs for the strip and for the stores in the strip.
The sign combines Renaissance Italian aesthetics and references to an English and early American public sphere in its name while situating these al-
lusions in the colonial landscapes of the Southwest (Fort Apache). This copiousness of signs indicates the desire to be rooted in time and place and,
at the same time, a profound uncertainty about whether any one memory
structure is up to the task of situating the lifestyle center in time and place.

Taken together, rooflessness, in-front-of-store parking, natural and local materials, and historicized details strive to connect lifestyle centers to
older versions of downtown. The lifestyle centers refer—without particular
rigor—to small town Main Street and urban shopping districts of older cities that once organized the suburban landscapes. Lifestyle centers leapfrog
over the regional mall back to a memorized landscape that seems built on
a more human scale, appears to express local conditions, and looks as if it
grew out of the local geography. In so doing, these centers are fairly precise responses to the kinds of agoraphobic anxieties raised by the mall and
the freeway. Rather than giant, abstract, placeless, modern forms the lifestyle centers analyzed here offer smaller-scale buildings, shrunken parking lots, and architectural details that help visitors orient themselves in
place and time.

Lifestyle Centers as Civic Space

This leapfrog to pre–World War II urban and small town forms, however, does more than humanize the shopping center. In drawing on urban, small town, and gentrified streetscapes, the lifestyle center makes possible its claim to be a downtown or civic space for new suburban developments. Just as every lifestyle center signifies its difference from the regional mall by removing the roof, so too each offers noncommercial gathering spaces that mirror or recall the civic spaces of downtowns and cities. Desert Ridge in suburban Phoenix offers a bandstand, a large, communal fireplace, and an interactive water feature that urges children to play in the cooling sprays. The District in suburban Las Vegas provides numerous pocket parks, and a grass- and tree-lined promenade (in the style of the great promenades in cities like Madrid and Barcelona). Aspen Grove in suburban Denver includes a small parklike space that divides the north and south parts of the mall and lies in the shadow of what looks like a water tower or grain silo (here is a reference to the pastoral central to residential developments). Or, in the lifestyle center portion of suburban Denver's FlatIron Crossing one end is anchored by a bandstand that hosts local musicians on the weekends, and the other offers a mini-park, sandlot, and picnic area. To explore this civicness, we turn to two noncommercial spaces in Centerra Promenade as representative anecdotes of the ways lifestyle centers strive to become suburbia's downtown.[39] In the Chapungu Sculpture Park and grassy Main Plaza, Centerra offers spaces that deftly weave culture, family, and consumerism into material enactments of consumer citizenship.

Drawing on Loveland's national reputation for the quantity and quality of its public sculpture and a decade's long attempt to connect retail and museum spaces, Centerra Promenade incorporates a sculpture park and a museum into its landscape. The Chapungu Cultural Arts Centre at Centerra is adjacent to the town square; the sculpture park is built into twenty-six acres just north of the shops and connected to the Promenade by bridges.[40] As the Centerra website proclaims, the sculpture park is, "A sanctuary from the everyday, the 26-acre Chapungu (pronounced cha-poon-goo) Sculpture Park is the only permanent exhibit of its kind in the U.S. Located east of The Promenade Shops, the public park features 82 African stone sculptures carved by artists from Zimbabwe. The artwork is positioned among water features, a 1.5 mile walking trail, benches for seating and community gathering areas."[41] The Centerra website positions the sculpture park as a public space containing not only sculptures but also seating and community gathering areas. The sculpture park also offers the kinds of cultural enrichment expected of the urban landscape. In the next paragraph, however, this "public park" is folded back into the economic imperatives of private development with the website offering the park as an ideal setting for fund-raisers and corporate or private events. The park is able to host over three hundred people with Centerra providing tents, power, and seating for the events.[42]

The sculpture park strives to intertwine consumption and civicness. More, though, the sculpture park, along with its supporting museum, attempts to locate these two strains of contemporary life squarely in the heteronormative white family. These spaces make these centering claims by creating a visual discourse that universalizes family, places this family in the marketplace, while distancing or exoticizing the African otherness of the sculptors and sculptures. The Chapungu Cultural Park's mission is, "To promote the Stone Sculptors of Zimbabwe, through worldwide exhibitions, documentation, workshops, preservation and sales."[43] As an interpretive vehicle, the Chapungu Sculpture Park works toward the marketing and preservation of the Zimbabwean culture by rhetorically constructing privileged narratives of authenticity and memory to audiences.[44] As Stephen A. King writes, "Appeals to authenticity often mirror a larger cultural struggle between powerful institutionalized voices and marginalized communities over the issues of representation and identity."[45] Centerra becomes a cultural authority, similar to a museum curator, which rhetorically crafts and packages an authentic heritage site that serves to solidify and privilege specific cultural memories.

Centerra has made it possible for people to experience the sculptors' cultural expressions through their artwork being displayed. This is Centerra's way of organizing a collective, mediated experience for shoppers who begin their journey here as tourists. King would call this "an example of 'niche tourism' . . . that capitalizes on the increasing efforts of whole communities to accentuate cultural heritage . . . to increase their tourism potential."[46] The sculpture park is a powerfully rhetorical tool that ultimately benefits Centerra financially and adds to its community-building functionality. Rather than simply having pictures of the art, the physically present representations of the art brings "tourists" closer to the people it represents and closer to one another as they experience the pieces of art selected for them. In this reading, the African sculptors are offered as an exotic other made visible through Centerra's display practices.[47]

Indeed, the sculpture park resonates with the imperialist nostalgia Renato

Rosaldo identified as central to the Western imagination. He writes, "Imperialist nostalgia revolves around a paradox: A person kills somebody, and then mourns the victim. In a more attenuated form someone deliberately alters a life form, and then regrets that things have not remained as they were prior to intervention. At one more remove, people destroy their environment, and then they worship nature. In any of its versions, imperialist nostalgia uses a pose of 'innocent yearning' both to capture people's imaginations and to conceal the complicity with often brutal domination."[48] This imperialist nostalgia offers a vision of a dynamic and ever-changing advanced society constantly revolving around the apparently static societies of savage others.[49] Even as contemporary, Western culture hurtles into a future of ever-expanding suburbs and along the networked nodes of late modernity, the Chapungu Sculpture Park names and represses the stabilities contemporary society has destroyed. It is not a mistake that the Chapungu Sculpture Park celebrates African markets and families, for the lifestyle center is a late modern vision of the intersections of family and commerce.

This nostalgic rendering of the marketplace and family was evident in 2008 in the Chapungu Museum. Directly under the name of the museum was inscribed the word "bazaar."[50] Bringing together bazaar and museum immediately blurs what the function of this space is supposed to be. Was this museum a cultural center dedicated to the African stone sculptors of Zimbabwe? Or was it a shop among the other shops where people can purchase representations of the art to be placed within their postmodern decorated homes? Strategically, the museum was both; the shop, or bazaar, disguised as a museum works as a marketing technique for the store. In learning about this other culture, people can feel better about themselves knowing that they are doing something good for humanity and the world. In short, the marketplace materializes modernity's liminality between commerce and culture.[51]

Liminality among commerce, culture, and family marks the Chapungu Sculpture Park. The park's exhibit is called "The Family—An African Perspective," which is really the selective worldview of its American founder, Roy Guthrie, and its developers, Poag & McEwen Lifestyle Centers. At the entrance to the Chapungu Sculpture Park, visitors are greeted by a welcome sign immediately prescribing that the sculptures will "elicit an experience that reminds the viewer of those matters so important in traditional African families and to all mankind." This immediate move from "traditional African families" to "all mankind" makes a crucial rhetorical shift. It lets visitors know that the park and the museum are not really designed to teach them about African families. Roland Barthes, writing about *The Family of Man* exhibit, argues that the exhibit's photographs offer a "myth of the human 'community,' which serves as an alibi to a large part of our humanism." This "mystification . . . always consists of placing Nature at the bottom of History."[52] Likewise, in the Chapungu Sculpture Park the histories of African families are stripped away to reveal an essential family, one that looks, in the end, remarkably suburban. The park is not about the African culture at all; instead, African culture becomes displaced by the need to evaluate and define US American culture. As the welcome sign asserts, the African values of "nature and the environment, village life, the role of women, the elders, the spirit world, customs and legend, the family and the children," become the naturalized values to be inhabited by visitors as a "contemporary way of 'making history.'"[53] The parallel between the sculptures' rhetoric and that of Centerra helps Centerra construct a seemingly authentic public memory and identity.

The connoted idea of family suggests cohesiveness and unity. The focus on the idea of family is the main vehicle for getting visitors to establish a collective identity. One specific sculpture is named "Togetherness in Family," captioned, "Held together by our spirits. We are strong and united in our numbers." This sculpture's meaning within the context of a lifestyle center would be apparent without its inscription. The sculpture's presence emphasizes the intertwining of individual and family in Africa and in suburban shopping. Parents can bring children here to teach lessons about family values and multiculturalism, but being at a place primarily reserved for consumption, the ultimate lesson being taught is how to be a valuable consuming citizen.

The representations of the art itself lends to the disguise of an altruistic multicultural view of the world. However, the idea of multiculturalism being sponsored here is a flimsy precautionary measure being taken to conceal the artwork's meaning of family. The connection has already been made clear that the artwork's espoused values are not different from its visitors, but are the same of all humans. The land donated to the park is adjacent to the shops at Centerra, which provides a backdrop for the artwork and a constant reminder of the larger cultural context. Many of the sculptures and their inscriptions face east, so that visitors must face west while observing the pieces. From this perspective, Macy's department store replaces the mountains that are usually so symbolic of Colorado life (figure 6.5). At Centerra, shopping and consumption are enforced as an American pastime and current way of life.

Figure 6.5. This Chapungu sculpture is of a mother and child enjoying their "time spent together," as revealed by its caption. Macy's structure fills the western background where the mountains can usually be seen. Photograph by Megan Beam.

The theme of family can also be identified as a metaphor for the American family. The caption, "Held together by our spirits. We are strong and united in our numbers," speaks to a most recent narrative used to bring people together in the wake of 9/11. "United We Stand" served as a campaign slogan to encourage people to band together in a time of tragedy. As united consumer citizens, Americans were asked to shop in hopes of bolstering a flagging, post 9/11 economy.[54] More, as Sturken asserts, the transmutation of politics into consumerism articulates with a culture of comfort in which consumers become "tourists of history." As tourists of history "the American public is encouraged to experience itself as the subject of history through consumerism, media images, souvenirs, popular culture, and museum and architectural reenactments, a form of tourism that has as its goal a cathartic 'experience' of history." This affective experience of history produces "the subjectivity of the tourist of history, for whom history is an experience once or twice removed, a mediated and reenacted experience, yet an experience nevertheless."[55] Chapungu Sculpture Park set next to Centerra Promenade Shops literalizes, concretizes, and materializes this experience of history. History, in the sculpture park, naturalizes the family, is mediated through imperialist nostalgia, and is offered as comforting relational and political structuring within an increasingly terrifying world.

As we move back from the sculpture garden and into the Promenade Shops, we are drawn again to the town square that separates the two blocks of small, lifestyle shops. Bordered by the Build-a-Bear store and the ice cream parlor, this other park returns us to the heartland of US culture (if we ever left). We can return to the grassy square, its large fire pit, the quaint gazebo, and plenty of seating on park benches. In this park space, shoppers can gather, exam their purchases, talk about the sculptures (or not), and decide where to go next. Nostalgically rendered and sewn into images of America, this space urges visitors to imagine themselves within warmly remembered relations of downtown and Main Street and thus becomes a public space in which to enact a suburban form of citizenship. Taken together, these two public spaces—the sculpture park and the town square—materially embody the lifestyle center's civic character.

Consumer Citizenship, Lifestyle Centers, and the Public Good Life

The lifestyle center offers a nostalgic vision of Main Street and urban retail districts. These centers strive to locate visitors in concretely understood relations of time and place. Further, they offer a vision of citizenship congruent with discourses of consumption, the structuring of suburbia into consumer culture, and of centering the heteronormative family as the first and last unit of citizenship. None of this should really surprise us. Over the course of the last one hundred years, consumer culture has increasingly become the site of citizenship, what Lizabeth Cohen has called consumer citizenship and the consumer's republic.[56]

First expressed in the 1880s, the connection between consumer capitalism and democracy has become deeply seated in the US consciousness.[57] In the post-World War II era, this connection was materialized in the new suburbs and then in the regional mall. What we have seen here, however, is the most recent embodiment of these centrally important connections. If the regional mall of the 1950s at first hoped to replace the town centers from which many suburbanites had fled, they quickly abrogated those roles. They did so in part for economic and political reasons; they did not in fact want to be held to the standards we hold urban public spaces. The mall's developers wanted to control speech and, to the extent they could, the types of people who might visit the malls.[58] At the same time, the regional mall did not provide the material or aesthetic resources suburbanites needed to truly feel at home in the spaces. Indeed, rather than offering a hometown for suburbia, malls were for many a site of anxiety and of homelessness created by the mall's abstractions and giganticism.

The lifestyle center deftly responds to these anxieties. These new centers artfully weave together images of Main Street and urban centers into new suburban developments. Removing roofs, inviting in cars and dogs, using historicist details, building with locally sourced materials, and offering noncommercial community spaces all remake the shopping center into the image of an older downtown. Here, then, is a space that at last fully expresses the rise of the consumer republic. Here are the streets, the lamps, and the parks, the cornerstones and the bandstands in which suburbanites can enunciate their (consumer) citizenship. In these new suburbs, devoid of traditional public spaces and where political action is often framed in terms of HOA covenants and around questions of property values, lifestyle centers offer idealized grammars for the contingent rhetorics of citizenship. If, as Benjamin Barber argues, too often democratic choice is refracted through brand choice (he writes: "Brand choice and, within brands, item choice [Crest Blue and Crest Regular], have been widely taken to constitute the essence of freedom in market societies and have even been sold to 'new democracies' as such"),[59] then consumer spaces turned into community and civic spaces turned again into consumer spaces (the sculpture park as ideal for corporate gatherings and for a price) makes perfect sense. Here you can park your car in front of the store, walk your dog on the sidewalk, attend a weekend conference, and buy the goods that express your free choices.

What is also important is that not only is a whole-built consumer space borrowing from and denuding democracy but this consumer space also intersects with the ways citizenship is framed as a consumer practice located in the family and the home. As Lynn Spigel argues, suburban residents develop "a position of meaning in the public sphere through their . . . social identities as private landowners."[60] In the first instance, then, suburbanites imagine their place in the public through a private action—namely, the buying and owning of their own home and their own plot of land. At the same time, contemporary neoliberal politics have consistently moved politics into the intimate spheres of the family and the home.[61] Politics increasingly is about the family and intimacy with arguments focusing on abortion, marriage, and genes, and stems from the family. Suburbanites imagine their stake in the public through the lens of home ownership while politics increasingly takes the home—and the relations home embodies—as the center and reason for its being. The lifestyle center, as a quasi-public memorialization of the kinds of town- and cityscapes suburbanites were fleeing and suburbia killed, is a form of imperialist nostalgia of which Renato Rosaldo writes and which the Chapungu Sculpture Park literalizes.[62] The lifestyle center hopes to recover in form what has been lost in content. Just as what Dana Cloud calls therapeutic rhetoric, which "dislocates social and political conflicts onto individuals or families, privatizes both the experience of oppression and possible modes of resistance to it, and translates political questions into psychological issues to be resolved through personal, psychological change," the lifestyle center offers the public space for this privatization, individualization, and familization of politics.[63] It should be no surprise, then, that the publicness of the lifestyle center is offered in spaces like Chapungu Sculpture Park that offers an imperialist nostalgia of the African family. Nor is it a stretch anymore to see the city square bordered by Build-a-Bear with its own reference (through Theodore Roosevelt) to imperialism and its own play on nostalgia. It is in this sense that the lifestyle center looks awry at the urban scene from which it draws.[64]

While dependent on images of the city and recalling the city scene that suburbia has already vehemently rejected, the lifestyle center at once points to and ignores or represses the dangers of the city. This pointing to and looking away from dangerous pasts and places is familiar by now. Suburban films critique suburbs as stultifying and boring and offer risky allegiances as affectively powerful responses to this banality. And yet, in the end, the individual returns to the center of the family and the security of the whitewashed, picket-fenced suburb. Likewise, the megachurch offers a public forgetting of sacred spaces and practices, a forgetting that clears mnemonic space for Christianity to fully involve itself in the pleasures of the mall. And here, in the lifestyle center, are offered visions of older urban space. But this new space is privatized, removing the risks of public encounters that might be challenging. This vision of civic action is made possible only and exclusively through the structures of consumer capitalism. And the modes of affiliation offered are not those of a community built of difference, but those built out of the smallest units imaginable: the individual and the nuclear family. The city—and its diversity and civic potentiality—is raised and then is immediately and obsessively denied. In this looking at and looking away is an embodied affective relationship to the lost city, the lost hometown. The lifestyle center returns the suburbanite to these lost homes. It does so through the affective longings of nostalgia (longings, as argued throughout this book, for the time and place of home). In this version, nostalgia recalls scenes of desire but—as Slavoj Žižek teaches us—the closer we get to the real of our desire, the more anxious we become.[65] Nostalgia, which is itself at once pleasurable and painful, allows us to approach the desired city scene while also always scrim the desired scene so as to reduce its anxieties. The rough-hewn walls, textured walkways, adjacent art displays, and the Main Street–style parking all remind us of and help us to remember these cities and towns to which we (do not) wish to return.

Apparent, then, is the desire for civic engagement and community connection. Hidden, left out, or repressed are the possibilities of an older, democratic, nonconsumerist vision of civic action. Even as the lifestyle center reaches out to the absent city, it reinforces the walls and gates of the domestic landscape. Rather than contradicting the aesthetics of safety with a rough and tumble city scene, the lifestyle center leavens this aesthetic with a spatial imaginary of the city. Like Marita Sturken's tourists of history, the shoppers in the Promenade Shops at Centerra in Loveland, Colorado; the District in Henderson, Nevada; or Desert Ridge Marketplace in suburban Phoenix gaze upon images of civic culture and community action, buying its legacy, and hoping for comfort without the promise of change. The lifestyle center brings this project full circle. From the fear of the city, through the suburban spatial imaginary, into the homes, restaurants, churches of the suburb, we have returned again to the city, that is, an image of the city, comforting, clean, and always for sale.

Remembering and Rethinking Suburbs

The lifestyle centers' rhetorical force lies in the fact that it is a memorial to the city and to Main Street. Its brick-fronted stores, open fire pits, pedestrian-friendly sidewalks, and civic squares recall older forms of gathering and community making. Leapfrogging over the immediate past of placeless architecture and soulless design they publicly draw on and produce an image of the city as it once and never was. As memorials to the city, these new spaces express the desire to recover the objects of civic contentment. In their use of memory, their appeals to locality, and their carefully constructed aesthetics of safety, lifestyle centers are topoi for making meaning in the early twenty-first century. They spatialize and materialize an otherwise abstract argument—namely, that past and place can serve as useful rhetorical resources out of which people can build meaningful lives in the face of the twenty-first century's challenges and opportunities.

But lifestyle centers are not the only rhetorical landscapes available for suburbanites seeking to make a good life. Megachurches, chain restaurants, residential neighborhoods, and suburban films are all starting places and hortatory forms that shape the dreaming and imagining, materializing and performing of the suburban good life. While the particular rhetorical modes of address and the specific actions and values these landscapes materialize are diverse, they all draw on the resources of memory and locality, and each strives to create seemingly safe, secure, and compelling suburban spaces. These suburban landscapes, then, are built out of the rhetorical spatialities of memory, locality, and safety, offering to residents these resources as topoi from which they can construct their particular versions of the suburban good life. What, then, might be the rhetorical consequences of these suburban topoi?

Memory

Suburbs, often built into apparently empty land and rapidly spreading away from the urban centers, have little claim to the well-worn traditions that can suture people into space and time. Building in new forms and on new land presents powerful possibilities. Symbolizing and materializing a new start and the potential of invention and reinvention, new lands and buildings hold out the promise of reconstruction and renewal. In fact, this is precisely the rhetoric of the megachurch. By materializing a public forgetting of nineteenth- and twentieth-century progressive and conservative calls for personal and social transformation, the megachurch built as a shopping mall or professional office articulates a religion free of guilt and, in many ways, free of responsibilities. Even as megachurches eschew memory appeals, housing developments, lifestyle centers, and chain restaurants all draw on mnemonic inventional resources. Often referring to European forms, the suburban built environment is nearly obsessed with memory. And memory is exactly the right term, for public memory is produced in and for the present out of materials that appear to be about the past. Memory of this sort offers the possibility of connecting present concerns, values, and performances into a solidifying lineage. Importantly, memory's users often understand that the memories constructed in a particular site may be false or fake, and still the memories—or perhaps the memory of memory—can have powerful affective pull. Visitors to the Mary Queen of Scotts House in Scotland fully understood that Mary may never have slept in the house; nevertheless, they found the house inspiring and meaningful. So also visitors to MonteLago in suburban Las Vegas are surely aware that they are not in a Renaissance Italian hill town and yet the site's mnemonics affectively ground visitors in an appealing memorializing aesthetic.

Of course, memory is not only important in new suburbs. In fact, the draw of gentrified neighborhoods like those of Old Pasadena or Chicago's Wicker Park is founded on rhetorical memories.[1] The difference, of course, is that these older landscapes can make apparently more authentic claims to memory as the landscapes are, in fact, older. Nonetheless, these spaces are linked to new suburbs as fully constituted memoryscapes and, because of this, a richer understanding of memory's function in contemporary cities and suburbs can enliven the ways we live in these spaces. In fact, rhetorically, the differences between the two forms of memory may not be as different as they appear. In both cities and suburbs, the repetition of mnemonic forms responds to loss and emptiness. Eric Gordon, for example, argues that the contemporary push for urban historic preservation embodies desires that "are dictated by social factors, specifically the perceived loss of history."[2] In the city and the suburbs history returns as repeated memory and is designed for spectatorship. In the city there is a continual—if spectral—return of the past in spaces like Faneuil Hall in Boston. In the suburbs, the city itself returns in the lifestyle center, which is modeled on these same logics of repetition, spectatorship, and loss. In each case, these rhetorically constructed and materially enacted memories make present spatial timeliness and offer affective possibilities of connecting present and past. More, however, the memories enacted and materialized urge particular relations to the past and the present and so help ground specific values and attitudes.

Locality

If memory is one way of grounding values and attitudes, so also are appeals to specific places. Of course, the problem of locating ourselves in the world is not particularly new, nor does it only impact the suburbs. Nonetheless, the apparent newness and placelessness of suburban spaces raises the difficulties and possibilities of location in specific ways. Because locality depends on a sense of situatedness in place and time, suburbia's newness and placelessness demands and makes difficult appeals to locality. There are few readily apparent rhetorical props for locality in these new suburbs, and so we see appeals to a wild mix of European, US American, and regionally specific geographic aesthetics. This lack of obvious geographic markers is one reason why suburbia so easily taps into modernity's anxieties, like the uncanny, agoraphobia, and the painful longings of nostalgia. Modernity's estrangement of familiar (familial) landscapes is at the heart of these anxieties. More, these anxieties circulate around the home even as the home is offered as one of the most powerful s/cites of locality.[3] And so suburbs are tasked with creating familiar and familial homes but doing so in land without a history of intensive middle-class settlement and, thus, without the well-worn pathways that can make home seem secure. Locality builds concrete geographical references to settle people into space and enacts memory to suture residents into time. This is why lifestyle centers use apparently natural and sometimes local-sourced materials, restaurants consistently refer to specific places like northern Italy, and homes are often built in geographically specific styles (Mission or Provençal, for example) while drawing on pastoral images to embed home into productive and recognizable landscapes.

Meanwhile, the locality produced in the landscapes of the suburbs is not homogenous. For example, housing developments depend on pastoralism. This is a particularly powerful aesthetic in the US American imaginary, but it is also one that, at least in housing developments, emphasizes roots and walls that resist stretching out into the world. The chain restaurants I studied produce a more globalized vision of locality offering the "world on a plate."[4] The restaurants enact forms of locality that recognize and cover the global systems that bring food and families to the table. While restaurants may connect suburbs to the world—or at least to commodified images of ethnicity—lifestyle centers work hard to connect suburbs to the image of the city and the small town, thus (re)extending the suburb into the spaces it quite explicitly hybridizes. The megachurch appears to work at cross-purposes to these localizing landscapes as it studiously avoids both historical and geographic references. And yet, by offering a banal suburban space explicitly referencing the most placeless and achronic forms in the surrounding landscape, the megachurch thoroughly instantiates the suburb to which it ministers while performing intersecting consumerist popular culture with a metaphysical narrative that can justify suburbia's values.

Locality as a concept and a rhetorical practice helps suburban analysts recognize the ways many suburban spaces acknowledge and even celebrate their worldliness and their explicit insertion in global economic and cultural systems. At the same time the suburbs work hard to connect these global opportunities and risks to a sense of place and time that can make the global more legible. Clearly, many of the aesthetic modes that do this work—the simplified Italian forms and food, the referencing of the city through in-front-of-store parking—just barely connects the global and the local through a kind of thin or stretched aesthetics that not only empties and then reanimates difference but also covers many of the deep contradictions of globality.[5] Nonetheless, the locality offered in these suburbs is not only always inward looking and reduced to simple parochialism. Instead, locality is one way of negotiating the difficult and pleasurable relations between local and global and the need to find oneself in place and time.

Locality, however, functions in urban as well as suburban spaces. For example, recent Starbucks redesigns in cities like Seattle eschew corporate branding for a vision of a neighborhood or local coffee shop. Community tables, rough-hewn wood-covered walls, expanded neighborhood announcement boards, regular coffee cuppings or tastings, and café names that reference the café's street address instead Starbucks are all communicative constructions of locality.[6] Built first into gentrifying neighborhoods, Starbucks efforts to regain its soul through references to both time and place suggests an overarching concern with and importance of locality in late modernity. Understanding the specific rhetorical modes by which contemporary spaces create locality can ground richer conceptualizations of the built environment, both urban and suburban.

Safety and Risk

Locating oneself in time and place responds to a fundamental requirement of personal and social identity.[7] While there can be pleasure in being lost, with its frisson of unexpected encounters and new experiences, this pleasure comes in relation to a more fundamental sense of locatedness. Memory and locality serve as ways of negotiating the relationship between safety and risk. In suburban films, suburbs are imagined as banal because suburbs are overly safe. In contrast, the films offer unexpected, risky encounters with nonsuburban or nonfamiliar people as a compensatory gesture. While the films offer salutary risk, the suburban built environment emphasizes safety and comfort. The housing developments' pastoralism—along with the walls, gates, and Westcorp Security signs—produce an affective aesthetic of safety.

But safety and risk are also at stake in the other landscapes. Restaurants with their extension into the world through ethnic food work to link the abstractions of the global food chain (an abstraction that can raise anxieties) into familial traditions. At the same time, as miniature trips out of the suburbs and into Tuscan hills, Olive Garden and Macaroni Grill enable the slightest tinges of touristic adventure. Likewise, the lifestyle center's referencing of old-fashioned city downtowns obliquely reference urban landscapes of fear even as all possibilities of risk are scrubbed from the privately held landscapes. Meanwhile, the megachurch is explicitly about safety. By obsessively integrating itself into the banalities of suburbia, it cossets parishioners in familiar consumer morality. Guilt and duty are expunged and the oddities and demands of older forms of Christianity left behind through a forceful public forgetting. Meanwhile, the narrative spun by the building and its services provides an overarching frame for the suburban good life, locating the values of suburban popular culture not in time or place but in a justifying religious story.

The suburban good life's contours, as expressed in these buildings, neighborhoods, and visual texts are rendered in memory and geography, time and place, history and locality. In the first chapter I argued that the good life is a project, not a product, and that ethos—imagined as a rhetorical and material dwelling and haunting—neatly captures the material and spatial concerns embedded in performing the good life. In its earliest senses, ethos referred to the natural and ingrained haunts and habits of animals. While, as Charles Chamberlain argues, ethos shifted meaning from the haunts of animals to the character of individuals and societies, it never left behind these ancient meanings.

The suburban invocation of a pastoral aesthetic well illustrates competing forms of haunting.[8] Memories of a pastoral scene powerfully connect place, time, and the pastoral scene in a spatial mnemonic—that is, it is a mnemonic that is compellingly materialized in space—even as the pastoral is itself a memory of a space-time relation. And, for my purposes, it is a memory of a haunt, or a memory of an apparently natural setting for humans. Like the horse's pasture of which Chamberlain writes, the suburban pastoral references to and enactment of a landscape built out of the natural world for the care and feeding of humans is one material and aesthetic form of the suburban ethos.[9] This ethos expresses a motivating need to connect the natural world and, at the same time, a hesitancy in doing so without the comforting boundaries of the pasture's cultivation and fence. Olive Garden and Macaroni Grill bring the goods of global pastures to the local table, situating selves in the blended space of the pastoral. And the pastoral returns—but in a somewhat different sense of the word—in the megachurch where pastoral care and community is formed, suturing the home, restaurants, and shopping centers into a justifying religious narrative.

This suburban good life is a returning to or a repetition of imagined former modes of the good life. For Marialisa Calta, in the good family life, everyone has a place at the table and thus in the world. The produced ethnicity of the restaurants sutures eaters into well-worn and generations-old habits of family. The consistent references to the pastoral landscape tie homeowners into imagined relations with family, others, and the land and into eighteenth- and nineteenth-century visions of America. The historicism of the lifestyle centers (re)connects suburbanites with both the urban centers and the small (often rural) towns suburbanites have rejected. And the megachurch—even as it rejects its church history and refuses to make the same demands on its worshippers as do other versions of US American Christianity—fully embeds itself in this other religion: that of the suburban consumer popular culture.

In this sense these suburbs are, in complex ways, nostalgic. That is, they materialize a deep longing for a missing home. But unlike the longings one has of actually occurring if missing objects, this nostalgia is linked as much to melancholia as grief. Mourning the loss of a never-existing object is particularly difficult—in fact, nearly impossible—for it is difficult for the subject to separate from an object that has always only been an internalized fantasy. Grief, on the other hand, can be resolved as it responds to the loss of a remembered, real object and is a process by which the subject detaches from the lost object.[10] There is a real sense in which the homes longed for have never really existed and so, we, along with *Pleasantville's*

David, at once recognize and refuse to recognize that "there is no right house, no right car." This mournful nostalgia urges us to consistently circulate around the missing, and possibly never existing, object, in this case around the locatable and localizable familial home responsive to, and securing within, an age of terror.[11]

But this mournful nostalgia is also, at least partly, why our haunts are sometimes haunted. Certainly, *haunt* means the place and people we belong to, but in a specifically US American connotation, it also refers to the residence of ghosts.[12] What makes the haunted house so frightening is the uncanny contrast between the comforts of familiar haunts and the haunting visions caused by the return of dead and nearly forgotten others. The haunting of our homes caused by the return of the repressed and produced by the familiar-out-of-place is the precise form of the uncanny.[13] Caught between the comfort and the anxiety of haunt, the suburbs consistently try to push away unhomely ghosts with memories of a comforting place while suburban anxieties are shifted into the spatial imaginary of films, television shows, and other creative texts. Haunts, haunted, and haunting: the suburbs are at once a home away from the anxieties of late modernity and the (at least possible) locale of these same anxieties. The ghosts of a demanding religion stalk but are submerged in the megachurch; the fears of placelessness are covered with historicist domestic and commercial architecture; the seemingly destroyed familiar familial patterns are replaced with memorized images of familial space and ethnic foodways in chain restaurants; the banalities of everyday suburban life are compellingly represented, rejected, and recovered in suburban films. This suburban good life, then, while always an ongoing project, is also often a defensive construct. With roots and walls as its major material tropes and longing and fear its central affective constructs, the suburban good life seems ill-prepared to imagine a progressive future.[14]

Constructing the Suburban Good Life

Perhaps it is this haunting, mournful inability to nondefensively imagine the good life that is undermining outer-ring suburbs and pushing people into cities and older suburbs. Perhaps many are recognizing that in the attempt to solve a whole series of problems to which the modern city gave rise, the outer-ring suburbs produced their own troubling difficulties. By refusing the densities of the city, suburbs solved (for suburban residents at least) some of the city's pressing problems. But the solution created new threats to physical and social health.[15] Throughout the book I have alluded to the centrality of automobiles to the design and functioning of suburbs. Many older communities' most important physical manifestations, including the integration of multiple spatial functions into a neighborhood, were unmade by the car-dependent suburb. In the older, preautomobile city, schools, shops, offices, and residences were, of necessity, easily accessed by foot or mass transportation.[16] In contrast to the social connections fostered by dense walkable neighborhoods, car dependence reduces the amount of exercise suburbanites get and can lead to social isolation. Those most affected by suburban car culture are the young, the old, the sick, and the poor. Without ready access to public transportation and with social services and opportunities located miles away from their homes, the young, poor, and elderly can experience isolation.

Car dependence combines with expanding food deserts—those vast regions within both cities and outer-ring suburbs underserved by supermarkets and overserved by mini-marts and fast food—to foster rising public health problems. Public health scholars argue that these transformations are so dramatic that the current generation may be the first in decades with shorter life expectancy than their parents.[17] Surely the good life as a project ought not to lead to the rising rates of obesity, Type II diabetes, and the raft of other health problems characteristic of our rebuilt suburban environment.

This shortened life expectancy, however, is not just a factor of reduced exercise caused by car dependency. It is also partially due to shifting social landscapes that can be ever more isolating. For example, in 1974, over 60 percent of US American children biked to school, but by 2000 only 13 percent did.[18] Surely the shift has multiple causes, at the base of which is a built environment deeply inhospitable to biking by children and adults. For schoolchildren, distances from home to school (and other child-friendly spaces like parks) are too great for easy biking. Suburban roads often do not include bike lanes or sidewalks, and school administrators and city planners declare that intersections near schools are too complicated and dangerous for children to walk and bike to school.[19] More, however, the fear of crime that partially drives suburban development also limits children's bike riding. In short, for many the suburban good life is increasingly isolated and defensive as children are taxied from one appointment to the next, strapped into the back seats of cars, held at arm's length from their natural and social environment.

It is against this death-producing material and social landscape that lifestyle centers react. In place of the huge regional mall, lifestyle centers serve a smaller population and, more importantly, are often planned and sometimes executed as mixed-use landscapes with residential, office, and retail spaces located within easy walking distance of each other. While responding (as I argued in chapter 6) to economic demands, the mixed-use lifestyle center is a distinctly nonsuburban vision of the good life. Drawing on influences of New Urbanism, which also argues for (but seldom enacts) mixed-use, pedestrian-friendly designs, lifestyle centers materially, socially, and culturally envision densely settled suburban landscapes in which workers, shoppers, and residents mingle. Of course, these new visions of suburban locality are still fraught. Many lifestyle centers are not mixed use, relying on just one or two economic activities and drawing most consumers from relatively long distances. Nonetheless, the lifestyle center is one enactment of the increasingly popular vision of a more compact, more walkable, and more heterogeneous way of living. In fact, these are precisely the characteristics inner-ring suburbs use to draw outer-ring suburbanites in toward the urban centers.[20] It is possible that young adults beginning to move from their parents' homes will find these inner- and outer-ring suburban mixed-use spaces appealing and thus are supporting building new, fully functioning downtowns.

More salutary than the window dressing of the lifestyle center is the rapid growth of farmers' markets in the last twenty years. After a period of rapid decline in the 1960s and 1970s, grower-only farmers' markets have rebounded and have done so in cities and in old and new suburbs. While in the 1970s, the suburbs—and the attendant social, cultural, and economic changes—undermined the importance of the farmers' market, in the twenty-first century, these same suburbs play a significant role in the markets' recent renaissance. In the metro areas I studied, a significant number of the farmers' markets are located in newer, outer-ring suburbs rather than in urban centers. Not surprisingly, some of these markets are hosted by recently built lifestyle centers. In suburban Denver, farmers sell produce to Littleton residents at Aspen Grove, while in Northglenn, The Orchard Town Center hosts a local farmers' market.[21] Locating farmers' markets in lifestyle centers reinforces lifestyle centers' downtown and small town aesthetics and emphasizes shifting aesthetic imperatives for suburbs.

In fact, farmers' markets offer different aesthetic, cultural, and social experiences from the world-on-a-plate ethnicity of the chain restaurant. In most markets—especially those that are certified farmers' markets where sellers affirm they are also the growers—the stands are staffed by the actual growers and the produce comes from identifiable and identifiably close market gardens and farms. In place of the chain restaurant's carefully controlled and managed images of locality that create epistemic barriers between consumers and farmers, grower-only farmers' market customers interact with the growers themselves, buying carrots and beets still laden with local loam.[22] While lifestyle centers offer planned versions of ritual and revelry, farmers' markets offer less planned, more dispersed, and seasonally dependent rituals. Over the years, farmers' market attendees come to depend on the stand that offers tastes of meltingly ripe peaches in July, the grower who roasts poblano chiles in late August, and the gardener who offers bushels of tomatoes for freezing and canning as the days shorten in September.

Of course, like the rest of the suburbs, the cultural consequentiality of the market is rhetorically constructed, and it too responds directly to the disconcerting difficulties of globalization. In fact, the farmers' market is a particularly powerful suburban response to late modernity. The suburbs are often built into land that had been or is close to productive farmland, situating suburban landscapes closer to—often in the very midst of—farmers. This proximal relation, with its reduced travel distances, times, and costs, makes grower-only markets economically viable. At the same time, dividing once-rural land into smaller suburban parcels remakes agricultural production in areas adjacent to cities. Large farms are subdivided into smaller parcels, some of which are ideal for growing the vegetables and fruits in demand at farmers' markets even as these plots lose their value for producing grain or livestock. Finally, farmers' markets materialize one already-available powerful version of the suburban good life—namely, a good life tinged with pastoral scenes and imagined as a hybrid space between urban and rural cultures and landscapes. The farmers' market—and other cultural institutions that offer handmade, locally produced, or vintage cultural and material goods—points to a different, less abstracted, more dispersed, and more networked urban and suburban response to late modernity's opportunities and risks.[23]

Perhaps, in the second decade of the twenty-first century, outer- and inner-ring suburbs and urban centers are building new forms of locality. These forms continue to rely on and respond to global networks of economies, cultures, and power, but they can also more clearly and materially connect to the local. Crucially, spaces like farm to fork restaurants and cafés and grower-only farmers' markets provide spaces for (re)imaging local communities. Taking the farmers' market as one particular version of this new/old vision, we can see old and young, rich and poor (as farmers' markets increasingly accept state and federal food aid), grower and consumer connect over the basics of daily life: our food. Perhaps, as Calta argues, families need to eat dinner together so that children can find their place in the world.[24] But it may also be that community members can find their place in the world as they wander the stalls of the farmers' markets, drink coffee at the local coffee shop, and buy jewelry from a local artisan.

While this vision continues to imagine citizenship through the lens of consumerism, it also sees these consumer spaces—like the agoras and marketplaces of the Classical and Renaissance city—as sites of congregation and conversation, spaces of communication that can reinvigorate and more fully materialize the local in a global world, that can teach the "skills necessary for association beyond private life."[25] What all of this suggests is that we cannot give up on efforts to create a comforting sense of locality in suburbs. While the suburban topoi of creating and materializing locality I have investigated here seem thin and defensive, hardly rich or complex enough to sustain individuals, families, and communities within late modernity's globalization, a sense of place and time—of rootedness in Simone Weil's sense—must animate new visions of the built environment.[26] We desperately need a "public realm which is legible, trusted, and well-tried" and that relies on a rich, fully embodied collective memory, etched into stone, rendered in brick and mortar, located in a recognizable place, and lived in a compelling and compellingly difficult everyday life.[27]

As important as a legible, trusted, and well-tried public space may be, the anomie represented (and then repressed) in the suburban films I wrote about in chapter 2 suggests that we also need much more affectively compelling spaces, spaces that connect us in ways that are other than rational, readable, and reliable. At least some of our spaces also need to attend to our embodied and affective ways of moving through space. These spaces—I admit I am not a designer and cannot know exactly what this space might look like—might fold past, present, and future together in nonlinear ways, in ways that better represent how our bodies and our souls actually move through the world. In our daily lives, in the not-fully-conscious ways we make our way from street to building to house to bedroom is not rational or fully cognitive. Perhaps suburban and urban spaces, rather than simply calling on obvious if contradictory memories to found our present, can urge us to imagine new futures more consonant with the world in which we live. Maybe these spaces can remake the landscapes of our memory, connecting us to pasts and presents that might be repressed, denied, only visible if seen sideways. These new spaces might engage us not only as rational or even consuming beings but also as beings fully embedded in a sensory world of position and orientation.[28] Might the farmers' market be just this sort of place? Might the tiny backyard garden that comes into the public for just a few weeks with curly garlicscapes at once disrupt the present of the multinational food conglomerates with new/old foodways? Might the acrid and powerful smell of roasting green chiles return actual scent to the suburban landscape, pulling us up short in an otherwise sanitized world?[29] No, the farmers' market is not a panacea, but its spatial and cultural dis- and reorienting force may offer one way of producing landscapes of memory powerful enough to help us reimagine our world. We need, in short, a way of thinking and building space that offers a folding together of time and place, of past and future, which acknowledges that any moment is always a hinge between what was and what will be. Or better, that reminds us that *was* and *will be* mutually inflect each other, are complexly and powerfully co-present and co-constructing.

And we need a way of imagining, building, and experiencing space that rests on this fundamental fact: into the suburbs, into the city, into the countryside and world, we take our whole selves. We take with us always our cognitive selves worried about mapping and clearly delineating here from there, now from then. But we also take our embodied, sensorial, affective selves in which all of these places and times get mixed up, reworked, unmolded, and refolded. What might this suburban space look like? Or differently, what might this suburban space feel like, sound like, smell like? In this book I have attempted to attend to what the current suburb looks, smells, feels like to provide starting places—topoi—for this next conversation. Already, in simply thinking the affective and the material alongside the cognitive and symbolic, we can come to experience our own spaces more richly, with our senses more awake, aware, and alive to the places of our daily life. It is only as we reawaken our whole selves to the spaces we currently live in that we can hope to reimagine them in more fully, more powerful, and, in the end, in ways better suited to dreaming well the good life.

Notes

Introduction

1. Kevin M. Kruse and Thomas J. Sugure, "Introduction: The New Suburban History," in *The New Suburban History*, ed. Kevin M. Kruse and Thomas J. Sugure (Chicago: University of Chicago Press, 2006), 8.

2. During this same time period, urban growth surged and did so both in newer cities like Los Angeles and in older cities like New York. Nonetheless, suburban growth—even in those suburban areas where growth has slowed the most—still outpaces urban growth. In short, even in the midst of the foreclosures and home price declines, suburbs remain the most popular places to settle. William H. Frey, "Texas Gains, Suburbs Lose in 2010 Census Preview," Brookings: State of Metropolitan America, no. 12, June 25, 2010, http://www.brookings.edu/opinions/2010/0625_population_frey.aspx. Accessed March 23, 2011.

3. Amy Maria Kenyon, *Dreaming Suburbia: Detroit and the Production of Postwar Space and Culture* (Detroit: Wayne State University Press, 2004), 1.

4. Edward Casey, *The Fate of Place: A Philosophical History* (Berkeley: University of California Press, 1997), 50–73.

5. Ian Buchanan, "Heterophenomenology, or de Certeau's Theory of Space," *Social Semiotics* 6 (1996): 112–16; Michel de Certeau, *The Practice of Everyday Life*, trans. Steven Rendall (Berkeley: University of California Press, 1984), 97–98.

6. Frances Yates, *The Art of Memory* (Chicago: University of Chicago Press, 1966), 46.

7. Greg Dickinson, "Memories for Sale: Nostalgia and the Construction of Identity in Old Pasadena," *Quarterly Journal of Speech* 83 (1997): 3–4.

8. Gaston Bachelard, *The Poetics of Space*, trans. Maria Jolas (Boston: Beacon Press, 1994), 5–9. Intriguingly, Frances Yates briefly summarizes Aristotle's discussion of dreams and memory and intersects this discussion with topos such that, Aristotle suggests, rhetorically trained memories can shape and organize our dreams. Yates, *Art of Memory*, 46.

9. The literature on spatiality in rhetoric is large and growing, and it is explicitly linked to the "spatial turn" in the humanities and the social sciences. Carole Blair, Greg Dickinson, and Brian L. Ott, "Introduction: Rhetoric/Memory/Space," in *Places of Public Memory: The Rhetoric of Museums and Memorials*, ed. Greg Dickinson, Carole Blair, and Brian L. Ott (Tuscaloosa: University of Alabama Press, 2011), 22–25; Barney Warf and Santa Arias, "Introduction: The Reinsertion of Space into the Social Sci-

ences and the Humanities," in *The Spatial Turn: Interdisciplinary Perspectives*, ed. Barney Warf and Santa Arias (London: Routledge, 2009), 1–10.

10. Pierre Bourdieu, *Outline of a Theory of Practice*, trans. Richard Nice (Cambridge: Cambridge University Press, 1977); Michel de Certeau, *The Practice of Everyday Life*, trans. Steven Rendall (Berkeley: University of California Press, 1984); Michel Foucault, *Discipline and Punish: the Birth of the Prison*, 2nd Vintage Books ed., trans. Alan Sheridan (New York: Vintage Books, 1995); Henri Lefebvre, *The Social Production of Space*, trans. Donald Nicholson-Smith (Oxford: Blackwell, 1991); Meaghan Morris, *Too Soon, Too Late: History in Popular Culture* (Bloomington: University of Indiana Press, 1998). For a trenchant critique of these authors, see Doreen Massey, *For Space* (London: Sage Publications, 2005).

11. Blair, Dickinson, and Ott, "Introduction," 2–3.

12. John Archer, *Architecture and Suburbia: From English Villa to American Dream House, 1690–2000* (Minneapolis: University of Minnesota Press, 2005), 73–80.

13. Leo Marx, *The Machine in the Garden: Technology and the Pastoral Ideal in America* (New York: Oxford University Press, 1964), 5.

14. Ibid.

15. Blair, Dickinson, and Ott, "Introduction," 2.

16. Yates, *Art of Memory*, 1–2.

17. Ibid., 39–48, 82–104. Mary J. Carruthers, T*he Book of Memory: A Study of Memory in Medieval Culture* (Cambridge: Cambridge University Press, 1990), 222, 253–56.

18. Yates, *Art of Memory*, 129–59, 199–230; Charles Burroughs, *From Signs to Design: Environmental Process and Reform in Early Renaissance Rome* (Cambridge, MA: MIT Press, 1990), 20; Anthony Vidler, *The Architectural Uncanny Essays in the Modern Unhomely* (Cambridge, MA: MIT Press, 1992), 177–79; Lawrence W. Rosenfield, "Central Park and the Celebration of Civic Virtue," in *American Rhetoric: Context and Criticism*, ed. Thomas Benson (Carbondale: Southern Illinois University Press, 1989), 249–50; Richard Sennett, *The Conscience of the Eye: The Design and Social Life of Cities* (New York: W. W. Norton, 1990), 152–58.

19. Patrick H. Hutton, *History as an Art of Memory* (Hanover, NH: University Press of New England, 1993), 61; Richard Terdiman, *Present Past: Modernity and the Memory Crisis* (Ithaca, NY: Cornell University Press, 1993), 241.

20. Bachelard, *Poetics of Space*, 9.

21. Ibid., 7.

22. Ibid., xxxiv.

23. Richard Terdiman calls modernity's memory desire "nostalgia for memory." Terdiman, *Present Past*, 39.

24. Steve Macek, *Urban Nightmares: The Media, the Right, and the Moral Panic over the City* (Minneapolis: University of Minnesota Press, 2006), xv.

25. Setha Low, *Behind the Gates: Life Security, and the Pursuit of Happiness in Fortress America* (New York: Routledge, 2003), 9–10; see also Edward J. Blakely and Mary Gail Snyder, *Fortress America: Gated Communities in the United States* (Washington, DC: Brookings Institution Press, 1997), 15.

26. Christopher Leinberger, "The Death of the Fringe Suburb," *New York Times*, November 25, http://www.nytimes.com/2011/11/26/opinion/the-death-of-the-fringe-suburb.html?_r=1&ref=suburbs. Accessed January 2, 2011.

27. Ibid.

28. Frey, "Texas Gains, Suburbs Lose in 2010 Census Preview."

29. Morris, *Too Soon, Too Late*, xxiii.

30. Barbara A. Biesecker and John Louis Lucaites, eds., *Rhetoric, Materiality, and Politics* (New York: Peter Lang, 2009); Jeremy Packer and Stephen B. Crofts Wiley, eds., *Communication Matters: Materialist Approaches to Media, Mobility, and Networks* (London: Routledge, 2011).

31. Hans Ulrich Gumbrecht, *Production of Presence: What Meaning Cannot Convey* (Stanford, CA: Stanford University Press, 2004), 17.

32. Carole Blair, "Reflections on Criticism and Bodies: Parables from Public Places," *Western Journal of Communication* 65 (2001): 271–94.

33. Kenneth Burke, *Permanence and Change: An Anatomy of Purpose*, 3rd ed. (Berkeley: University of California Press, 1984).

34. Barry Brummett, "Rhetorical Theory as Heuristic and Moral: A Pedagogical Justification," *Communication Education* 33, no. 2 (1984): 103.

Chapter 1

1. Amy Maria Kenyon, *Dreaming Suburbia: Detroit and the Production of Postwar Space and Culture* (Detroit: Wayne State University Press, 2004), 1.

2. For a review of postwar criticisms of suburbs, see Becky Nicolaides, "How Hell Moved from the City to the Suburbs: Urban Scholars and Changing Perceptions of Authentic Community," in *The New Suburban History*, eds. Kevin M. Kruse and Thomas J. Sugure (Chicago: University of Chicago Press, 2006), 80–98.

3. Class is, according to many, a driving factor in suburban migration. Suburbs are populated by—and are imagined as—home of middle-class aspirations. William F. Frey, "Black Populations Dropping in Big Cities," Brookings: State of Metropolitan America, 27, March 22, 2011. Accessed March 23, 2011; Andrew Wiese, " 'The House I Live In': Race, Class, and African American Suburban Dreams in the Postwar United States," in *The New Suburban History*, eds. Kevin M. Kruse and Thomas J. Sugure (Chicago: University of Chicago Press, 2006), 110–19.

4. Lizabeth A. Cohen, *Consumer's Republic: The Politics of Mass Consumption in Postwar America* (New York: Alfred A. Knopf, 2003); Nicolaides, "How Hell Moved from the City to the Suburbs," 97.

5. Kevin M. Kruse and Thomas J. Sugure, "Introduction: The New Suburban History," in *The New Suburban History*, ed. Kevin M. Kruse and Thomas J. Sugure (Chicago: University of Chicago Press, 2006), 3.

6. While the insidious practices of redlining that enforced race and class exclusions in the suburbs throughout much of the twentieth century are now illegal, suburbs continue to trade on these exclusions. Some of these exclusions are remnants of the redlining practices, as these rules deeply diminished the growth of wealth for nonwhite US citizens. By restricting home ownership to whites from the 1920s through the 1960s, the single most important way for individuals and families to obtain and pass on equity was removed from black and Latino/a families. Meanwhile, a series of other practices like restrictive covenants and homeowner association rules strive to maintain the exclusions of suburbs. See George Lipsitz, *The Possessive Investment in Whiteness: How White People Profit from Identity Politics* (Philadelphia: Temple University Press, 2006), 1–23; George Lipsitz, *How Racism Takes Place* (Philadelphia: Temple University Press,

2011), 15, 29–30; Setha Low, *Behind the Gates: Life Security, and the Pursuit of Happiness in Fortress America* (New York: Routledge, 2003), 10; Wiese, "The House I Live In," 118.

7. Suburban observers are certainly not in agreement on the suburb's moral worth. The literature is too large to capture here, but a selective list includes M. P. Baumgartner, *The Moral Order of a Suburb* (New York: Oxford University Press, 1988); Robert A. Beauregard, *When America Became Suburban* (Minneapolis: University of Minnesota Press, 2006); Edward J. Blakely and Mary Gail Snyder, *Fortress America: Gated Communities in the United States* (Washington, DC: Brookings Institution Press, 1997); Renee Y. Chow, *Suburban Space: The Fabric of Dwelling* (Berkeley: University of California Press, 2002); Robert Fishman, *Bourgeois Utopias: The Rise and Fall of Suburbia* (New York: Basic Books, 1987); Dolores Hayden, *Building Suburbia: Green Fields and Urban Growth, 1820–2000* (New York: Pantheon Books, 2003); Kenneth T. Jackson, *Crabgrass Frontier: The Suburbanization of the United States* (New York: Oxford University Press, 1985); Kevin M. Kruse and Thomas J. Sugure, eds., *The New Suburban History* (Chicago: University of Chicago Press, 2006); Robert E. Lang and Jennifer B. LeFurgy, *Boomburbs: The Rise of America's Accidental Cities* (Washington, DC: Brookings Institution Press, 2007); Thomas J. St. Antoine, "Making Heaven out of Hell: New Urbanism and the Refutation of Suburban Spaces," *Southern Communication Journal* 72 (2007): 127–44; Lynn Spigel, *Welcome to the Dreamhouse: Popular Media and Postwar Suburbs* (Durham, NC: Duke University Press, 2001); Andrew Wiese, *Places of Their Own: African American Suburbanization in the Twentieth Century* (Chicago: University of Chicago Press, 2004).

8. Steve Macek, *Urban Nightmares: The Media, the Right, and the Moral Panic over the City* (Minneapolis: University of Minnesota Press, 2006), xv.

9. Charles Chamberlain, "From 'Haunts' to 'Character': The Meaning of Ethos and Its Relation to Ethics," *Helios* 11 (1984): 101–2; Michael J. Hyde, "Introduction: Rhetorically, We Dwell," in *The Ethos of Rhetoric*, ed. Michael J. Hyde (Columbia: University of South Carolina Press, 2004), xii.

10. I use *meaningful* in its two senses. First, suburban memories are legible and understandable, drawing on well-understood visual and material mnemonics. At the same time, these memories are affectively meaningful. See Carole Blair, Greg Dickinson, and Brian L. Ott, "Introduction: Rhetoric/Memory/Place," in *Places of Public Memory: The Rhetoric of Museums and Memorials*, ed. Greg Dickinson, Carole Blair, and Brian L. Ott (Tuscaloosa: University of Alabama Press, 2010), 3.

11. Evelyn S. Rupert, *The Moral Economy of Cities: Shaping Good Citizens* (Toronto: University of Toronto Press, 2006), 4–5. Rupert writes, "city making does indeed involve defining and articulating visions of the good city."

12. Baumgartner, *Moral Order of a Suburb*, 3.

13. John Archer, *Architecture and Suburbia: From English Villa to American Dream House, 1690–2000* (Minneapolis: University of Minnesota Press, 2005), 349–50.

14. Daniel C. Russell, *Plato on Pleasure and the Good Life* (New York: Oxford University Press, 2005), 20.

15. P. Christopher Smith, "Translator's Introduction," in *The Idea of the Good in Platonic-Aristotelian Philosophy*, by Hans-Georg Gadamer, trans. P. Christopher Smith (New Haven, CT: Yale University Press, 1986), xxviii.

16. See Maurice Charland, "Constitutive Rhetoric: The Case of the Peuple Québécois," *Quarterly Journal of Speech* 73 (1987): 133–50; Dana Cloud, "The Materiality of Discourse as Oxymoron: A Challenge to Critical Rhetoric," *Western Journal of Commu-*

nication 58 (1994): 141–63. Raymie McKerrow, "Critical Rhetoric: Theory and Praxis," *Communication Monographs* 56 (1989): 91–111; Ronald Greene, "Another Materialist Rhetoric," *Critical Studies in Mass Communication* 15 (1998): 21–41.

17. Michel de Certeau, *The Practice of Everyday Life*, trans. Steven Rendall (Berkeley: University of California Press, 1984); Henri Lefebvre, *The Social Production of Space*, trans. Donald Nicholson-Smith (Oxford: Blackwell, 1991).

18. Lefebvre, *Social Production of Space*, 216.

19. Certeau, *Practice of Everyday Life*, xix, 19, 97.

20. Rupert, *Moral Economy of Cities*, 5.

21. Chamberlain, "From 'Haunts' to 'Character': The Meaning of Ethos and Its Relation to Ethics," 97.

22. Ibid., 98.

23. Ibid., 101.

24. Ibid., 102–3.

25. Hyde, "Introduction: Rhetorically, We Dwell," xii.

26. Ibid., xxi. The passage continues:

Such a work of art thus assumes an epideictic function. With architecture in mind, one might also speak of the work as an 'edifying' discourse (in Latin 'to edify' is *aedificare*, from *aedes*, 'dwelling,' and *fiacre*, 'to make' or 'to build') whose communal character takes form as the artist uses materials (e.g., tropes, figures, topics, arguments, narratives, emotions) to attract attention, maintain our interest, and encourage us to judge the work as praiseworthy and persuasive.

27. Carole Blair makes clear the limitations, at least for those studying space, of a symbolic definition of rhetoric. See "Contemporary U.S. Memorial Sites as Exemplars of Rhetoric's Materiality," in *Rhetorical Bodies*, ed. Jack Selzer and Sharon Crowley (Madison: University of Wisconsin Press, 1999), 19.

28. Svetlana Boym, *The Future of Nostalgia* (New York: Basic Books, 2001), 3.

29. Ibid., 8.

30. Ibid., 8–9.

31. Ibid., 11. Boym joins others in asserting that nostalgia is a spatialized longing. For example, Fred Davis writes that contemporary nostalgia is a response to the "deep cultural and spatial disruption of contemporary society [which] has begun to dislodge man's [*sic*] deep psychological attachment to a specific house in a specific locality, in a specific region, which over the centuries had been fostered by the more settled and protracted arrangement of a primarily agricultural and small-town society." Fred Davis, *Yearning for Yesterday: A Sociology of Nostalgia* (New York: Free Press, 1979), 6. See also Anthony Vidler, *The Architectural Uncanny: Essays in the Modern Unhomely* (Cambridge: MIT Press, 1992), x.

32. Boym, *Future of Nostalgia*, 9.

33. In ibid., 25.

34. Vidler, *Architectural Uncanny*, 4.

35. Quoted in ibid., 4.

36. Ibid., 5.

37. Karl Marx and Friedrich Engels, *The Communist Manifesto* (Arlington Heights, IL: Harlan Davidson, 1955), 13.

38. Karl Marx and Friedrich Engels, *The Communist Manifesto*, trans. Terrell Carver, in

The Communist Manifesto: New Interpretations, ed. Mark Cowling (Edinburgh: Edinburgh University Press, 1998), 14. http://web.a.ebscohost.com.ezproxy2.library.colostate.edu :2048/ehost/ebookviewer/ebook/bmxlYmtfXzk3NjdfX0FO0?sid=c46b1d89-d2b4 –4291–8fbb-cab2d6b7eb42@sessionmgr4002&vid=1&format=EB&lpid=lp_III&rid =0. Accessed February 25, 2014.

39. Ibid.

40. Richard Terdiman, *Present Past: Modernity and the Memory Crisis* (Ithaca, NY: Cornell University Press, 1993), 39.

41. Ibid., 44.

42. Anthony Vidler, *Warped Space: Art, Architecture, and Anxiety in Modern Culture* (Cambridge, MA: MIT Press, 2001), 26–28.

43. Sitte quoted in Vidler, *Warped Space*, 28.

44. Vidler, *Warped Space*, 25.

45. Gillian Brown, "The Empire of Agoraphobia," *Representations* 20 (Fall 1987): 136.

46. Vidler, *Warped Space*, 26.

47. Edward L. Glaser, *The Triumph of the City: How Our Greatest Invention Makes Us Richer, Smarter, Greener, Healthier, and Happier* (New York: Penguin Press, 2011).

48. Ibid., 6.

49. Kathy Peiss, *Cheap Amusements: Working Women and Leisure in Turn-of-the-Century New York* (Philadelphia: Temple University Press: 1985).

50. Patricia Pringle, "Spatial Pleasures," *Space and Culture* 8 (2005): 142.

51. Ibid., 142. See also John F. Kasson, *Amusing the Million: Coney Island at the Turn of the Century* (New York; Hill and Wang, 1978).

52. Marc Aúge, *Non-Places: Introduction to an Anthropology of Supermodernity*, trans. John Howe (London: Verso, 1995); Anthony Giddens, *Modernity and Self-Identity: Self and Society in the Late Modern Age* (Stanford, CA: Stanford University Press, 1991).

53. Pico Iyer, *The Global Soul: Jet Lag, Shopping Malls, and the Search for Home* (New York: Alfred A. Knopf, 2000), 18–20.

54. I was struck, in the late 1990s, when sitting at a Coffee People coffee shop in Portland by a group of hipsters sitting at the next table. Like me, they were visiting from Southern California. "This is like," they said, "LA the way it used to be." The memory, nostalgia, and implosion of places are wrapped up in this simple assertion.

55. Giddens, *Modernity and Self-Identity*, 17–18. Within communication studies, Andrew Wood has explored the implosion of spaces in a series of essays on what he calls "omnitopia." See Andrew Wood, " 'What Happens [in Vegas]': Performing the Post-Tourist Flâneur in 'New York' and 'Paris,' " *Text and Performance Quarterly* 25 (2005): 315–33; Andrew Wood, " 'Are We There Yet?': Searching for Springfield and the Simpsons' Rhetoric of Omnitopia," *Critical Studies in Media Communication* 22 (2005): 207–22; Andrew Wood, "A Rhetoric of Ubiquity: Terminal Space as Omnitopia," *Communication Theory* 13 (2003): 324–44.

This view of the dissolution of place within postmodernity is not without its critics. Most trenchant and persuasive is that of Doreen Massey, who argues that material space remains crucial both to analysis and to individuals' everyday experiences. See Doreen Massey, *For Space* (London: Sage Publications, 2005), 126–42.

56. Giddens, *Modernity and Self-Identity*, 19.

57. Nan Ellin, "Shelter from the Storm or Form Follows Fear and Vice Versa," in *Architecture of Fear*, ed. Nan Ellin (New York: Princeton Architectural Press, 1997), 35;

Low, *Behind the Gates*, 9–10. Michael Dear, "Beyond the Post-Fordist City," *Contention* 5 (1995): 72. George Lipsitz, *Time Passages: Collective Memory and American Popular Culture* (Minneapolis: University of Minnesota Press, 1990), 5–6. Low, *Behind the Gates*, 21–22. Laura Pulido, "Rethinking Environmental Racism: White Privilege and Urban Development in Southern California," *Annals of the Association of American Geographers* 90 (2000): 12.

58. Jim Collins, *Architectures of Excess: Cultural Life in the Information Age* (New York: Routledge, 1995), 33–44.

59. Victor Burgin, *In/Different Spaces: Place and Memory in Visual Culture* (Berkeley: University of California Press, 1996), 190. Massey, *For Space*, 177–180.

60. Massey, *For Space*, 177–95.

61. Jessie Stewart and Greg Dickinson, "Enunciating Locality in the Postmodern Suburb: FlatIron Crossing and the Colorado Lifestyle," *Western Journal of Communication* 72 (2008): 299.

62. Joan Faber McAlister explores the problem of contemporary rootlessness and rhetorics of place in midwestern suburbs through the philosophy of Simone Weil and analysis of marketing materials for new suburban developments in Illinois, Iowa, and Minnesota. These "subdivisions," she writes, "simulate historical permanence, stability, and continuity. In other words, they create an instant sense place by means of a particular aesthetic whose rhetorical effect is temporal." Joan Faber McAlister, "Material Aesthetics in Middle America: Simone Weil, the Problem of Roots, and the Panoptic Suburb," in *Rhetoric, Materiality, and Politics*, ed. Barbara A. Biesecker and John Louis Lucaites (New York: Peter Lang, 2009), 109.

63. Ellin, "Shelter from the Storm or Form Follows Fear and Vice Versa," 25.

64. Marita Sturken, *Tourists of History: Memory, Kitsch, and Consumerism from Oklahoma City to Ground Zero* (Durham, NC: Duke University Press, 2001), 7.

65. M. Christine Boyer, *The City of Collective Memory: Its Historical Imagery and Architectural Entertainments* (Cambridge, MA: MIT Press, 1996), 1; Greg Dickinson, "Memories for Sale: Nostalgia and the Construction of Identity in Old Pasadena," *Quarterly Journal of Speech* 83 (1997): 2; Andreas Huyssen, *Present Pasts: Urban Palimpsests and the Politics of Memory* (Stanford, CA: Stanford University Press, 2003), 15; Michael Sorkin, "See You in Disneyland," in *Variations on a Theme Park: The New American City and the End of Public Space*, ed. Michael Sorkin (New York: Noonday Press, 1992), 205; Sharon Zukin, *Landscapes of Power: From Detroit to Disney World* (Berkeley: University of California Press, 1991), 233–41.

66. Beauregard, *When America Became Suburban*, 17; Macek, *Urban Nightmares*, 37–70.

67. Hayden, *Building Suburbia*, 4–5, 45–50.

68. Archer, *Architecture and Suburbia*, xvi.

69. Hayden, *Building Suburbia*, 71; Owen D. Gutfreund, *Twentieth-Century Sprawl: Highways and the Reshaping of the American Landscape* (New York: Oxford University Press, 2004), 7–60. Gutfreund compellingly argues that the federalization of the highway system and the development of free rather than toll roads ("freeways") throughout the twentieth century was distinctly antiurban and constituted a significant shift of tax dollars from cities to rural and suburban areas and from public transportation to private transportation. On the importance of the street to suburbs, see Cynthia L. Girling and Kenneth I. Helphand, *Yard, Street, Park: The Design of Suburban Open Space* (New York: John Wiley and Sons, 1994), 34–37.

70. Federal loan guarantees not only enabled middle-class individuals to obtain mortgages, the restrictive redlining within the loan practices ensured the desired homogeneity within suburban spaces. Jackson, *Crabgrass Frontier*, 202–15.

71. Gutfreund, *Twentieth-Century Sprawl*, 7–60; Fishman, *Bourgeois Utopias*, 15, 55; Girling and Helphand, *Yard, Street, Park*, 34; Hayden, *Building Suburbia*, 4;

72. Janet L. Abu-Lughod, *Race, Space, and Riots in Chicago, New York, and Los Angeles* (Oxford: Oxford University Press, 2007).

73. Macek, *Urban Nightmares*, xii–xv.

74. Kenyon, *Dreaming Suburbia*, 47–49.

75. Nicolaides, "How Hell Moved from the City to the Suburbs," 97.

76. Kenyon, *Dreaming Suburbia*, 2.

77. Joel Garreau, *Edge City: Life on the New Frontier* (New York: Doubleday, 1991); Hayden, *Building Suburbia*, 4–5, 181–86; Fishman, *Bourgeois Utopias*, 17, 155.

78. As Meaghan Morris argues, modernist malls go to some lengths to create a sense of place. Meaghan Morris, *Too Soon, Too Late: History in Popular Culture* (Bloomington: Indiana University Press, 1998), 86–90. They at times strive to create place through references to memory. As we will see, however, early twenty-first-century production of consumer spaces argues that earlier versions of the mall were overly abstract, too removed from both time and place. See also Margaret Morse, "An Ontology of Everyday Distraction: The Freeway, the Mall, and Television," in *Logics of Television: Essays in Cultural Criticism*, ed. Patricia Mellencamp (Bloomington: Indiana University Press, 1990), 197.

79. Kathryn Milun, *Pathologies of Modern Urban Space: Empty Space, Urban Anxiety, and the Recovery of the Public Self* (New York: Routledge, 2007), xi.

80. Low, *Behind the Gates*, 11.

81. Diana I. Agrest, *Architecture from Without: Theoretical Framings for a Critical Practice* (Cambridge, MA: MIT Press, 1991), 112; Charles Burroughs, *From Signs to Design: Environmental Process and Reform in Early Renaissance Rome* (Cambridge, MA: MIT Press, 1990), 19; Lawrence W. Rosenfield, "Central Park and the Celebration of Civic Virtue," in *American Rhetoric: Context and Criticism*, ed. Thomas Benson (Carbondale: Southern Illinois University Press, 1989), 226–29; Frances A. Yates, *The Art of Memory* (Chicago: University of Chicago Press, 1966), 129–59.

82. Dickinson, "Memories for Sale," 2–4.

83. Vidler, *Warped Space*, 177, 186.

84. Yates, *Art of Memory*, 129–59.

85. Rosenfield, "Central Park and the Celebration of Civic Virtue," 226–29.

86. Paul Oskar Kristeller, *Renaissance Thought and Its Sources* (New York: Columbia University Press, 1979), 29–31, 242–59.

87. In fact, tracing the history of these relations could easily take us back to the beginnings of both rhetoric and of memory in the Western world. See Dickinson, "Memories for Sale," 304.

88. Gaston Bachelard, *The Poetics of Space*, trans. Maria Jolas (Boston: Beacon Press, 1994).

89. Ibid., 9. Memory, Bachelard asserts, is not so much interested or connected to time but to place.

Memories are motionless, and the more securely they are fixed in space, the sounder they are. To localize a memory in time is merely a matter for the biographer and only corresponds to a sort of external history, for external use, to be communicated to others. But hermeneutics, which is more profound than biography, must determine the centers of fate by ridding history of its conjunctive temporal tissue, which has no action on our fates. For a knowledge of intimacy, localization in the spaces of our intimacy is more urgent than the determination of dates.

Chapter 2

1. *Pleasantville*, directed by Gary Ross (Los Angeles: New Line Cinema, 1998).

2. Victor Burgin, *In/Different Spaces: Place and Memory in Visual Culture* (Berkeley: University of California Press, 1996), 190.

3. Yi-Fu Tuan, "Images and Mental Maps," *Annals of the Association of American Geographers* 65 (1975): 211.

4. Ibid.

5. Henri Lefebvre, *The Social Production of Space*, trans. Donald Nicholson-Smith (Oxford: Blackwell, 1991), 39.

6. Charles Jenks, *The Language of Postmodern Architecture*, 5th ed. (New York: Rizzoli, 1987), 39–80; Darryl Hattenhauer, "The Rhetoric of Architecture: A Semiotic Approach," *Communication Quarterly* 32 (1984): 71–77.

7. Carole Blair, Greg Dickinson, and Brian Ott, "Introduction: Rhetoric/Memory/Place," in *Places of Public Memory: The Rhetoric of Museums and Memorials* (Tuscaloosa: University of Alabama Press, 2010), 15–16; Sara Ahmed, *The Cultural Politics of Emotion* (New York: Routledge, 2004), 11–13.

8. Brian L. Ott, "The Visceral Politics of *V for Vendetta*: On Political Affect in Cinema," *Critical Studies in Media Communication* 27 (2010): 49.

9. Lefebvre, *Social Production of Space*, 42.

10. As Lauren Berlant argues, contemporary considerations of the relations among aesthetics, affect, and embodiment de-universalize the site of analysis, engaging these relations in particular space and time. Lauren Berlant, "Critical Inquiry, Affirmative Culture," *Critical Inquiry* 30 (2004): 448.

11. Edward S. Casey, *Getting Back into Place: Toward a Renewed Understanding of the Place-World* (Bloomington: Indiana University Press, 1993), x. Sara Ahmed directly connects the post-9/11 fear as a political organization of emotion where home is "mobilised as a defense against terror." Ahmed, *Cultural Politics of Emotion*, 74.

12. Berlant, "Critical Inquiry, Affirmative Culture," 448.

13. Lawrence Grossberg, *We Gotta Get Out of This Place: Popular Conservatism and Postmodern Culture* (New York: Routledge, 1992), 80; Erika Doss, "Affect," *American Art* 23 (2009): 9–11.

14. Lefebvre, *Social Production of Space*, 33. David Harvey renames Lefebvre's representations of space *spatial imagination* and defines it this way: "Spaces of representation are mental inventions (codes, signs, 'spatial discourses,' utopian plans, imaginary landscapes, and even material constructs such as symbolic spaces, particular built environments, paintings, museums, and the like) that imagine new possibilities for spatial practices." David Harvey, *The Condition of Postmodernity: An Inquiry into the Origins of Social Change* (Cambridge, MA: Blackwell, 1989), 218–19.

15. Phillip E. Wegner, *Imaginary Communities: Utopia, the Nation, and the Spatial Histories of Modernity* (Berkeley: University of California Press, 2002), 15–17.

16. Ibid.

17. Ibid., 45.

18. In this sense, the spatial imaginary is part of the visual "mental image" of the city Kevin Lynch wrote about in *The Image of the City* (Cambridge, MA: MIT Press, 1960), 1–2. Writing of the city landscape, Lynch asserts, "At every instant, there is more than the eye can see, more than the ear can hear, a setting or a view waiting to be explored. Nothing is ever experienced by itself, but always in relations to its surroundings, the sequences of events leading up to it, the memory of past experiences" (1). While Lynch is clearly concerned primarily with our past experiences with our built environment, it is not much of a stretch to say that our image of the city or suburb "is soaked in memories and meanings" from a full range of spatial texts.

19. Burgin, *In/Different Spaces*, 28.

20. Anthony Vidler, *The Architectural Uncanny: Essays in the Modern Unhomely* (Cambridge, MA: MIT Press, 1992), 179–80; Wegner, *Imaginary Communities*, xvi.

21. Michael J. Hyde, "Introduction: Rhetorically, We Dwell," in *The Ethos of Rhetoric*, ed. Michael J. Hyde (Columbia: University of South Carolina Press, 2004), xii.

22. Ibid.

23. Michel de Certeau, *The Practice of Everyday Life*, trans. Steven Rendall (Berkeley: University of California Press, 1984), 115–30. For Certeau, "spatial stories" are not limited to verbal enactments of and about space. Instead, spatial stories include the "enunciation" of space through practices like walking, cooking, dwelling, shopping, reading.

24. Michel de Certeau and Luce Giard, "A Practical Science of the Singular," in *The Practice of Everyday Life*, vol. 2, *Living and Cooking*, ed. Michel de Certeau, Luce Giard, and Pierre Mayol; trans. Timothy J. Tomasik (Minneapolis: University of Minnesota Press, 1998), 254–55.

25. Hyde, "Introduction: Rhetorically, We Dwell," xii.

26. In the post–World War II years, Kenyon argues, we dreamed ourselves to be American, dreams that figured Americans as suburban and white. These dreams hid the social exclusions upon which suburbia was built, and yet these dreams find their concretization within suburbia itself. Amy Maria Kenyon, *Dreaming Suburbia: Detroit and the Production of Postwar Space and Culture* (Detroit: Wayne State University Press, 2004), 2–3.

27. Television, like film, has engaged suburbia as both setting and topic. While many television shows laud suburbia, recent shows like *Desperate Housewives* and *Weeds* try to look at the darker underbelly of the suburbs. Both of these shows reinforce the visualization of suburbia that I will be addressing in the rest of this essay. The title sequence of *Weeds* is instructive. The show opens with a stylized aerial map of Agrestic, the suburban development that is the geography of the show. As the map—which could be from a brochure for the development—fills in, Malvina Richards begins to sing her 1960s antisuburbs song "Little Boxes." As the song lampoons the stultifying sameness of the suburbs, we see repeated images of nearly identical houses, runners in the same clothes, and indistinguishable Land Rovers driving out of the development. In this opening sequence is offered the contradiction between the utopic visions of suburbia as a place of security and beauty and dystopic visions of suburbia as a site of profound and soul-killing blandness. *Weeds*, of course, turns on the story of a single mom trying to keep her perfect suburban life together by dealing pot, pot she buys from an

African American, inner-city family. The title, then, refers to the illicit drug but also to the invasion of illicit plants into the apparently perfect lawns of contemporary suburban developments. Both *Weeds* and *Desperate Housewives* suggest that hidden behind suburbia's perfect facades or below their weedless and preternaturally green lawns lay disturbing values and identities. And yet neither, in serious ways, offers alternative visions to the safety and comfort of the suburbs that the shows disturb and always return the viewer into the arms of a white, heteronormative family. I point to these television shows to indicate that the visualization and narrativization of suburbia is a central focus of current popular culture. As important as television is for understanding what the *Pleasantville* effect might be, in-depth analysis of these shows is beyond the scope of this study. For analysis of televisual representations of suburbia, see Kenyon, *Dreaming Suburbia*, and Lynn Spigel, *Welcome to the Dream House: Popular Media and Postwar Suburbs* (Durham, NC: Duke University Press, 2001). On *Desperate Housewives*, see Janet McCabe and Kim Akass, *Reading* Desperate Housewives: *Beyond the White Picket Fence* (New York: I. B. Taurus, 2006).

28. Douglas Muzzio and Thomas Halper, "Pleasantville? The Suburb and Its Representation in American Movies," *Urban Affairs Review* 37 (2002): 544.

29. *American Beauty*, directed by Sam Mendes (Universal City, CA: Dreamworks SKG, 1999); *Edward Scissorhands*, directed by Tim Burton (Century City, CA: 20th Century Fox, 1990); *Far from Heaven*, directed by Todd Haynes (New York: Focus Features, 2002); *In the Land of Women*, directed by Jon Kasden (Beverly Hills, CA: Castle Rock Entertainment, 2007); *Little Children*, directed by Todd Field (Los Angeles: New Line Cinema, 2006); *The Truman Show*, directed by Peter Wier (Hollywood, CA: Paramount Pictures, 1998).

30. I am not arguing that these films are primarily memory texts; rather, the films use memory as one of their rhetorical modes. Some of the movies are more clearly centered on memory (*Pleasantville*, for example), in others the appeal to memory is more subtle (*The Truman Show*, for example).

31. Cynthia L. Girling and Kenneth I. Helphand, *Yard, Street, Park: The Design of Suburban Open Space* (New York: John Wiley and Sons, 1994), 21; Virginia Scott Jenkins, *The Lawn: A History of an American Obsession* (Washington, DC: Smithsonian Institution Press, 1994), 5.

32. Girling and Helphand argue that the automobile is central to making the visual and experiential landscape of the suburbs. "To the traditional interplay of city and country, dwelling and nature, has been added mobility and the street. The dialectic of culture-nature is now a triad of culture-nature-mobility." Girling and Helphand, *Yard, Street, Park*, 34.

33. The clockwork coming and going of men in *Edward Scissorhands* is repeated in *Pleasantville*, though in *Pleasantville*, most of the men seem to walk to work. The walking in 1950s Pleasantville (which is not repeated, except as a moment of "rebellion" in *American Beauty*) is another mark of *Pleasantville*'s nostalgia. *In the Land of Women* first introduces us to the suburb Carter is moving to in images of tree-lined streets and then through the windshield of a Mazda 3. The title sequence of *Weeds* offers a line of Land Rovers winding out of the suburb. Turning point scenes in *Little Children* occur in cars and vans.

34. The importance of the yard and yard work is reinforced in other suburban movies. Notable for its variations on the theme is *My Blue Heaven*, where we know that

Steve Martin—an East Coast mobster relocated to the suburbs of Southern California as part of being in the witness relocation program—is beginning his adjustment to suburban life when he mows his lawn, though he does so in one of his many suits (*My Blue Heaven*, directed by Herbert Ross [Burbank, CA: Warner Brothers, 1990]). The narrative of *Far from Heaven* circulates around the relationship between an African American gardener and a white homeowner. Here—in signifying that this is a wealthier suburb—the yard work is done by hired help, and the yards are bigger and more complex. Nonetheless, yards remain important to the image of the suburb.

35. After the single-family home, the white picket fence is the most prevalent sign of suburbia in these films.

36. Dolores Hayden, *Building Suburbia: Green Fields and Urban Growth, 1820–2000* (New York: Pantheon Books, 2003), 17, 26–35.

37. Girling and Helphand, *Yard, Street, Park*, 23.

38. Indeed, the gendering of the lawns and lawn work in the films absolutely reinforces Jenkins's argument. Women, to the extent they are figured as concerned about lawns, are concerned with beauty over technique and control. Carolyn Burnham is the only woman seen working in the yard in these films, and she is tending red roses (a motif in *American Beauty*). See Jenkins, *The Lawn*, 118–21.

39. Muzzio and Halper, "Pleasantville? The Suburb and Its Representation in American Movies," 547.

40. As indicated above, *Weeds* makes explicit the racial segregation that marks suburbia. In the suburban neighborhood nearly everyone is white. Nancy Botwin, the lead character and pot dealer, buys her supply from a black family in a neighborhood clearly coded as inner city. The house's yard is weed infested, there are bars on the windows and, in one episode, it is sprayed by gunshots in a drive-by shooting.

41. As I will argue below, race reappears in the soundtracks and on the margins of many of these films. Krin Gabbard argues that race often "appears" in US American films in these very ways. He calls these appearances, "black magic." Krin Gabbard, *Black Magic: White Hollywood and African American Culture* (New Brunswick, NJ: Rutgers University Press, 2004), 6. These films' visual and narrative development of white space intersects with the development of white spaces in other contexts. See Ronald L. Jackson II, "White Space, White Privilege: Mapping Discursive Inquiry into the Self," *Quarterly Journal of Speech* 85 (1999): 39; Thomas K. Nakayama and Robert L. Krizek, "Whiteness: A Strategic Rhetoric," *Quarterly Journal of Speech* 81 (1995): 291; Laura Pulido, "Rethinking Environmental Racism: White Privilege and Urban Development in Southern California," *Annals of the Association of American Geographers* 90 (2000): 13; Raka Shome, "Space Matters: The Power and Practice of Space," *Communication Theory* 13 (2003): 42.

42. In *Better Luck Tomorrow* (2003) the film opens and closes with two of the film's protagonists crawling along the carefully mown lawn toward the sound of the beeping of a pager. In the opening sequence, the characters dig up the hand of an obviously dead body. Finding the hand sets the story in motion and is framed by a voice-over: "You never forget the sight of a dead body. I had never seen a dead body before. But then again I was experiencing a lot of things for the first time. I guess it is just part of growing up." Here the metaphor of sins hidden underneath the beauty of the pastoral scene is literalized.

The pastoral as theme of the suburban landscape will be central to my argument in the next chapter.

43. As I discuss below, Sarah has nearly completed, but given up on, a PhD in English literature. This opening voice-over, then, at once places Sarah at a distance from the other mothers but at a distance from her own past.

44. She most roundly criticizes the neighbor who returned to work when her child was still too young and offers unasked-for advice. Most important—in setting the tone for the film—is that the other mothers should be like her and her husband who have a date to have sex every Tuesday evening "whether they feel like it or not"—advice that Sarah parrots under her breath with disgust. In this advice for regulated sex—sex behind the white picket fence—is captured the stultifying rhetoric of suburbia.

45. The film intercuts the discussion of the book with images of Sarah and Brad having (anal, we presume) sex. The visual movement between the relatively sedate discussion of Emma's passion in a suburban living room and the passionate sex in Sarah's attic clearly indicates at visual and affective levels the near consubstantiality of Emma and Sarah.

46. We need to remember, of course, that Emma Bovary committed suicide at the end of the novel. As we will see, the narratives of *Madame Bovary* and *Little Children* could not have more different conclusions.

47. The film is framed through Lester's voice-over as a story of a man who has lost his sense of identity. It is clear that the present has forsaken him and that the past offers amelioration; he has, to paraphrase Burgin, lost his place in time (*In/Different Spaces*, 190). The audience is invited to, like Lester, find his or her place in time in an idealized image of the past.

48. Lawrence Grossberg, *We Gotta Get Out of This Place: Popular Conservatism and Postmodern Culture* (New York: Routledge, 1992), 208–10.

49. Setha Low, *Behind the Gates: Life Security, and the Pursuit of Happiness in Fortress America* (New York: Routledge, 2003), 16–22.

50. Muzzio and Halper, "Pleasantville? The Suburb and Its Representation in American Movies," 549–50.

51. A nearly identical distinction between suburbia and the world outside of suburbia motivates a turning point in *Land of Women*. Carter, in talking with Lucy—the teenage daughter who lives across the street from Carter's mom and is developing a crush on Carter—tells her that "there's a big fucking world out there. It's messy, and it's chaotic, and it's never ever the thing you'd expect. It is OK to be scared but you cannot allow your fears to turn you into an asshole when it comes to the people that really love you, the people that need you." Like David, Carter is the experienced man, teaching the inexperienced woman about the outside world. This world is scary and difficult but one that is also real and even appealing.

52. For example, Jennifer's first attempts to seduce Skip are set to Pat Boone's "Mr. Blue." As the movie shifts to scenes of the town's teens following Jennifer and Skip's lead in their convertibles on lover's lane, the music shifts to the rhythm-and-blues influenced "Be-Bop-a-Lula." The next scene shifts to the soda fountain as David comes to work. A teenager drops a coin in the jukebox and selects "Lawdy Miss Clawdy," a song performed and written by black men. This shift from white pop to black rhythm and blues corresponds with the deepening shift in identities within the movie. The music

shifts from white to black, from suburb to urban, as the young people become more aware of their own feelings and their passions. My reading of the use of black music in *Pleasantville* closely follows Krin Gabbard's argument in *Black Magic*. See 90–104.

53. Ibid., 97–99.

54. Ibid., 98.

55. It is important to note that only David leaves the new and improved Pleasant-ville. We are left to assume that colorized Pleasantville is, in some senses, ideal. Further, the knowledge that David gains from his time in Pleasantville provides him resources for living in the present. The nostalgic landscapes of Pleasantville, then, are pedagogical.

56. Thomas DiPiero, *White Men Aren't* (Durham, NC: Duke University Press: 2002), 20, 148–50. DiPiero writes that whiteness depends on a "maneuver of externalizing fragmentation or division onto another while simultaneously demanding of that other knowledge of white masculinity." In short, whiteness demands that "others" reflect back whiteness's own identity. In this scene, Cathy seems unsure of her identity, her place in the world. Raymond, on the other hand, sees clearly, and his clear vision resets the boundaries of white and black.

57. With the phrase *perverse space* I am pointing, more or less obliquely, to Elizabeth Grosz's *Space, Time, and Perversion: Essays on the Politics of Bodies* (New York: Routledge, 1995). Throughout the book, Grosz explores the intersections among masculinist epis-temologies, built space, and perverse desire. Perversity ambiguously suggests dominant response to nonheterosexual sexualities and spaces while also suggesting the progres-sive potential of "perversity." In "Women, Chora, Dwelling," Grosz writes that West-ern philosophy and architecture expels all difference, shifting all that is "not male" to Other spaces that are then rejected, denied, hidden. Perverse spaces serve as the outside necessary to the making and maintenance of an inside. While I am trying to point to perversity as a mode of boundary making, I am not rendering a normative judgment about that perversity.

58. George Chauncey, *Gay New York: Gender, Urban Culture, and the Making of the Gay Male World, 1890–1940* (New York: Basic Books, 1994), 26; Gordon Brent Ingram, "Marginality and the Landscape of Erotic Alien(n)ations," in *Queers in Space: Commu-nities, Public Spaces, Sites of Resistance*, ed. Gordon Brent Ingram, Anne-Marie Bouthil-lette, and Yolanda Retter (Seattle: Bay Press, 1997), 27–29.

59. Eve Kosofsky Sedgwick, *Epistemology of the Closet* (Berkeley: University of Cali-fornia Press, 1990): 1, 10, 65, 67; see also Lee Edelman, "Men's Room," in *Stud: Ar-chitectures of Masculinity*, ed. Joel Saunders (New York: Princeton Architectural Press, 1996), 152.

60. Several collections can serve as good introductions to the spatialization of sexu-ality, including David Bell and Gill Valentine, eds., *Mapping Desire: Geographies of Sexu-alities* (London and New York: Routledge, 1995); Beatriz Colomina, ed., with Jennifer Bloomer, *Sexuality and Space* (New York: Princeton Architectural Press, 1992); Gordon Brent Ingram, Anne-Marie Bouthillette, and Yolanda Retter, eds., *Queers in Space: Com-munities, Public Spaces, Sites of Resistance* (Seattle: Bay Press, 1997).

61. Chauncey, *Gay New York*, 331–54.

62. Ingram, "Marginality and the Landscape of Erotic Alien(n)ations," 27.

63. Chauncey, *Gay New York*, 25.

64. George Chauncey, "'Privacy Could Only Be Had in Public': Gay Uses of the

Streets," in *Stud: Architectures of Masculinity*, ed. Joel Saunders (New York: Princeton Architectural Press, 1996), 224, 259; Joel Saunders, "Introduction," in ibid., 12–15.

65. Nathan Stormer, "Addressing the Sublime: Space, Mass Representation, and the Unpresentable," *Critical Studies in Media Communication* 21 (2004): 234.

66. DiPiero, *White Men Aren't*, 99.

67. It is worth noting, as does Gabbard, that the film opens with contemporary problems defined as issues like AIDS and ozone depletion. At the end of the film, the problem is David's mother's breakup with her boyfriend. Gabbard, *Black Magic*, 103.

68. Marita Sturken, *Tourists of History: Memory, Kitsch, and Consumerism from Oklahoma City to Ground Zero* (Durham, NC: Duke University Press, 2001): 5–12.

Chapter 3

1. Gaston Bachelard, *The Poetics of Space*, trans. Maria Jolas (1964; Boston: Beacon Press, 1994), 46–47 (epigraph). Bachelard writes:

> In the life of man, the house thrusts aside contingencies, its councils of continuity are unceasing. Without it, man would be a dispersed being. It maintains him through the storms of the heavens and through those of life. It is body and soul. It is the human being's first world. Before he is 'cast into the world,' as claimed by certain hasty metaphysics, man is laid in the cradle of the house. And always, in our daydreams, the house is a large cradle. A concrete metaphysics cannot neglect this fact, this simple fact, all the more since this fact is a value, an important value, to which we return in our daydreaming. Being is already a value. Life begins well, it begins enclosed, protected, all warm in the bosom of the house. (ibid., 6–7)

2. Addressing several suburbs in metropolitan Denver, Las Vegas, and Phoenix, I cannot claim generalizability. As I argued in chapter 1, however, there are some significant advantages to focusing careful critical attention on fewer sites, for doing so allows a careful, detailed, and rich analysis of the very specific material means by which suburbs construct the good life. Thus the analysis will provide topoi for understanding other spaces. At the same time, I will intersect my analysis with the work of other suburban scholars to indicate similarities and differences between the suburbs I work in and other suburbs and suburban discourses.

3. John Lukács, "Bourgeois Interior," *American Scholar* 39 (1970): 624.

4. The classic text on the rise of the nuclear family in modernity is Lawrence Stone, *The Family, Sex, and Marriage in England, 1500–1800*, abridged ed. (New York: Harper Torchbooks, 1979). What I am calling the *intimate family*, Stone refers to as the "affective family" in which there is growing equality and greater emphasis on affection between spouses, more freedom for children, and a growing separation between the family and larger kinship networks and the community at large. See, for example, page 149.

5. Witold Rybczynski, *Home: A Short History of an Idea* (New York: Penguin Books, 1986), 47–48. The separating of the married couple from the family takes another turn in the contemporary suburb as the couple's bedroom is increasingly distanced from the rest of the house. As Joan Faber McAlister argues, "The location of the master bed-

room at a distance from the other rooms (and never directly over one) in suburban houses facilitates the uninhibited use of this space for intimate encounters." Joan Faber McAlister, "Figural Materialism: Renovating Marriage through the American Family Home," *Southern Communication Journal* 76 (2011): 293.

6. Rybczynski, *Home: A Short History of an Idea*, 48.

7. Dolores Hayden, *The Grand Domestic Revolution: A History of Feminist Designs for American Homes, Neighborhoods, and Cities* (Cambridge, MA: MIT Press, 1981), 22–23.

8. Lynn Spigel, "The Suburban Home Companion: Television and the Neighborhood Ideal in Postwar America," in *Sexuality and Space*, ed. Beatriz Colomina and Jennifer Bloomer (New York: Princeton Architectural Press, 1992), 186.

9. Ibid.

10. Ibid. On these contradictions, see also Setha Low, *Behind the Gates: Life Security, and the Pursuit of Happiness in Fortress America* (New York: Routledge, 2003), 10.

11. Lauren Berlant, *The Queen of America Goes to Washington City: Essays on Sex and Citizenship* (Durham, NC: Duke University Press, 1997), 1; Dana L. Cloud, *Control and Consolation in American Culture and Politics: Rhetorics of Therapy* (Thousand Oaks, CA: Sage, 1998), xv, xxi, 2.

12. Cloud, *Control and Consolation in American Culture and Politics,* xxi.

13. As I argued in chapter 1, *nostalgia* is a complicated term that circulates around home. It takes home as its subject and its object and can offer both progressive and regressive opportunities. Crucially, the home as nostalgia at once offers comforting images of warmly remembered pasts but brings with it as well the disturbing tang of loss. On rhetoric, memory, nostalgia, and the built environment, see Greg Dickinson, "Memories for Sale: Nostalgia and the Construction of Identity in Old Pasadena," *Quarterly Journal of Speech* 83 (1987): 1–27.

14. Theano S. Terkenli, "Home as a Region," *Geographical Review* 85 (1995): 325–26.

15. The problem of roots and of connecting residents to time and geography is at the heart of Joan Faber McAlister's argument about midwestern subdivisions and Simone Weil. Weil, writing in the immediate aftermath of the German occupation of France, identifies rootlessness as a fundamental and deeply disturbing characteristic of modern life and is particularly endemic to the United States, with its history of migration and immigration. As McAlister points out, suburban developments confront this sense of rootlessness head on and through material aesthetics. Joan Faber McAlister, "Material Aesthetics in Middle America: Simone Weil, the Problem of Roots, and the Panoptic Suburb," in *Rhetoric, Materiality, and Politics*, ed. Barbara A. Biesecker and John Louis Lucaites (New York: Peter Lang, 2009), 105–9.

16. Steve Macek, *Urban Nightmares: The Media, the Right, and the Moral Panic over the City* (Minneapolis: University of Minnesota Press, 2006), xv.

17. Sigmund Freud, "The Uncanny," in *The Uncanny*, trans. David McLintock (London: Penguin Books, 2003), 123–62.

18. Ibid., 126. Interestingly, *heimlich* means a *tame* as opposed to a *wild* animal—an animal that is friendly with humans. Compare this with the ancient sense of *ethos* I discussed in chapter 1, where ethos means something like the haunts of animals; that is, the natural or wild places and states of animals. This sense of *haunt* as wild or untamed appears again in the haunted house. Here, however, haunting seems unnatural, and yet, as I will argue, haunting—or the uncanny—is an affect caused by the repression of humans' constitutive (bisexual) drives, the fear of castration and of death.

19. Ibid., 132.

20. Ibid., 148.

21. "Every affect arising from an emotional impulse—of whatever kind—is converted into fear by being repressed." Ibid., 147.

22. Ibid., 151.

23. Ibid., 144.

24. Hugh Haughton, introduction to Sigmund Freud, *The Uncanny*, trans. David McLintock (London: Penguin Books, 2003), lii–liii.

25. While Vienna was never directly attacked during the battles of World War I, the Great War deeply traumatized the city. Already a diverse city, the flood of soldiers and refugees remade the city and did so in ways that caused significant anxiety. What is more, these anxieties circulated around troubled relations between home or home front and hinterland. The war, in short, remade Vienna as city and as home. Maureen Healy, *Vienna and the Fall of the Hapsburg Empire: Total War and Everyday Life in World War I* (Cambridge: Cambridge University Press, 2004), 5.

26. Martin Heidegger, "Letter on Humanism," trans. Frank A. Cappuzi, in collaboration with J. Glenn Gray, in *Basic Writings*, ed. David Farrell Krell (New York: Harper and Row, 1977), 243. In this passage, Heidegger goes on to write: "What Marx recognized in an essential and significant sense, though derived from Hegel, as the estrangement of man has its roots in the homelessness of modern man" (243). In fact, *estrange* and *estrangement* are—at least conceptually—related to the uncanny. In archaic and obsolete meanings from the sixteenth to nineteenth centuries, *estrange* can mean to make a person a stranger to a place or to "withhold from knowledge," "to render 'foreign,'" or "to render strange or unfamiliar in appearance." Oxford English Dictionary, online.

27. McAlister, "Material Aesthetics," 108.

28. Suburban subdivisions are typically understood as single-use, residential neighborhoods, developed by a single company and governed by restrictive covenants and homeowner associations. See Robert Fogelson, *Bourgeois Nightmares: Suburbia, 1870–1930* (New Haven, CT: Yale University Press, 2005), 17–24.

29. Ibid., 109.

30. Bachelard, *Poetics of Space*, xxxvii, 9. Bachelard, writing of memory, asserts, "For a knowledge of intimacy, localization in the spaces of our intimacy is more urgent than the determination of dates" (9).

31. Hans Ulrich Gumbrecht, *Production of Presence: What Meaning Cannot Convey* (Stanford, CA: Stanford University Press, 2004), 2, 17. "To speak of 'production of presence' implies that the (spatial) tangibility effect coming from the communication media is subjected, in space, to movements of greater or lesser proximity, and of greater or lesser intensity" (17).

32. McAlister, "Material Aesthetics," 100.

33. Yi-Fu Tuan, "Images and Mental Maps," *Annals of the Association of American Geographers* 65 (1975): 211.

34. Eric Avila, *Popular Culture in the Age of White Flight: Fear and Fantasy in Suburban Los Angeles* (Berkeley: University of California Press, 2004); Kenneth T. Jackson, *Crabgrass Frontier: The Suburbanization of the United States* (New York: Oxford University Press, 1985); Amy Maria Kenyon, *Dreaming Suburbia: Detroit and the Production of Postwar Space and Culture* (Detroit: Wayne State University Press, 2004).

35. The Meadows. http://meadowscastlerock.com. Accessed July 30, 2004.

36. Jackson, *Crabgrass Frontier*, 238–43.

37. Under the open space headline, the copy reads: "Open space areas filled with native grasses and foliage meet stunning ridgelines, where large areas of natural beauty are reserved for the whole community's enjoyment." The Meadows.

38. Country Homes. http://www.mcstain.com/the_parks/countryhomes.htm. Accessed November 12, 2002.

39. McStain Colonial. http://www.mcstain.com/the_parks/countryhomes/aspen _house.htm. Accessed November 12, 2002.

40. Sheffield Homes Grand Opening. http://www.sheffieldhomes.com/grand _opening.htm. Accessed November 12, 2002.

41. Brookhaven Lane. http://www.brookhavenlane.com/brookhaven_main.shtml. Accessed November 12, 2002.

42. Villa Avignon Toast. http://www.brookhavenlane.com/va_default.htm. Accessed November 12, 2002. This image stands out because it is the only image of non-Euro-Americans on all of the sites I visited. Many sites showed no people at all. When they did, however, they were, with just this one exception, white.

43. George Lipsitz, *How Racism Takes Place* (Philadelphia: Temple University Press, 2011), 14.

44. Roland Barthes, *Mythologies* (New York: Hill and Wang, 1972), 123.

45. McAlister, "Good Neighbors," 288.

46. Lipsitz, *How Racism Takes Place*, 29.

47. John Beck, "Without Form and Void: The American Desert as Trope and Terrain," *Nepantla: Views from the South* 2 (2001): 63–83.

48. Ibid., 74.

49. In northwest Las Vegas.

50. In east Aurora, Colorado.

51. In Commerce City, Colorado.

52. Reunion. http://www.reunionco.com/index.php?c=56&d=57&a=39&w=2&r =Y. Accessed December 9, 2006.

53. Clearly *pastoral* and *agrarian* have somewhat different meanings, with pastoral being more complex and including forms of music and painting, a way of seeing landscapes, images of shepherding, taking care of or being located in pasture lands. Agrarian more directly points to the cultivation of land and, more particularly, the cultivation of land by landowners. While different, the terms point to similar cultural values, in particular the beauty and fecundity of nature bent to human needs. As we will see, suburbs use distinctly agrarian images to build a pastoral landscape. I more carefully develop my argument about the pastoral below.

54. There are, of course, regional differences in this vernacular. Developments in New Mexico are much more likely to directly refer to the adobe dwellings of Native American heritage, with less emphasis on the Mission style that dominates Southern California.

55. Geographers are at the forefront of theorizing and critically assessing place, and in fact, place is a constitutive concept of contemporary cultural geography. For some *place* has come to mean local and progressive sites of resistance to the ravages of modernity. But as Doreen Massey argues, this misunderstands both the conceptual power of place and the material politics of living in late modernity. Rather than making a particular or theoretical definition about the ontological status of place, the argument

here is that suburban developments make claims to a sense of place—that is, a sense of locality, including a connection to geographic contours and cultural structures of particular place. Place, in this context, becomes a cultural and material site in which residents negotiate the contradictions, difficulties, and opportunities of late modernity. See Doreen Massey, *For Space* (London: Sage Publications, 2005), 5–6; Timothy Oakes, "Place and the Paradox of Modernity," *Annals of the Association of American Geographers* 87 (1997): 510, 519–20.

56. These are all developments of Pardee Homes in greater Las Vegas. Coyote Springs is a wholly new suburb developed by Pardee Homes fifty miles north of Las Vegas. See http://www.pardeehomes.com/index.php?startat=%2Fprovidence.php%3F. Accessed December 10, 2006. Phoenix and Denver suburbs are also dominated by these same naming strategies. In Phoenix, for example, Lennar is developing Estates at Carefree Crossing, Estates at Coquito Trails, and Inaugurals at Desert Cedars, and in Surprise they are building Signatures at Greer Ranch; see Standard Pacific Homes, Lennar. http://www.lennar.com/findhome/city.aspx?CITYID=PHO&BRANDID=USH. Accessed December 10, 2006. Finally, in Denver, Standard Pacific Homes is building the Townhomes at Hunters Run. http://standardpacifichomes.com/findhome/NeighborhoodIntro.aspx?NID=899. Accessed December 10, 2006. D. R. Horton is offering Balterra at Sterling Hills, Bristlecone at Tallgrass, and Landing at Cherry Creek. http://www.drhorton.com/corp/DivisionSplash.do?divId=Y5. Accessed December 10, 2006.

57. Whatever rockwood is, it clearly is something in the carbon-based part of human experience.

58. Castle Rock Wine Fest. http://www.castlerockwinefest.com/. Accessed December 10, 2006.

59. Highlands Ranch, Parks and Trails. http://www.highlandsranch.com/custom/ParksAndTrails.html?top=comm. Accessed December 13, 2006.

60. Thomas E. Cronin, "What Do Coloradoans Believe?" *Denver Post*, August 27, 2006. LexisNexis. Accessed December 13, 2006. Associated Press, "Economy Passes Growth as Coloradoans Biggest Concern," September 25, 2004. LexisNexis. Accessed December 13, 2006.

61. The development of suburbs rich in open land is also an aesthetic and material mode of creating exclusion. For a detailed study of how aestheticized nature protects and hides exclusionary class and race practices, see James S. Duncan and Nancy G. Duncan, "The Aestheticization of the Politics of Landscape Preservation," *Annals of the Association of American Geographers* 91 (2001): 387–409.

62. The lifestyle center and shopping strips bring the consumer culture amenities into suburbs.

63. John Archer, *Architecture and Suburbia: From English Villa to American Dream House, 1690–2000* (Minneapolis: University of Minnesota Press, 2005), 216.

64. The History of Highlands Ranch. http://www.highlandsranch.com/custom/HrHistory.html. Accessed December 14, 2006.

65. Ibid.

66. Leo Marx, *The Machine in the Garden: Technology and the Pastoral Ideal in America* (New York: Oxford University Press, 1964), 6.

67. Ibid., 141.

68. Ibid., 128.

69. Ibid., 226, 364–65.

70. Archer, *Architecture and Suburbia*, 170.

71. Loren Baritz, *The Good Life: The Meaning of Success for the American Middle Class* (New York: Alfred A. Knopf, 1989), 11.

72. Archer, *Architecture and Suburbia*, xvi.

73. Ibid., 3.

74. Baritz, *Good Life*.

75. Archer, *Architecture and Suburbia*, 46–61, 146–48, 166–68.

76. In fact, in some cases land that was in a mid-sized family farm has been sold, made into smaller plots for suburban or ex-urban homes but with enough land for the owner to do some hobby farming. It is for this reason that while the number of mid-sized family farms is dramatically shrinking, the total number of farms is on the rise. People living on the subdivided farm land raise vegetables for a local market or produce honey for a local food co-op and thus are considered farmers. See Les Christie, "Farming for Fun," CNNMoney, January 6, 2005. http://money.cnn.com/2005/01/04/real _estate/buying_selling/hobbyfarms/. Accessed June 19, 2011.

77. Las Vegas suburbs seem the least attached to agricultural metaphors. Certainly there are a number of developments with "ranch" in the name, but few go beyond the basic naming to visual or other forms of agricultural referencing.

78. New Urbanist developments are the most likely to include direct references to farm houses or small-town, midwestern homes. By emphasizing porches and placing garages behind the homes off of alleys, New Urbanist designs can more easily accommodate closer references to past styles. For examples in Colorado of New Urbanist planning that includes significant referencing of rural and small-town architecture, see Prospect NewTown, http://www.prospectnewtown.com/; and High Plains Village at Centerra, http://www.mcstain.com/Page-917.htm?CommunityID=1.

79. On the centrality of safety in creating residential spaces, see Edward J. Blakely and Mary Gail Snyder, *Fortress America: Gated Communities in the United States* (Washington, DC: Brookings Institution Press, 1997); and Low, *Behind the Gates*.

80. Kevin Lynch summarizes the falseness of separating time and place in the title of his 1972 book on meaning-making in cities. *What Time Is This Place?* (Cambridge, MA: MIT Press, 1972).

81. On gated residential developments, see Blakely and Snyder, *Fortress America*, and Low, *Behind the Gates*.

82. Low, *Behind the Gates*, 11.

83. Ibid., 10–11.

84. New Urbanism strives to reverse this trend by placing the garage in the back off of an alley and re/placing the porch in the front.

85. Svetlana Boym, *The Future of Nostalgia* (New York: Basic Books, 2001), 8–11.

86. Marx, *Machine in the Garden*.

87. Joan Faber McAlister, "Domesticating Citizenship: The Kairotopics of America's Post-9/11 Home Makeover," *Critical Studies in Media Communication* 27 (2010): 91.

88. Low, *Behind the Gates*, 9–10.

89. Ibid., 9–15.

90. McAlister, "Good Neighbors," 280, 284–85.

91. McAlister, "Figural Materialism," 294–95.

92. David Seamon, "Gaston Bachelard's Topoanalysis in the 21st Century: The Lived Reciprocity between Houses and Inhabitants as Portrayed by American Writer

Louis Bromfield," in *Phenomenology 2010*, ed. Lester Embree (Bucharest, Romania: Zeta Books, 2010). http://ksu.academia.edu/DavidSeamon/Papers/169389/Gaston_Bachelards _Topoanalysis_in_the_21st_Century_The_Lived_Reciprocity_between_Houses_and _Inhabitants_as_Portrayed_by_American_Writer_Louis_Bromfield. Accessed June 28, 2011.

93. Alain de Botton, *The Architecture of Happiness* (New York: Pantheon Books, 2006), 107.

94. Indeed, in his long meditation on home, de Botton sidetracks into Christian and Islamic sacred architecture (ibid., 117).

95. Carole Blair, "Contemporary U.S. Memorial Sites as Exemplars of Rhetoric's Materiality," in *Rhetorical Bodies*, ed. Jack Selzer and Sharon Crowley (Madison: University of Wisconsin Press, 1999), 19. Greg Dickinson, "Joe's Rhetoric: Finding Authenticity at Starbucks," *Rhetoric Society Quarterly* 32 (2002): 22.

96. I use *sense* here very specifically to mean the ways the body senses space, a sense that is at once symbolically scrimmed and affectively registered. Brian Ott has written about this embodied relationship between the symbolic and the affective as a movement from the experiencing (or, sensing) body and the body of experience (or, the sense-making body). Brian L. Ott, "The Visceral Politics of *V for Vendetta*: On Political Affect in Cinema," *Critical Studies in Media Communication* 27 (2010): 49. See also Brian Massumi, "The Autonomy of Affect," *Cultural Critique* 31 (1995): 85. Massumi begins his analysis of the autonomy of affect with a distinction between *intensity*, which he will link to affect, and *qualification,* which he will link to signification and emotion.

97. Massumi, "The Autonomy of Affect," 85; Hans Ulrich Gumbrecht, *Production of Presence: What Meaning Cannot Convey* (Stanford, CA: Stanford University Press, 2004), 2.

98. By gesturing to both here and now, the affective aesthetics of safety are kairotopic. Kairotopic analysis allows the rhetorical critic to simultaneously engage how rhetoric functions through time and space. McAlister, "Domesticating," 91. McAlister argues that visions of the contemporary home as a safe space outside of the maelstrom of post-9/11 terror depend on exporting and forgetting domestic terrorism against women within the house and also the violence of poverty located in urban, suburban, and rural landscapes.

99. Jane Bennett, "The Force of Things: Steps Toward an Ecology of Matter," *Political Theory* 32 (2004): 354.

100. Massumi, "The Autonomy of Affect," 85.

101. McAlister, "Domesticating," 90–93.

102. Ian Cook and Philip Crang, "The World on a Plate: Culinary Culture, Displacement, and Geographical Knowledges," *Journal of Material Culture* 1 (1996): 131–53.

Chapter 4

1. Sarah Karnasiewicz, "Eating Dinner as a Family Puts Priorities of the Home in Order," Catholic Online. http://www.catholic.org/hf/family/story.php?id=18802. Accessed January 6, 2010.

2. Heather Mason Kiefer, "Empty Seats: Fewer Families Eat Together," Gallup Online, January 24, 2004. http://www.gallup.com/poll/10336/empty-seats-fewer-families -eat-together.aspx. Accessed July 6, 2011.

3. The National Center on Addiction and Drug Abuse at Columbia University, "The Importance of Family Dinners, VI," September 2010. http://www.casacolumbia.org/upload/2010/20100922familydinners6.pdf. Accessed July 6, 2011.

4. *Globalization* along with its root term *global* and its attendant terms *globality* and *globalism* are contested. For my purposes, I am taking globalization as the processes associated with international and transnational capitalism. These processes are themselves contested. As one of the popular prophets of globalization, Thomas Friedman, argues, under the conditions of globalization the world is flat or at least flattening. This flattening, Friedman argues, is the result of the interconnectedness fostered by service and information economies along with transportation and communication technologies that serve to increasingly connect disparate parts of the globe. Harm J. De Blij reads globalization differently, asserting the globalization functions in and creates a rough landscape, a roughness that interrupts the smooth flows of capital and information. Arjun Appadurai argues that modernity is marked by a remaking of the imagination, a remaking influenced by and responsive to the speed and mobility encoded in globalizing electronic media and new transportation systems. Regardless, globalization can be taken to mean the processes by which capital and information flow and how these global flows remake the world. Globality can be thought of as the resulting and constituting cultural manifestations of globalization. See Arjun Appadurai, *Modernity at Large: Cultural Dimensions of Globalization* (Minneapolis: University of Minnesota Press, 1996); Harm J. De Blij, *The Power of Place: Geography, Destiny, and Globalization's Rough Landscape* (Oxford: Oxford University Press, 2009), ix; Thomas L. Friedman, *The World Is Flat: A Brief History of the Twenty-First Century* (New York: Picador, 2007).

5. Ian Cook and Philip Crang, "The World on a Plate: Culinary Culture, Displacement, and Geographical Knowledges," *Journal of Material Culture* 1 (1996): 131.

6. Ibid., 131.

7. The flavor of food is created out of the complex interactions of taste, smell (with smell the single most important sensation in the "flavor image"), touch, sight, and sound. The five tastes that the tongue apprehends matter in making flavor, but so too do a full range of embodied, memorized, and emotionally redolent responses to the food experience. Gordon M. Shepherd, *Neurogastronomy: How the Brain Creates Flavor and Why It Matters* (New York: Columbia University Press, 2012), 4–5, 104–30.

8. Eric King Watts and Mark P. Orbe, "The Spectacular Consumption of 'True' African American Culture: 'Whassup' with the Budweiser Guys?" *Critical Studies in Media Communication* 19 (2002): 4. I am drawing here on Watts's and Orbe's conceptualization of "spectacular consumption." "A key rhetorical resource in the economy of spectacular consumption," they write

> is the paradoxical tension between the 'different' and the widely available. On the one hand, the pleasure of consuming otherness is advanced by the Other's uniqueness. On the other hand, in a mass consumer culture, commodity value rises to a sufficient level only when the Other undergoes massive replication.

9. Clearly there are a wide range of chain restaurants that line the streets of the suburbs. These restaurants draw on diverse aesthetics for the appeal. Southern comfort food influences Black-Eyed Pea and Cracker Barrel, hometown grill or burger joint founds Applebee's and Red Robin. Chili's draws together vaguely identified Tex-Mex

with a burger joint aesthetics. And, though I will pay most attention to Macaroni Grill and Olive Garden, there are other chains that address Italian styles. I have chosen to attend primarily to Olive Garden and Macaroni Grill to crystalize a series of important material and aesthetic relations present in many of these other restaurants: the importance of family, appeals to authenticity, the return of ethnicity, and pastoralism. I will intersect my close analysis of these two chains—and particular instances of each—with other chain restaurants to check for similarities and differences across the genre.

10. Leda Cooks, "You are What You (Don't) Eat? Food, Identity, and Resistance," *Text and Performance Quarterly* 29 (2009): 98–100.

11. Michel de Certeau, Luce Giard, and Pierre Mayol, *The Practice of Everyday Life*, vol. 2, *Living and Cooking* (Minneapolis: University of Minnesota Press, 1998).

12. Pierre Bourdieu, *Distinction: A Social Critique of the Judgment of Taste*, trans. Richard Nice (Cambridge, MA: Harvard University Press, 1984). While food as a mode of distinction is a significant theme throughout the book, see in particular the first part of the chapter, "The Habitus and the Space of Life-Styles," 169–200.

13. Claude Lévi-Strauss, *The Raw and the Cooked: Introduction to a Science of Mythology: I*, trans. John and Doreen Weightman (New York: Harper and Row, 1969).

14. Mary Douglas, *Purity and Danger: An Analysis of Concepts of Pollution and Taboo* (London: Routledge and Kegan Paul, 1966). See also Mary Douglas, "Food as a System of Communication," in *In the Active Voice* (London: Routledge and Kegan Paul, 1982), 82–124.

15. Luce Giard, "Doing-Cooking," in *The Practice of Everyday Life*, vol. 2, *Living and Cooking*, ed. Michel de Certeau, Luce Giard, and Pierre Mayol (Minneapolis: University of Minnesota Press, 1998), 171.

16. Pierre Mayol, "Living," in ibid., 141.

17. Theodore C. Humphrey and Lin T. Humphrey, *We Gather Together: Food and Festival in American Life* (Ann Arbor: UMI Research Press, 1988).

18. On the continued gendering of food on the Food Network, see Rebecca Swenson, "Domestic Divo? Televised Treatments of Masculinity, Femininity, and Food," *Critical Studies in Media Communication* 26 (2009): 38–41. While men and women star in Food Network shows, women are far more likely to offer domestic and familial visions of food, men more likely to star in shows that emphasize competition, leisure, or professional abilities.

19. For example, some believe they can predict children's successes in school on the number of meals eaten at home. Some research has suggested a correlation between family dinner and illicit drug use. Fewer family dinners is correlated with greater drug use. Increased drug use by children and teenagers is correlated with lower grades in school. The National Center on Addiction and Substance Abuse at Columbia University, "The Importance of Family Dinners," 2009. http://casafamilyday.org/familyday/. Accessed January 5, 2010.

20. Karnasiewicz, "Eating Dinner as a Family Puts Priorities of the Home in Order."

21. Barbara Kingsolver, Steven, L. Hopp, and Camille Kingsolver, *Animal, Vegetable, Miracle: A Year of Food Life* (New York: HarperCollins, 2007); Michael Pollan, *The Omnivore's Dilemma: A Natural History of Four Meals* (New York: Penguin Press, 2006); Michael Pollan, *In Defense of Food: An Eater's Manifesto* (New York: Penguin Press, 2008), Eric Schlosser, *Fast Food Nation: The Dark Side of the All-American Meal* (Boston: Houghton

Mifflin, 2001); Ann Vileisis, *Kitchen Literacy: How We Lost Knowledge of Where Food Comes From and Why We Need to Get It Back* (Washington, DC: Island Press/Shearwater Books, 2008).

22. Elspeth Probyn, *Carnal Appetites: FoodSexIdentities* (London and New York: Routledge, 2000), 3.

23. *Terroir* is notoriously difficult to translate from the French because the meaning is "embedded in French culture." The word is variously translated as "soil, locality, or part of a country." That said, terroir has become an important node in thinking food globally. Amy B. Trubeck, *The Taste of Place: A Cultural Journey into Terroir* (Berkeley: University of California Press, 2008), 9, 12. French tastemakers (like cookbook authors) and taste producers (like cheese makers and vintners), built the concept of terroir beginning in the early twentieth century. What these tastemakers and taste producers "said may have embraced the timeless and essential notion of mother Earth, but what they did was create a vision of agrarian rural France and convincingly put it in people's mouths" (22).

24. For example, Paula Deen's cookbooks, and her show on the Food Network, connect the South with family through the lens of nostalgia. Paula Deen and Melissa Clark, *Paula Deen's the Deen Family Cookbook* (New York: Simon and Schuster, 2009).

25. Greg Dickinson and Casey Maugh, "Placing Visual Rhetoric: Finding Material Comforts in Wild Oats Marketplace," in *Defining Visual Rhetorics*, ed. Charles A. Hill and Marguerite Helmers (New York: Lawrence Erlbaum Associates, 2004), 259–75.

26. Cook and Crang, "The World on a Plate," 131.

27. Pollan, *The Omnivore's Dilemma*; Schlosser, *Fast Food Nation*.

28. Cook and Crang, "The World on a Plate," 132.

29. Ibid.

30. Ibid., 133.

31. Ibid, 133–34.

32. Diane Negra, "Ethnic Food Fetishism: Whiteness and Nostalgia in Recent Film and Television," *Velvet Light Trap* 50 (2002): 69.

33. Watts and Orbe, "The Spectacular Consumption of 'True' African American Culture," 1–20; Helena Shugart, "Sumptuous Texts: Consuming 'Otherness' in Food Film Genre," *Critical Studies in Media Communication* 25 (2008): 68–90.

34. Watts and Orbe, "The Spectacular Consumption of 'True' African American Culture," 3.

35. Shugart, "Sumptuous Texts," 69.

36. bell hooks, "Eating the Other," in *Black Looks: Race and Representation* (Boston: South End Press, 1992), 31. hooks writes, "Currently, the commodification of difference promotes paradigms of consumption wherein whatever difference the Other inhabits is eradicated, via exchange, by a consumer cannibalism that not only displaces the Other but denies the significance of the Other's history in the process of decontextualization" (31).

37. Families eat, on average, 5.7 meals a week away from home. Gretchen Kurtz, "Mommy This Restaurant Rocks: Sample Our Menu of Eateries That Are Friendly to Both Grown-Ups and the Crayon Set," DenverPost.Com. http://www.denverpost .com/food/ci_3084262. Accessed October 8, 2005.

38. Giard, "Doing-Cooking," 171.

39. Restaurant Industry Facts. http://www.restaurant.org/research/ind_glance.cfm. Accessed October 1, 2005.

40. Kurtz, "Mommy This Restaurant Rocks."

41. Lizabeth Cohen, "From Town Center to Shopping Center: The Reconfiguration of Community Marketplaces in Postwar America," *American Historical Review* 101 (1996): 1052–53; Robert Fishman, *Bourgeois Utopias: The Rise and Fall of Suburbia* (New York: Basic Books, 1987); Dolores Hayden, *Building Suburbia: Green Fields and Urban Growth, 1820–2000* (New York: Pantheon Books, 2003).

42. Andrew Hurley, "From Hash House to Family Restaurant: The Transformation of the Diner and Post–World War II Consumer Culture," *Journal of American History* 83 (1997): 1293–99.

43. Ibid., 1299.

44. Ibid., 1306.

45. Negra, "Ethnic Food Fetishism," 65.

46. Donna J. Haraway, *Modest_Witness@Second_Millennium.FemaleManÓ_Meets_OncoMouseä: Feminism and Technoscience* (New York: Routledge, 1997), 1–3; Rosi Braidotti, *Nomadic Subjects: Embodiment and Sexual Difference in Contemporary Feminist Theory* (New York: Columbia University Press, 1994), 41–56; Susan M. Squier, "Reproducing the Posthuman Body: Ectogenetic Fetus, Surrogate Mother, Pregnant Man," in *Posthuman Bodies*, ed. Judith Halberstam and Ira Livingston (Bloomington: Indiana University Press, 1995), 113–32; Jacquelyn N. Zita, *Body Talk: Philosophical Reflections on Sex and Gender* (New York: Columbia University Press, 1998), 76–79.

47. Zita, *Body Talk*, 8–9.

48. Judith Butler, *Gender Trouble: Feminism and the Subversion of Identity* (1990; New York: Routledge, 2000); Judith Butler, *Bodies That Matter: On the Discursive Limits of "Sex"* (New York: Routledge, 1993).

49. Henri Lefebvre, *The Social Production of Space*, trans. Donald Nicholson-Smith (Cambridge: Blackwell, 1991), 170, 194.

50. David A. Kessler, *The End of Overeating: Controlling the Insatiable American Appetite* (New York: Rodale, 2009), 13–21. Kessler argues that the food industry's emphasis on fat, salt, and sugar creates foods that are "highly rewarding stimuli." In short, the more fat, sugar, and salt a consumer eats, the more fat, sugar, and salt the consumer wants to eat. In fact, the brain's response to food occurs in the same region of the brain as those activated by the cravings involved in drug abuse.

51. Cook and Crang, "The World on a Plate," 131.

52. Scott Lasch, *Critique of Information* (London: Sage Publications, 2002), 23–25; Ali Yakhlef, "Global Brands as Embodied 'Generic Spaces': The Example of Branded Chain Hotels," *Space and Culture* 7 (2004): 237.

53. In fact, it is likely the case that the generic spaces of the 1990s are no longer as appealing as they once were. The recent redesigns of Starbucks stores to more fully integrate into the local neighborhood and to more carefully embody a sense of authenticity is one of many examples of global institutions attempting to make generic a sense of locality. Claire Cain Miller, "Now at Starbucks: A Rebound," *New York Times*, January 20, 2010, nytimes.com. Accessed December 31, 2010. Similarly, Giorgia Aiello has been arguing that current design practices in Europe are at once generic and, rather than aesthetically thin, provide resources of thinking and covering over diversity. Giorgia

Aiello, "The Appearance of Diversity: Visual Design and the Public Communication of EU Identity," in *European Union Identity: Perceptions from Asia and Europe*, ed. Jessica Bain and Martin Holland (Baden-Baden: Nomos, 2007), 159–60; Giorgia Aiello, "From Wound to Enclave: The Visual-Material Performance of Urban Renewal in Bologna's Manifattura delle Arti," *Western Journal of Communication* 75 (2011): 359.

54. Jane Brody, in her *New York Times* Personal Health column, reported on a recently published study of weight gain in over 100,000 people. Increased consumption of French fries accounted for over three pounds of weight gain over four years. Red meat, along with sweets, refined starches, and sugared drinks are also strongly linked to weight gain. Red Robin's abundance of French fries and red meat also leads to abundance of embodied weight. Jane E. Brody, "Still Counting Calories? Your Weight-Loss Plan May Be Outdated," *New York Times*, July 19, 2011. http://www.nytimes.com/2011/07/19/health/19brody.html?ref=science. Accessed July 21, 2011.

55. Red Robin Food. http://www.redrobin.com/food/. Accessed February 4, 2010. Just below this headline is a picture of seven burgers, arranged in a wedge so that the last two seem to be far in the distance. Each burger is overstuffed with melting cheese, onion rings, chicken patties, bacon slices, lettuce, tomatoes, and, of course, the huge beef patty in the center. As is typical of images on menus and websites, the food overfills the image frame, further emphasizing the abundance of the food for the burger (or the pasta or the steak) is too big for even a web page to contain. Just for interest's sake, the Bleu Ribbon Burger with blue cheese, onion straws, beef burger patty, chipotle mayo, and other fixings, has 1,052 calories, 63 grams of fat, and over 1,000 mgs of sodium. Red Robin Food. http://www.redrobin.com/food/. Accessed February 4, 2010.

56. TGI Friday's "Good Things Happen in Threes." http://www.tgifridays.com/promos/3course.aspx. Accessed February 4, 2010.

57. Olive Garden RevItalia. http://www.ramskiandcompany.com/portfolio/hospitality/olive-garden/. Accessed February 9, 2010.

58. Ibid.

59. Negra, "Ethnic Food Fetishism," 62, Shugart, "Sumptuous Texts," 69.

60. Frances Mayes, *Under the Tuscan Sun* (San Francisco: Chronicle Books, 1996).

61. Davide Girardelli, "Commodified Identities: The Myth of Italian Food in the United States," *Journal of Communication Inquiry* 28 (2004): 307.

62. Olive Garden. "Our Passion." http://www.olivegarden.com/ourpassion/CITbook_p2.asp. Accessed October 18, 2005.

63. Greg Dickinson, "Joe's Rhetoric: Finding Authenticity at Starbucks," *Rhetoric Society Quarterly* 32 (2002): 12.

64. Similarly, food films banish the sterility of the modern supermarket. Negra, "Ethnic Food Fetishism," 63; Shugart, "Sumptuous Texts," 83. The disconnect between the image of homemade, fresh food in the front of the restaurant and the trucks and farmer labors that undergird this image is related to the epistemic barriers Michael Carolan has been studying in regard to both sustainable agriculture and the production of cheap food. Michael S. Carolan, "Do You See What I See?: Examining the Epistemic Barriers to Sustainable Agriculture," *Rural Sociology* 71 (2006): 232–60. For Carolan, epistemic distance and epistemic barriers arise when "socio-biophysical objects, effects, and relationships . . . are beyond direct perception." Many elements in the food production process "cannot be perceived—that is, tasted, touched, heard, smelled, or seen—through our senses alone" (235).

65. Cook and Crang, "The World on a Plate," 132.

66. References to recognizable places like Tuscany can help locate the restaurant in its global networks. But this aesthetic can work in another direction as well, as local restaurants will occasionally take on the thinned aesthetics of chain restaurants to enhance their appeal. Take, for example, Enzio's in Old Town Fort Collins. Part of a locally owned collection of restaurants, Enzio's uses the aesthetics of Olive Garden and Macaroni Grill to broaden its appeal. The colors of its signage are almost the exact same palate as Olive Garden's, and it assertion of Italianicity through its collection of family recipes from the Italian countryside is very familiar. Indeed, it would be hard to distinguish Enzio's from other Italian chains, except for a small logo on the upper right side of Enzio's web page that asserts that the restaurant is "local, genuine" and serves "fresh food made from scratch." Even here, the message is only slightly different from that of the other restaurants I have investigated. In fact, the appeals to Fort Collins are thinner in Enzio's than in the local Applebee's, which includes photographs of Fort Collins as part of its decorations. What is clear is that the aesthetics of global networks and local landscapes intertwine and interanimate. This is precisely the rhetorical form of locality: the twining of local and global in rhetorical efforts to suture specific landscapes into complex networks of time and place.

67. Sarah LeTrent, "Yes, Skeptics, Olive Garden Does Have a Tuscan Culinary Institute." CNN Living. http://www.cnn.com/2010/LIVING/homestyle/05/10/olive.garden.culinary.institute/. Accessed December 18, 2012.

68. Girardelli, "Commodified Identities," 319.

69. Marialisa Calta, Barbarians at the Plate: Taming and Feeding the Modern American Family (New York: Perigree Books, 2005), 1.

70. Ibid., 1.

71. Negra, "Ethnic Food Fetishism," 69.

72. As Lawrence Grossberg argues, popular culture articulates affective relations. Lawrence Grossberg, We Gotta Get Out of This Place: Popular Conservatism and Postmodern Culture (New York: Routledge, 1992), 79–87.

73. Ibid.

74. Sarah Ahmed, The Promise of Happiness (Durham, NC: Duke University Press, 2010), 5.

75. Cook and Crang, "The World on a Plate," 132.

Chapter 5

1. Martin Luther King Jr., "I've Been to the Mountaintop." http://www.americanrhetoric.com/speeches/mlkivebeentothemountaintop.htm. Accessed March 14, 2007.

2. Dana L. Cloud, Control and Consolation in American Culture and Politics: Rhetorics of Therapy (Thousand Oaks, CA: Sage, 1998), xxi.

3. Carole Blair, Greg Dickinson, and Brian L. Ott, "Introduction: Rhetoric/Memory/Place," in Places of Public Memory: The Rhetoric of Museums and Memorials, ed. Greg Dickinson, Carole Blair, and Brian L. Ott (Tuscaloosa: University of Alabama Press, 2010), 9–10.

4. Ibid., 28. This limiting of memory's proliferation, conversely, also suggests the importance of the memory places actually realized.

5. Ibid., 19–20.

6. Bradford Vivian, *Public Forgetting: The Rhetoric and Politics of Beginning Again* (University Park: Pennsylvania State University Press, 2010), 48.

7. As in the rest of this book, I use *meaningful* to refer both to legibility and to an emotional or affective dimension that allows this legibility to matter. Blair, Dickinson, and Ott, "Introduction: Rhetoric/Memory/Place," 3.

8. Vivian, *Public Forgetting*, 166.

9. Brian L. Ott, Eric Aoki, and Greg Dickinson, "Ways of (Not) Seeing Guns: Presence and Absence at the Cody Firearms Museum," *Communication and Critical/Cultural Studies* 8 (2011): 228.

10. Greg Dickinson, Brian L. Ott, and Eric Aoki, "Spaces of Remembering and Forgetting: The Reverent Eye/I at the Plains Indian Museum," *Communication and Critical/Cultural Studies* 3 (2006): 29–31.

11. Ibid., 31.

12. http://www.radiantchurch.com/history.asp. Accessed October 13, 2006. Jonathan Mahler, "The Soul of the New Exurb," *New York Times Magazine*, March 27, 2005. http://www.nytimes.com/2005/03/27/magazine/327MEGACHURCH.html ?_r=0. Accessed September 28, 2014.

13. Anne C. Loveland and Otis B. Wheeler, *From Meetinghouse to Megachurch: A Material and Cultural History* (Columbia: University of Missouri Press, 2003), 1–2.

14. Mark Chaves, "2005 Paul Douglas Lecture: All Creatures Great and Small: Megachurches in Context," *Review of Religious Research* 47 (2006): 333.

15. Ibid., 333, 338.

16. Ibid., 342-344. Chaves argues that the most compelling single factor driving the rise of the megachurch is an economy of scale. Church attendees are demanding more and more services. These services are expensive. Larger churches have the financial resources to provide these services.

17. James B. Twitchell, *Branded Nation: The Marketing of Megachurch, College, Inc., and Museumworld* (New York: Simon and Schuster, 2004), 84.

18. Loveland and Wheeler, *From Meetinghouse to Megachurch*, 123.

19. Jeanne Halgren Kilde, *When Church Became Theatre: The Transformation of Evangelical Architecture and Worship in Nineteenth-Century America* (New York: Oxford University Press, 2002), 11.

20. Ibid.

21. Loveland and Wheeler, *From Meetinghouse to Megachurch*, 7.

22. Ibid., 5–7.

23. Kilde, *When Church Became Theatre*, 32–33; Loveland and Wheeler, *From Meetinghouse to Megachurch*, 28.

24. Ibid.

25. Ibid., 168.

26. Ibid., 215.

27. Ibid., 216.

28. Lizabeth Cohen, "From Town Center to Shopping Center: The Reconfiguration of Community Marketplaces in Postwar America," *American Historical Review* 101 (1996): 1052–53.

29. Another form of informality: the pastor goes by his first rather than last name, his name a mix of formal "pastor," and informal "Lee."

30. http://www.radiantchurch.com/. Accessed October 18, 2006.

31. Jay R. Howard and John M. Streck, "The Splintered Art World of Contemporary Christian Music," *Popular Music* 15 (1996): 42.

32. Bob Millard quoted in ibid., 45.

33. Loveland and Wheeler, *From Meetinghouse to Megachurch*, 257.

34. One of the characteristics of at least some megachurches is the intersection of men and biker culture. The head pastors of two of the churches to which I paid the most attention—Radiant Church and Timberline Community Church in Fort Collins, Colorado—spoke often of riding Harley Hogs. On the Radiant Church website, for example, they offer a video of a father's day sermon in which pastor Lee rides into the auditorium on a Harley, while the first picture in the photo slide tour is of a gaggle of Harleys under a tent outside of the church building. See http://www.welcometoradiant.com/northcampus/default.htm. Accessed October 21, 2006.

35. Kilde writes that the late nineteenth-century church architects were also often busy designing the theaters and concert halls, which were gaining popularity. The church, theater, and concert hall shared the same problem: seating larger numbers of people, while offering each an intimate experience of the entertainment offered on the stage. Kilde, *When Church Became Theatre*, 113. Even as the size of the buildings hampered intimacy, the largeness was a crucial part of the architectural rhetoric and indicated a cultural importance and popularity. Loveland and Wheeler, *From Meetinghouse to Megachurch*, 34–35.

36. In fact, one large church in Fort Collins regularly opens the auditorium for basketball games.

37. http://www.radiantchurch.com/welcome/kids.asp. Accessed October 26, 2006.

38. Ibid.

39. Twitchell, *Branded Nation*, 65.

40. http://www.radiantchurch.com/adults.asp. Accessed October 26, 2006.

41. In his sermon on homosexuality, McFarland asserts that homosexuals choose their sexuality, and with the help of God and the support of Celebrate Recovery, formerly gay members of Radiant have been able to "recover" from their sinful lifestyle. Lee McFarland, "What to Tell Your Gay Friend," http://www.radiantchurch.com/media/messages/audio/70.mp3. Accessed October 23, 2006.

42. http://www.radiantchurch.com/welcome/kids.asp Accessed October 27, 2006.

43. Ibid.

44. Kilde, *When Church Became Theatre*, 159.

45. Ibid., 161.

46. Ibid., 162–63.

47. Ibid., 219.

48. David Chaney, "Authenticity and Suburbia," in *Imagining Cities: Scripts, Signs, Memory*, ed. Sallie Westwood and John Williams (London: Routledge, 1997), 142–43.

49. Mark A. Shibley, "Contemporary Evangelicals: Born-Again and World Affirming," *Annals of the American Academy of Political and Social Science* 558 (1998): 74.

50. Shibley argues that contemporary evangelicals are not necessarily culturally conservative, pointing, for example, to Metropolitan Community Church, which openly embraces homosexuality. Shibley is certainly right about neo-evangelicals' diversity. Megachurches I studied were open to popular culture forms like rock music, coffee shops, and tight t-shirts, but were still conservative on family and gender values. See Shibley, "Contemporary Evangelicals," 85.

51. Shibley argues that contemporary evangelicals—while clearly not feminist—can

be considered postfeminist. Member needs drive these changing visions of the family. Not only are neo-evangelicals more likely to be college educated than are fundamentalists or Pentecostals, but also the continued move of women into professions shifts the economic condition of the family. Shibley, "Contemporary Evangelicals," 72–74.

52. Dana L. Cloud, "The Rhetoric of <Family Values>: Scapegoating, Utopia, and the Privatization of Social Responsibility," *Western Journal of Communication* 62 (1998): 388.

53. Joel Osteen, *Your Best Life Now: 7 Steps to Living at Your Full Potential* (New York: Warner, 2004); Rick Warren, *The Purpose Driven Life: What on Earth Am I Here For?* (Grand Rapids: Zondervan, 2002).

54. Shibley, "Contemporary Evangelicals," 75.

55. Kilde, *When Church Became Theatre*, 215, 217.

56. Alain de Botton, *The Architecture of Happiness* (New York: Pantheon Books, 2006), 107–8.

Chapter 6

1. Bloomberg News, "Fed Says Consumer Debt Rose in December," *New York Times* February 8, 2000, C2. LexisNexis. Accessed April 15, 2010. Richard W. Stevenson, "Fed Reports Family Gains from Economy," *New York Times*, January 19, 2000, C1. LexisNexis. Accessed April 15, 2010. Bloomberg News, "Pace of '99 Retail Sales Fastest in 15 Years," January 14, 2000. LexisNexis. Accessed April 15, 2010.

2. Louis Uchittle, "Equity Shrivels as Homeowners Borrow and Buy," *New York Times*, January 19, 2001, A1. LexisNexis. Accessed April 15, 2010. Article reports that equity in homes is at its lowest level as homeowners borrow more against their homes to fund consumer spending.

3. Greg Lindsay, "Say Goodbye to the Mall," *Advertising Age* 77 (40): 2006. Ebscohost Academic Search Premier. Accessed August 22, 2008. Paragraphs 3–4.

4. Lizabeth Cohen, "From Town Center to Shopping Center: The Reconfiguration of Community Marketplaces in Postwar America," *American Historical Review* 101 (1996): 1051–52.

5. As argued in the introduction, the postwar suburb depended on a number of government subsidies, including the building of roads and interstates. These roads not only opened new lands for domestic settlement but were also central to developing the large regional malls.

6. On the shift from Fordist to post-Fordist economies and the spatial consequences, see David Harvey, *The Condition of Postmodernity: An Enquiry into the Origins of Cultural Change* (Oxford: Blackwell, 1989). On the place destroying logics of postindustrial economics, see Sharon Zukin, *Landscapes of Power: From Detroit to Disneyland* (Berkeley: University of California Press, 1991).

7. Steve Macek, *Urban Nightmares: The Media, the Right, and the Moral Panic over the City* (Minneapolis: University of Minnesota Press, 2006), xv. For a historical analysis of white flight in Los Angeles, see Eric Avila, *Popular Culture in the Age of White Flight: Fear and Fantasy in Suburban Los Angeles* (Berkeley: University of California Press, 2004).

8. Cohen, "From Town Center to Shopping Center," 1052–53.

9. For a detailed analysis of how the car shaped both a city and shopping, see Richard Longstreth, *From City Center to Regional Mall: Architecture, the Automobile, and Retailing in Los Angeles, 1930–1950* (Cambridge, MA: MIT Press, 1998).

10. In fact, orienting shopping buildings toward the automobile was evolutionary, as

Longstreth points out. In the late 1920s, for example, Bullocks Wilshire—a brand new Art Deco department store in Los Angeles—began to draw shoppers out of the urban core and onto the horizontally conceptualized city streets of the new city. It signified this in part by including a large (for the time) parking lot behind the store and orienting the store toward the parking lot.

11. Cohen, "From Town Center to Shopping Center," 1068–71.

12. Reyner Banham, *Los Angeles: The Architecture of Four Ecologies* (Berkeley: University of California Press, 2001), 195.

13. Owen D. Gutfreund, *Twentieth-Century Sprawl: Highways and the Reshaping of the American Landscape* (New York: Oxford University Press, 2004).

14. Kathryn Milun, *Pathologies of Modern Urban Space: Empty Space, Urban Anxiety, and the Recovery of the Public Self* (New York: Routledge, 2007), 100.

15. Andrew F. Wood, *City Ubiquitous: Place, Communication, and the Rise of Omnitopia* (Cresskill, NJ: Hampton Press, 2009), 137–41.

16. Margaret Morse, "An Ontology of Everyday Distraction: The Freeway, the Mall, and Television," in *Logics of Television: Essays in Cultural Criticism*, ed. Patricia Mellencamp (Bloomington: Indiana University Press, 1990), 197.

17. Ibid., 195.

18. Ibid.

19. Milun, *Pathologies of Modern Urban Space*, 126.

20. Ibid., 23.

21. Parija Bhatnagar, "Not a Mall, It's a Lifestyle Center: Developers Are Embracing These Cozy, High-End Urban Centers in Lieu of Traditional Big Box Formats," CNNMoney.com. January 12, 2005. http://money.cnn.com/2005/01/11/news /fortune500/retail_lifestylecenter/. Accessed September 10, 2007.

22. Lindsay, "Say Goodbye to the Mall," 14–16.

23. Quoted in ibid., 7.

24. Ibid., 6.

25. Slavoj Žižek, "Looking Awry," *October* 50 (1989): 30–55; Slavoj Žižek, *Looking Awry: An Introduction to Jacques Lacan through Popular Culture* (Cambridge, MA: MIT Press 1992), 11–12; Brian L. Ott, Eric Aoki, and Greg Dickinson, "Ways of (Not) Seeing Guns: Presence and Absence at the Cody Firearms Museum," *Communication and Critical/Cultural Studies* 8 (2011): 228–29.

26. Daniel Makagon, "Bring on the Shock Troops: Artists and Gentrification in the Popular Press," *Communication and Critical/Cultural Studies* 7 (2011): 26–52; Giorgia Aiello, "From Wound to Enclave: The Visual-Material Performance of Urban Renewal in Bologna's Manifattura delle Arti," *Western Journal of Communication* 75 (2011): 341–66; Sharon Zukin, *Loft Living: Culture and Capital in Urban Change* (New York: Routledge, 1989).

27. See Greg Dickinson, "Memories of Sale: Nostalgia and the Construction of Identity in Old Pasadena," *Quarterly Journal of Speech* 83 (1997): 1–27.

28. For a communication perspective on New Urbanism, see Thomas J. St. Antoine, "Making Heaven out of Hell: New Urbanism and the Refutation of Suburban Spaces," *Southern Communication Journal* 72 (2007): 127–44.

29. Ibid., 131–32.

30. D. W. Meinig, "Symbolic Landscapes: Some Idealizations of American Communities," in *The Interpretation of Ordinary Landscapes: Geographical Essays*, ed. D. W. Meinig (New York: Oxford University Press, 1979), 167.

31. Richard V. Francavigilia, *Main Street Revisited: Time, Space, and Image Building in Small Town America* (Iowa City: University of Iowa Press, 1996), 162.

32. James J. Farrell, *One Nation under Goods: Malls and the Seductions of American Shopping* (Washington, DC: Smithsonian Books, 2003), 35.

33. Ibid., 36.

34. Edward Relph, *The Modern Urban Landscape* (Baltimore: Johns Hopkins University Press, 1987), 254.

35. Build-A-Bear Workshop, Inc., 2008, About Us. http://www.buildabear.com /shopping/contents/content.jsp?catId=3100004&id=10100029&sc_hpan=footer&sc _hpdr=footer_veryleft. Accessed October 4, 2014.

36. Marita Sturken, *Tourists of History: Memory, Kitsch, and Consumerism from Oklahoma City to Ground Zero* (Durham, NC: Duke University Press, 2001), 7.

37. Jessie Stewart and Greg Dickinson, "Enunciating Locality in the Postmodern Suburb: FlatIron Crossing and the Colorado Lifestyle," *Western Journal of Communication* 72 (2008): 291–94.

38. On the importance of street lighting to making the city as experienced in the twentieth century, see Wolfgang Schivelbusch, *Disenchanted Night: The Industrialization of Light in the Nineteenth Century*, trans. Angela Davies (Berkeley: University of California Press, 1988), 79–134. Thanks to Giorgia Aiello for pointing me to this cite.

39. Kenneth Burke, *A Grammar of Motives* (Berkeley: University of California Press, 1969), 59–61.

40. The cultural center is no longer part of the Centerra Promenade; the space has been taken over by retail shops and its traces completely erased.

41. Chapungu Sculpture Park. http://centerracolorado.com/contentPages/display /56. Accessed November 23, 2009. Paragraph 1.

42. Ibid., paragraph 2.

43. Chapungu: The Great Stone Sculptures of Africa. http://www .chapungusculpturepark.com/. Accessed July 28, 2011.

44. Stephen A. King, "Memory, Mythmaking, and Museums: Constructive Authenticity and the Primitive Blues Subject," *Southern Communication Journal* 71 (2006): 235.

45. Ibid.

46. Ibid., 236.

47. See bell hooks, "Eating the Other: Desire and Resistance," in *Eating Culture*, ed. Ron Scapp and Brian Seitz (Albany: State University of New York Press, 1998), 181–200.

48. Renato Rosaldo, *Culture and Truth: The Remaking of Social Analysis* (Boston: Beacon Press, 1989), 69–70.

49. Ibid., 70–71.

50. The appearance and then disappearance of the Chapungu Museum from Centerra Promenade Shops indicates one of the difficulties of writing about the built environment: though built of seemingly permanent materials, the landscape is constantly changing.

51. Zukin, *Landscapes of Power*, 41.

52. Roland Barthes, *Mythologies*, trans. Annette Lavers (New York: Hill and Wang, 1972), 100–101.

53. Tamar Katriel, "Sites of Memory: Discourses of the Past in Israeli Pioneering Settlement Museums," *Quarterly Journal of Speech* 80 (1994): 6.

54. Lizabeth Cohen, *A Consumer's Republic: The Politics of Mass Consumption in Postwar America* (New York: Alfred A. Knopf, 2003), 204.

55. Sturken, *Tourists of History*, 9.

56. Cohen, *A Consumer's Republic*.

57. Victoria de Grazia, "Empowering Women as Citizen-Consumers," in *The Sex of Things: Gender and Consumption in Historical Perspective*, ed. Victoria de Grazia with Ellen Furlough (Berkeley: University of California Press, 1996), 279.

58. Cohen, "From Town Center to Shopping Center," 1059.

59. Benjamin R. Barber, *Jihad vs. McWorld* (New York: Times Books, 1995): 72.

60. Lynn Spigel, "The Suburban Home Companion: Television and the Neighborhood Ideal in Postwar America," in *Sexuality and Space*, ed. Beatriz Colomina and Jennifer Bloomer (New York: Princeton Architectural Press, 1992), 186.

61. Lauren Berlant, *The Queen of America Goes to Washington City: Essays on Sex and Citizenship* (Durham, NC: Duke University Press, 1997), 26–27.

62. Rosaldo, *Culture and Truth*, 69–70. We don't want to equate the development of suburban shopping malls with the colonial destructions of which Rosaldo writes. We do want to note, however, that suburbia—and the policies and economics on which it is founded—is clearly aligned with the kinds of racial domination Rosaldo is concerned with.

63. Dana L. Cloud, *Control and Consolation in American Culture and Politics: Rhetorics of Therapy* (Thousand Oaks, CA: Sage, 1998), xxi.

64. Slavoj Žižek, *Looking Awry: An Introduction to Jacques Lacan through Popular Culture* (Minneapolis: University of Minnesota Press, 1997).

65. Ibid., 8.

Conclusion

1. Daniel Makagon, "Bring on the Shock Troops: Artists and Gentrification in the Popular Press," *Communication, Critical/Cultural Studies* 7 (2010): 26–52; Eric Gordon, *The Urban Spectator: American Concept Cities from Kodak to Google* (Hanover, NH: Dartmouth College Press, 2010), 153–55. Writing about the urban historic preservation movement that began in the late 1960s, Gordon notes, "The 'trauma' of renewal and historical/spatial displacement was met with a compulsion to relive, replay, and re-experience the lost object. . . . Historical preservation, once complemented by narrative through the design practices of New Urbanists and their predecessors, reframed the present city as a forum for the repetition of the past" (155).

2. Gordon, *Urban Spectator*, 155.

3. Gaston Bachelard, *The Poetics of Space*, trans. Maria Jolas (Boston: Beacon Press, 1994), xxxvii.

4. Ian Cook and Philip Crang. "The World on a Plate: Culinary Culture, Displacement, and Geographical Knowledges," *Journal of Material Culture* 1 (1996): 131–53.

5. Giorgia Aiello, "From Wound to Enclave: The Visual-Material Performance of Urban Renewal in Bologna's Manifattura delle Arti," *Western Journal of Communication* 75 (2011): 342.

6. Claire Cain Miller, "Now at Starbucks: A Rebound," *New York Times*, January 20, 2010. http://www.nytimes.com/2010/01/21/business/21sbux.html?sq=starbucks&st=nyt&adxnnl=1&scp=10&adxnnlx=1287943234-lfcRnEmDMOR2Y/5w5cbg7g.

Accessed December 31, 2010. This argument is based on work with Giorgia Aiello. Giorgia Aiello and Greg Dickinson, "Locality as/for Global Communication: A Material and Multi-Modal Analysis of Taste in the Redesign of Starbucks Stores," National Communication Association, San Francisco, California, 2010.

7. Alain de Botton, *The Architecture of Happiness* (New York: Pantheon Books, 2006), 106; Victor Burgin, *In/Different Spaces: Place and Memory in Visual Culture* (Berkeley: University of California Press, 1996), 190–91.

8. Charles Chamberlain, "From 'Haunts' to 'Character': The Meaning of Ethos and Its Relation to Ethics," *Helios* 11 (1984): 97–107.

9. Ibid., 98.

10. In psychoanalysis, *melancholia* is an unresolvable loss that is unresolvable in part because it may be a loss of something that never existed, or, differently, where the subject internalizes the lost object. *Grief*, on the other hand, can be resolved, as it responds to the loss of a remembered, real object and is a process in which the subject detaches himself or herself from the lost object. Joshua Gunn, "Mourning Speech: Haunting and the Spectral Voices of Nine-Eleven," *Text and Performance Quarterly* 24 (2004): 99.

11. Marita Sturken, *Tourists of History: Memory, Kitsch, and Consumerism from Oklahoma City to Ground Zero* (Durham, NC: Duke University Press, 2001), 5.

12. Oxford English Dictionary, http://o-www.oed.com.catalog.library.colostate.edu/view/Entry/84640?rskey=YWE25w&result=1&isAdvanced=false#eid. Accessed January 5, 2012.

13. In fact, for Freud the homely and unhomely—or the canny and the uncanny—are woven together in a tight if complex cloth. In some senses, homeliness will always depend on, or at least house, unhomeliness. Sigmund Freud, "The Uncanny," in *The Uncanny*, trans. David McLintock (London: Penguin Books, 2003), 124, 134. See also Gunn, "Mourning Speech," 98, 106.

14. Think, for example, of the constant and unfulfillable longings of the suburban film's main characters: Kathy Whitaker is farther from heaven at the end of the film than the beginning, we cannot imagine Pleasantville's David settling in nicely to his reconstructed suburban life, Edward returns to the castle on the hill alone while Kim—his almost-girlfriend—tells her regret-tinged story to her grandchild, and Truman's escape from his bubble is triumphant for his many audiences but is at best anticlimactic for him.

15. Howard Frumkin, Lawrence Frank, and Richard Jackson, *Urban Sprawl and Public Health: Designing, Planning, and Building for Healthy Communities* (Washington, DC: Island Press, 2004).

16. Few are more eloquent about the central importance of mixed-use, dense urban neighborhoods for social welfare than Jane Jacobs, *Death and Life of Great American Cities* (New York: Random House, 1961).

17. Jane D. Brody, "Communities Learn the Good Life Can Be a Killer," *New York Times*, February 20, 2012. http://well.blogs.nytimes.com/2012/01/30/communities-learn-the-good-life-can-be-a-killer/?scp=2&sq=Jane%20E.%20Brody%. Accessed February 2, 2012. Paragraph 3.

18. Ibid., paragraph 9.

19. These design factors lead to "hazard bussing" practices where children are bussed relatively short distances from home to school to avoid dangerous traffic patterns. Andrew L. Dannenberg, Richard J. Jackson, Howard Frumkin, Richard A. Schieber,

Michael Pratt, Chris Kochtitzky, and Hugh H. Tilson, "The Impact of Community Design and Land-Use Choices on Public Health: A Scientific Research Agenda," *American Journal of Public Health* 93 (2003): 1503.

20. Many urban planners and developers see mixed-use suburban in-fill as one area of building and economic growth of the next few years. While these in-fill projects are difficult, they seek to remake low-density, mono-use landscapes typical of suburbia into more urban-like landscapes with greater density, multiplicity of economic and cultural uses, and easier access to a variety of transportation options. Sam Newton, "Suburban Infill—Solving Infrastructure and Financing Issues," Urban Land Institute, November 10, 2011. http://urbanland.uli.org/Articles/2011/Nov/NewbergMinnesota. Accessed February 6, 2012.

21. Denver's Farmers Market. http://www.shopaspengrove.com/go/mallEvents .cfm?eventID=2145386486. Accessed January 27, 2012; Farmers Market at The Orchard. http://www.theorchardtowncenter.com/go/Poolb.cfm?MallID=876&FPURLID= 2129975056. Accessed January 27, 2012.

22. Michael S. Carolan, "Do You See What I See?: Examining the Epistemic Barriers to Sustainable Agriculture," *Rural Sociology* 71 (2006): 232–60; Thomas K. Tiemann, "Grower-Only Farmers' Markets: Public Spaces and Third Places," *Journal of Popular Culture* 41 (2008): 475–77.

23. The farmer's market can not only remake relations to place, as the food comes from nearby gardens and small farms, it can also remake the experience of time, as seasonality begins to return to the consciousness of consumers. See Carla R. Fjeld and Robert Sommer, "Regional-Seasonal Patterns in Produce Consumption at Farmer's Markets and Supermarkets," *Ecology of Food and Nutrition* (1982): 109–15.

24. Sarah Karnasiewicz, "Eating Dinner as a Family Puts Priorities of the Home in Order," Catholic Online. http://www.catholic.org/hf/family/story.php?id=18802. Accessed January 6, 2010. Paragraph 15.

25. Tiemann, "Grower-Only Farmers' Markets," 480. Jessie Stewart suggests that this form of consumerism could be considered "eloquent." A fully embodied and deeply committed social practice, eloquent consumer practices may be one way of reimagining community in late modernity. Personal conversation, February 7, 2012.

26. Joan Faber McAlister, "Material Aesthetics in Middle America: Simone Weil, the Problem of Roots, and the Panoptic Suburb," in *Rhetoric, Materiality, Politics*, ed. Barbara A. Biesecker and John Louis Lucaites (New York: Peter Lang, 2009), 105–6.

27. Michael Hebbert, "The Street as Locus of Collective Memory," *Environment and Planning D: Society and Space* 23 (2005): 593.

28. Brian Massumi, *Parables for the Virtual: Movement, Affect, Sensation* (Durham, NC: Duke University Press, 2002), 179. Massumi writes on the next page, "Cognitive mapping takes over where orientation stops."

29. Henri Lefebvre complains that modern spaces attempt to eliminate all odor, and that elimination is at once a denial of nature and of the human, perceiving body. Henri Lefebvre, *The Social Production of Space*, trans. Donald Nicholson-Smith (Oxford: Blackwell, 1991), 197–98.

Bibliography

Abu-Lughod, Janet L. *Race, Space, and Riots in Chicago, New York, and Los Angeles*. Oxford: Oxford University Press, 2007.

Agrest, Diana I. *Architecture from Without: Theoretical Framings for a Critical Practice*. Cambridge, MA: MIT Press, 1991.

Ahmed, Sara. *The Cultural Politics of Emotion*. New York: Routledge, 2004.

———. *The Promise of Happiness*. Durham, NC: Duke University Press. 2010.

Aiello, Giorgia, "The Appearance of Diversity: Visual Design and the Public Communication of EU Identity." In *European Union Identity: Perceptions from Asia and Europe*, edited by Jessica Bain and Martin Holland, 147–81. Baden-Baden: Nomos, 2007.

———. "From Wound to Enclave: The Visual-Material Performance of Urban Renewal in Bologna's Manifattura delle Arti." *Western Journal of Communication* 75 (2011): 341–66.

Aiello, Giorgia, and Greg Dickinson. "Locality as/for Global Communication: A Material and Multi-Modal Analysis of Taste in the Redesign of Starbucks Stores." National Communication Association, San Francisco, California, 2010.

Appadurai, Arjun. *Modernity at Large: Cultural Dimensions of Globalization*. Minneapolis: University of Minnesota Press, 1996.

Archer, John. *Architecture and Suburbia: From English Villa to American Dream House, 1690–2000*. Minneapolis: University of Minnesota Press, 2005.

Associated Press. "Economy Passes Growth as Coloradoans Biggest Concern." September 25, 2004. LexisNexis. Accessed December 13, 2006.

Aúge, Marc. *Non-Places: Introduction to an Anthropology of Supermodernity*. Translated by John Howe. London: Verso, 1995.

Avila, Eric. *Popular Culture in the Age of White Flight: Fear and Fantasy in the Suburban Los Angeles*. Berkeley: University of California Press, 2004.

Bachelard, Gaston. *The Poetics of Space*. Translated by Maria Jolas. 1964; Boston: Beacon Press, 1994.

Banham, Reyner. *Los Angeles: The Architecture of Four Ecologies*. Berkeley: University of California Press, 2001.

Barber, Benjamin R. *Jihad vs. McWorld*. New York: Times Books, 1995.

Baritz, Loren. *The Good Life: The Meaning of Success for the American Middle Class*. New York: Alfred A. Knopf, 1989.

Barthes, Roland. *Mythologies*. New York: Hill and Wang, 1972.

Baumgartner, M. P. *The Moral Order of a Suburb*. New York: Oxford University Press, 1988.

Beauregard, Robert A. *When America Became Suburban*. Minneapolis: University of Minnesota Press, 2006.

Beck, John. "Without Form and Void: The American Desert as Trope and Terrain." *Nepantla: Views from the South* 2 (2001): 63–83.

Bell, David, and Gill Valentine, eds. *Mapping Desire: Geographies of Sexualities*. London and New York: Routledge, 1995.

Bennett, Jane. "The Force of Things: Steps toward an Ecology of Matter." *Political Theory* 32 (2004): 347–72.

Berlant, Lauren. "Critical Inquiry, Affirmative Culture." *Critical Inquiry* 30 (2004): 445–51.

———. *The Queen of America Goes to Washington City: Essays on Sex and Citizenship*. Durham, NC: Duke University Press, 1997.

Bhatnagar, Parija. "Not a Mall, It's a Lifestyle Center: Developers Are Embracing These Cozy, High-End Urban Centers in Lieu of Traditional Big Box Formats." CNNMoney.com. January 12, 2005. http://money.cnn.com/2005/01/11/news/fortune500/retail_lifestylecenter/. Accessed September 10, 2007.

Biesecker, Barbara A., and John Louis Lucaites, eds. *Rhetoric, Materiality, and Politics*. New York: Peter Lang, 2009.

Blair, Carole. "Contemporary U.S. Memorial Sites as Exemplars of Rhetoric's Materiality." In *Rhetorical Bodies*, edited by Jack Selzer and Sharon Crowley, 16–57. Madison: University of Wisconsin Press, 1999.

Blair, Carole, Greg Dickinson, and Brian L. Ott, "Introduction: Rhetoric/Memory/Place." In *Places of Public Memory: The Rhetoric of Museums and Memorials*, edited by Greg Dickinson, Carole Blair, and Brian L. Ott, 1–55. Tuscaloosa: University of Alabama Press, 2010.

Blakely, Edward J., and Mary Gail Snyder. *Fortress America: Gated Communities in the United States*. Washington, DC: Brookings Institution Press, 1997.

Bloomberg News. "Fed Says Consumer Debt Rose in December." *New York Times*, February 8, 2000, C2. LexisNexis. Accessed April 15, 2010.

———. "Pace of '99 Retail Sales Fastest in 15 Years." January 14, 2000. LexisNexis. Accessed April 15, 2010.

Bourdieu, Pierre. *Distinction: A Social Critique of the Judgment of Taste*. Translated by Richard Nice. Cambridge, MA: Harvard University Press, 1984.

———. *Outline of a Theory of Practice*. Translated by Richard Nice. Cambridge: Cambridge University Press, 1977.

Boyer, M. Christine. *The City of Collective Memory: Its Historical Imagery and Architectural Entertainments*. Cambridge, MA: MIT Press, 1996.

Boym, Svetlana. *The Future of Nostalgia*. New York: Basic Books, 2001.

Braidotti, Rosi. *Nomadic Subjects: Embodiment and Sexual Difference in Contemporary Feminist Theory*. New York: Columbia University Press, 1994.

Brody, Jane E. "Communities Learn the Good Life Can Be a Killer." *New York Times*, February 20, 2012. http://well.blogs.nytimes.com/2012/01/30/communities-learn-the-good-life-can-be-a-killer/?scp=2&sq=Jane%20E.%20Brody%. Accessed February 2, 2012.

———. "Still Counting Calories? Your Weight-Loss Plan May Be Outdated." *New York*

Times, July 19, 2011. http://www.nytimes.com/2011/07/19/health/19brody.html ?ref=science. Accessed July 21, 2011.

Brookhaven Lane. http://www.brookhavenlane.com/brookhaven_main.shtml. Accessed November 12, 2002.

Brown, Gillian. "The Empire of Agoraphobia." *Representations* 20 (Fall 1987): 134–57.

Buchanan, Ian. "Heterophenomenology, or de Certeau's Theory of Space." *Social Semiotics* 6 (1996): 111–32.

Burgin, Victor. *In/Different Spaces: Place and Memory in Visual Culture.* Berkeley: University of California Press, 1996.

Burke, Kenneth. *A Grammar of Motives.* Berkeley: University of California Press, 1969.

Burroughs, Charles. *From Signs to Design: Environmental Process and Reform in Early Renaissance Rome.* Cambridge, MA: MIT Press, 1990.

Burton, Tim. *Edward Scissorhands.* Century City, CA: 20th Century Fox, 1990.

Butler, Judith. *Bodies That Matter: On the Discursive Limits of "Sex."* New York: Routledge, 1993.

———. *Gender Trouble: Feminism and the Subversion of Identity.* 1990; New York: Routledge, 2000.

Calta, Marialisa. *Barbarians at the Plate: Taming and Feeding the Modern American Family.* New York: Perigree Books, 2005.

Carolan, Michael S. "Do You See What I See?: Examining the Epistemic Barriers to Sustainable Agriculture." *Rural Sociology* 71 (2006): 232–60.

Carruthers, Mary J. *The Book of Memory: A Study of Memory in Medieval Culture.* Cambridge: Cambridge University Press, 1990.

Casey, Edward S. *The Fate of Place: A Philosophical History.* Berkeley: University of California Press, 1997.

———. *Getting Back into Place: Toward a Renewed Understanding of the Place-World.* Bloomington: Indiana University Press, 1993.

Castle Rock Wine Fest. http://www.castlerockwinefest.com/. Accessed December 10, 2006.

Certeau, Michel de. *The Practice of Everyday Life.* Translated by Steven Rendall. Berkeley: University of California Press, 1984.

Certeau, Michel de, and Luce Giard. "A Practical Science of the Singular." In *The Practice of Everyday Life.* Vol. 2, *Living and Cooking*, translated by Timothy J. Tomasik, 251–56. Minneapolis: University of Minnesota Press, 1998.

Certeau, Michel de, Luce Giard, and Pierre Mayol. *The Practice of Everyday Life.* Vol. 2, *Living and Cooking.* Translated by Timothy J. Tomasik. Minneapolis: University of Minnesota Press, 1998.

Chamberlain, Charles. "From 'Haunts' to 'Character': The Meaning of Ethos and Its Relation to Ethics. *Helios* 11 (1984): 97–107.

Chaney, David. "Authenticity and Suburbia." In *Imagining Cities: Scripts, Signs, Memory*, edited by Sallie Westwood and John Williams, 140–51. London: Routledge, 1997.

Chapungu: The Great Stone Sculptures of Africa. http://www.chapungusculpturepark .com/. Accessed July 28, 2011.

Chapungu Sculpture Park. http://centerracolorado.com/contentPages/display/56. Accessed November 23, 2009.

Charland, Maurice. "Constitutive Rhetoric: The Case of the Peuple Québécois." *Quarterly Journal of Speech* 73 (1987): 133–50.

Chauncey, George. *Gay New York: Gender, Urban Culture, and the Making of the Gay Male World, 1890–1940*. New York: Basic Books, 1994.

——. "'Privacy Could Only Be Had in Public': Gay Uses of the Streets." In *Stud: Architectures of Masculinity*, edited by Joel Saunders, 224–61. New York: Princeton Architectural Press, 1996.

Chaves, Mark. "2005 Paul Douglas Lecture: All Creatures Great and Small: Megachurches in Context." *Review of Religious Research* 47 (2005): 329–46.

Chow, Renee Y. *Suburban Space: The Fabric of Dwelling*. Berkeley: University of California Press, 2002.

Christie, Les. "Farming for Fun." CNNMoney. January 6, 2005. http://money.cnn.com/2005/01/04/real_estate/buying_selling/hobbyfarms/. Accessed June 19, 2011.

Cloud, Dana. *Control and Consolation in American Culture and Politics: Rhetorics of Therapy*. Thousand Oaks, CA: Sage, 1998.

——. "The Materiality of Discourse as Oxymoron: A Challenge to Critical Rhetoric." *Western Journal of Communication* 58 (1994): 141–63.

——. "The Rhetoric of Family Values: Scapegoating, Utopia, and the Privatization of Social Responsibility." *Western Journal of Communication* 62 (1998): 387–419.

Cohen, Lizabeth A. *Consumer's Republic: The Politics of Mass Consumption in Postwar America*. New York: Alfred A. Knopf, 2003.

——. "From Town Center to Shopping Center: The Reconfiguration of Community Marketplaces in Postwar America." *American Historical Review* 101 (1996): 1050–81.

Collins, Jim. *Architectures of Excess: Cultural Life in the Information Age*. New York: Routledge, 1995.

Colomina, Beatriz, ed., with Jennifer Bloomer. *Sexuality and Space*. New York: Princeton Architectural Press, 1992.

Cook, Ian, and Philip Crang. "The World on a Plate: Culinary Culture, Displacement, and Geographical Knowledges." *Journal of Material Culture* 1 (1996): 131–53.

Cooks, Leda. "You Are What You (Don't) Eat? Food, Identity, and Resistance." *Text and Performance Quarterly* 29 (2009): 94–110.

Country Homes. http://www.mcstain.com/the_parks/countryhomes.htm. Accessed November 12, 2002.

Cronin, Thomas E. "What Do Coloradoans Believe?" *Denver Post*, August 27, 2006. LexisNexis. Accessed December 13, 2006.

Dannenberg, Andrew L., Richard J. Jackson, Howard Frumkin, Richard A. Schieber, Michael Pratt, Chris Kochtitzky, and Hugh H. Tilson. "The Impact of Community Design and Land-Use Choices on Public Health: A Scientific Research Agenda." *American Journal of Public Health* 93 (2003): 1503.

Davis, Fred. *Yearning for Yesterday: A Sociology of Nostalgia*. New York: Free Press, 1979.

Dear, Michael. "Beyond the Post-Fordist City." *Contention* 5 (1995): 67–76.

De Blij, Harm J. *The Power of Place: Geography, Destiny, and Globalization's Rough Landscape*. Oxford: Oxford University Press, 2009.

De Botton, Alain. *The Architecture of Happiness*. New York: Pantheon Books, 2006.

Deen, Paula, and Melissa Clark. *Paula Deen's the Deen Family Cookbook*. New York: Simon and Schuster, 2009.

De Grazia, Victoria. "Empowering Women as Citizen-Consumers." In *The Sex of Things: Gender and Consumption in Historical Perspective*, edited by Victoria de Grazia with Ellen Furlough, 275–86. Berkeley: University of California Press, 1996.

Denver's Farmers Market. http://www.shopaspengrove.com/go/mallEvents.cfm?eventID =2145386486. Accessed January 27, 2012.

Dickinson, Greg. "Joe's Rhetoric: Finding Authenticity at Starbucks." *Rhetoric Society Quarterly* 32 (2002): 22.

———. "Memories for Sale: Nostalgia and the Construction of Identity in Old Pasadena." *Quarterly Journal of Speech* 83 (1997): 1–27.

Dickinson, Greg, and Casey Maugh. "Placing Visual Rhetoric: Finding Material Comforts in Wild Oats Marketplace." In *Defining Visual Rhetorics*, edited by Charles A. Hill and Marguerite Helmers, 259–75. New York: Lawrence Erlbaum Associates, 2004.

Dickinson, Greg, Brian L. Ott, and Eric Aoki. "Spaces of Remembering and Forgetting: The Reverent Eye/I at the Plains Indian Museum." *Communication and Critical/Cultural Studies* 3 (2006): 27–47.

DiPiero, Thomas. *White Men Aren't.* Durham, NC: Duke University Press, 2002.

Doss, Erika. "Affect." *American Art* 23 (2009): 9–11.

Douglas, Mary. *In the Active Voice.* London: Routledge and Kegan Paul, 1982.

———. *Purity and Danger: An Analysis of Pollution and Taboo.* London: Routledge and Kegan Paul, 1966.

Duncan, James S., and Nancy G. Duncan. "The Aestheticization of the Politics of Landscape Preservation." *Annals of the Association of American Geographies* 91 (2001): 387–409.

Edelman, Lee. "Men's Room." In *Stud: Architectures of Masculinity*, edited by Joel Saunders, 152–61. New York: Princeton Architectural Press, 1996.

Ellin, Nan. "Shelter from the Storm or Form Follows Fear and Vice Versa." In *Architecture of Fear*, edited by Nan Ellin, 13–45. New York: Princeton Architectural Press, 1997.

Farmers Market at The Orchard. http://www.theorchardtowncenter.com/go/Poolb.cfm ?MallID=876&FPURLID=2129975056. Accessed January 27, 2012.

Farrell, James J. *One Nation under Goods: Malls and the Seductions of American Shopping.* Washington, DC: Smithsonian Books, 2003.

Field, Todd. *Little Children.* Los Angeles: New Line Cinema, 2006.

Fishman, Robert. *Bourgeois Utopias: The Rise and Fall of Suburbia.* New York: Basic Books, 1987.

Fjeld, Carla R., and Robert Sommer. "Regional-Seasonal Patterns in Produce Consumption at Farmer's Markets and Supermarkets." *Ecology of Food and Nutrition* (1982): 109–15.

Fogelson, Robert. *Bourgeois Nightmares: Suburbia, 1870–1930.* New Haven, CT: Yale University Press, 2005.

Foucault, Michel. *Discipline and Punish: The Birth of the Prison.* 2nd Vintage Books ed. Edited and translated by Alan Sheridan. New York: Vintage Books, 1995.

Francavigilia, Richard V. *Main Street Revisited: Time, Space, and Image Building in Small Town America.* Iowa City: University of Iowa Press, 1996.

Frey, William F. "Black Populations Dropping in Big Cities." State of Metropolitan America, 27, March 22, 2011, Brookings.edu. Accessed March 23, 2011.

Freud, Sigmund Freud. "The Uncanny." In *The Uncanny.* Translated by David McLintock. London: Penguin Books, 2003. 123–62.

Friedman, Thomas L. *The World Is Flat: A Brief History of the Twenty-First Century.* New York: Picador, 2007.

Frumkin, Howard, Lawrence Frank, and Richard Jackson. *Urban Sprawl and Public Health: Designing, Planning, and Building for Healthy Communities*. Washington, DC: Island Press, 2004.

Gabbard, Krin. *Black Magic: White Hollywood and African American Culture*. New Brunswick, NJ: Rutgers University Press, 2004.

Garreau, Joel. *Edge City: Life on the New Frontier*. New York: Doubleday, 1991.

Giard, Luce. "Doing-Cooking." In The Practice of Everyday Life. Vol. 2, *Living and Cooking*, Michel de Certeau, Luce Giard, and Pierre Mayol, 149–238. Translated by Timothy J. Tomasik. Minneapolis: University of Minnesota Press, 1998.

Giddens, Anthony. *Modernity and Self-Identity: Self and Society in the Late Modern Age*. Stanford, CA: Stanford University Press, 1991.

Girardelli, Davide. "Commodified Identities: The Myth of Italian Food in the United States." *Journal of Communication Inquiry* 28 (2004): 307–24.

Girling, Cynthia L., and Kenneth I. Helphand. *Yard, Street, Park: The Design of Suburban Open Space*. New York: John Wiley and Sons, 1994.

Glaser, Edward L. *The Triumph of the City: How Our Greatest Invention Makes Us Richer, Smarter, Greener, Healthier, and Happier*. New York: Penguin Press, 2011.

Gordon, Eric. *The Urban Spectator: American Concept Cities from Kodak to Google*. Hanover, NH: Dartmouth College Press, 2010.

Greene, Ronald. "Another Materialist Rhetoric." *Critical Studies in Mass Communication* 15 (1998): 21–41.

Grossberg, Lawrence. *We Gotta Get Out of This Place: Popular Conservatism and Postmodern Culture*. New York: Routledge, 1992.

Grosz, Elizabeth. *Space, Time, and Perversion: Essays on the Politics of Bodies*. New York: Routledge, 1995.

Gumbrecht, Hans Ulrich. *Production of Presence: What Meaning Cannot Convey*. Stanford, CA: Stanford University Press, 2004.

Gunn, Joshua. "Mourning Speech: Haunting and the Spectral Voices of Nine-Eleven." *Text and Performance Quarterly* 24 (2004): 99–114.

Gutfreund, Owen D. *Twentieth-Century Sprawl: Highways and the Reshaping of the American Landscape*. New York: Oxford University Press, 2004.

Haraway, Donna J. *Modest_Witness@Second_Millennium.FemaleMan©_Meets_OncoMouse™: Feminism and Technoscience*. New York: Routledge, 1997.

Harvey, David. *The Condition of Postmodernity: An Inquiry into the Origins of Social Change*. Cambridge, MA: Blackwell, 1989.

Hattenhauer, Darryl. "The Rhetoric of Architecture: A Semiotic Approach." *Communication Quarterly* 32 (1984): 71–77.

Haughton, Hugh. Introduction to Sigmund Freud, *The Uncanny*, translated and edited by David McLintock, vii–lv. New York: Penguin Books, 2003.

Haunt. Oxford English Dictionary. http://o-www.oed.com.catalog.library.colostate.edu/view/Entry/84640?rskey=YWE25w&result=1&isAdvanced=false#eid. Accessed January 5, 2012.

Hayden, Dolores. *Building Suburbia: Green Fields and Urban Growth, 1820–2000*. New York: Pantheon Books, 2003.

———. *The Grand Domestic Revolution: A History of Feminist Designs for American Homes, Neighborhoods, and Cities*. Cambridge, MA: MIT Press, 1981.

Haynes, Todd. *Far from Heaven*. New York: Focus Features, 2002.

Healy, Maureen. *Vienna and the Fall of the Hapsburg Empire: Total War and Everyday Life in World War I*. Cambridge: Cambridge University Press, 2004.

Hebbert, Michael. "The Street as Locus of Collective Memory." *Environment and Planning D: Society and Space* 23 (2005): 593.

Heidegger, Martin, "Letter on Humanism." Translated by Frank A. Cappuzi in collaboration with J. Glenn Gray. In *Basic Writings*, Martin Heidegger and David Farrell Krell, 213–66. New York: Harper and Row, 1977.

Highlands Ranch. Parks and Trails. http://www.highlandsranch.com/custom/ParksAndTrails.html?top=comm. Accessed December 13, 2006.

History of Highlands Ranch. http://www.highlandsranch.com/custom/HrHistory.html. Accessed December 14, 2006.

hooks, bell, "Eating the Other." In *Black Looks: Race and Representation*, 21–39. Boston: South End Press, 1992.

Howard, Jay R., and John M. Streck. "The Splintered Art World of Contemporary Christian Music." *Popular Music* 15 (1996): 37–53.

Humphrey, Theodore C., and Lin T. Humphrey. *We Gather Together: Food and Festival in American Life*. Ann Arbor, MI: UMI Research Press, 1988.

Hurley, Andrew. "From Hash House to Family Restaurant: The Transformation of the Diner and Post–World War II Consumer Culture." *Journal of American History* 83 (1997): 1282–1308.

Hutton, Patrick H. *History as an Art of Memory*. Hanover, NH: University Press of New England, 1993.

Huyssen, Andreas. *Present Pasts: Urban Palimpsests and the Politics of Memory*. Stanford, CA: Stanford University Press, 2003.

Hyde, Michael J. "Introduction: Rhetorically, We Dwell." In *The Ethos of Rhetoric*, edited by Michael J. Hyde, xii–xxviii. Columbia: University of South Carolina Press, 2004.

Ingram, Gordon Brent. "Marginality and the Landscape of Erotic Alien(n)ations." In *Queers in Space: Communities, Public Spaces, Sites of Resistance*, edited by Gordon Brent Ingram, Anne-Marie Bouthillette, and Yolanda Retter, 27–52. Seattle: Bay Press, 1997.

Ingram, Gordon Brent, Anne-Marie Bouthillette, and Yolanda Retter, eds. *Queers in Space: Communities, Public Spaces, Sites of Resistance*. Seattle: Bay Press, 1997.

Iyer, Pico. *The Global Soul: Jet Lag, Shopping Malls, and the Search for Home*. New York: Alfred A. Knopf, 2000.

Jackson, Kenneth T. *Crabgrass Frontier: The Suburbanization of the United States*. New York: Oxford University Press, 1985.

Jackson, Ronald L., II. "White Space, White Privilege: Mapping Discursive Inquiry into the Self." *Quarterly Journal of Speech* 85 (1999): 36–54.

Jacobs, Jane. *Death and Life of Great American Cities*. New York: Random House, 1961.

Jenks, Charles. *The Language of Postmodern Architecture*. 5th ed. New York: Rizzoli, 1987.

Karnasiewicz, Sarah. "Eating Dinner as a Family Puts Priorities of the Home in Order." Catholic Online. http://www.catholic.org/hf/family/story.php?id=18802. Accessed January 6, 2010.

Kasden, Jon. *In the Land of Women*. Beverly Hills, CA: Castle Rock Entertainment, 2007.

Kasson, John F. *Amusing the Million: Coney Island at the Turn of the Century*. New York: Hill and Wang, 1978.

Katriel, Tamar. "Sites of Memory: Discourses of the Past in Israeli Pioneering Settlement Museums." *Quarterly Journal of Speech* 80 (1994): 1–20.

Kessler, David A. *The End of Overeating: Controlling the Insatiable American Appetite.* New York: Rodale, 2009.

Kenyon, Amy Maria. *Dreaming Suburbia: Detroit and the Production of Postwar Space and Culture.* Detroit: Wayne State University Press, 2004.

Kiefer, Heather Mason. "Empty Seats: Fewer Families Eat Together." Gallup Online, January 24, 2004. http://www.gallup.com/poll/10336/empty-seats-fewer-families-eat-together.aspx. Accessed, July 6, 2011.

Kilde, Jeanne Halgren. *When Church Became Theatre: The Transformation of Evangelical Architecture and Worship in Nineteenth-Century America.* New York: Oxford University Press, 2002.

King, Martin Luther, Jr. "I've Been to the Mountaintop." http://www.americanrhetoric.com/speeches/mlkivebeentothemountaintop.htm. Accessed March 14, 2007.

King, Stephen A. "Memory, Mythmaking, and Museums: Constructive Authenticity and the Primitive Blues Subject." *Southern Communication Journal* 71 (2006): 235–50.

Kingsolver, Barbara, Steven, L. Hopp, and Camille Kingsolver. *Animal, Vegetable, Miracle: A Year of Food Life.* New York: HarperCollins, 2007.

Kristeller, Paul Oskar. *Renaissance Thought and Its Sources.* New York: Columbia University Press, 1979.

Kruse, Kevin M., and Thomas J. Sugure, *The New Suburban History.* Chicago: University of Chicago Press, 2006.

———. "Introduction: The New Suburban History." In *The New Suburban History*, edited by Kevin M. Kruse and Thomas J. Sugure, 1–10. Chicago: University of Chicago Press, 2006.

Kurtz, Gretchen. "Mommy This Restaurant Rocks: Sample Our Menu of Eateries That Are Friendly to Both Grown-Ups and the Crayon Set." DenverPost.Com. http://www.denverpost.com/food/ci_3084262. Accessed October 8, 2005.

Landing at Cherry Creek. http://www.drhorton.com/corp/DivisionSplash.do?divId=Y5. Accessed December 10, 2006.

Lang, Robert E., and Jennifer B. LeFurgy. *Boomburbs: The Rise of America's Accidental Cities.* Washington, DC: Brookings Institution Press, 2007.

Lasch, Scott. *Critique of Information.* London: Sage Publications, 2002.

Lefebvre, Henri. *The Social Production of Space.* Translated by Donald Nicholson-Smith. Oxford: Blackwell, 1991.

Leinberger, Christopher. "The Death of the Fringe Suburb." *New York Times*, November 26, 2011. http://www.nytimes.com/2011/11/26/opinion/the-death-of-the-fringe-suburb.html. Accessed January 2, 2012.

Lennar. Townhomes at Hunters Run. http://www.lennar.com/findhome/city.aspx?CITYID=PHO&BRANDID=USH. Accessed December 10, 2006.

LeTrent, Sarah. "Yes, Skeptics, Olive Garden Does Have a Tuscan Culinary Institute." CNN Living. http://articles.cnn.com/2010–05–10/living/olive.garden.culinary.institute_1_riserva-di-fizzano-chefs-tuscan-cuisine?_s=PM:LIVING. Accessed December 18, 2012.

Lévi-Strauss, Claude. *The Raw and the Cooked: Introduction to a Science of Mythology: I.* Translated by John and Doreen Weightman. New York: Harper and Row, 1969.

Lin, Justin. *Better Luck Tomorrow.* Glendale, CA: Cherry Sky Films, 2003.

Lindsay, Greg. "Say Goodbye to the Mall." *Advertising Age* 77 (40): 2006. Ebscohost Academic Search Premier. Accessed August 22, 2008.

Lipsitz, George. *How Racism Takes Place.* Philadelphia: Temple University Press, 2011.

——. *The Possessive Investment in Whiteness: How White People Profit from Identity Politics.* Philadelphia: Temple University Press, 2006.

——. *Time Passages: Collective Memory and American Popular Culture.* Minneapolis: University of Minnesota Press, 1990.

Longstreth, Richard. *From City Center to Regional Mall: Architecture, the Automobile, and Retailing in Los Angeles, 1930–1950.* Cambridge, MA: MIT Press, 1998.

Loveland, Anne C., and Otis B. Wheeler. *From Meetinghouse to Megachurch: A Material and Cultural History.* Columbia: University of Missouri Press, 2003.

Low, Setha. *Behind the Gates: Life Security, and the Pursuit of Happiness in Fortress America.* New York: Routledge, 2003.

Lukács, John. "Bourgeois Interior." *American Scholar* 39 (1970): 620–30.

Lynch, Kevin. *Image of the City.* Cambridge, MA: MIT Press, 1960.

——. *What Time Is This Place?* Cambridge, MA: MIT Press, 1972.

Makagon, Daniel. "Bring on the Shock Troops: Artists and Gentrification in the Popular Press." *Communication and Critical/Cultural Studies* 7 (2011): 26–52.

Macek, Steve. *Urban Nightmares: The Media, the Right, and the Moral Panic over the City.* Minneapolis: University of Minnesota Press, 2006.

Mahler, Jonathan. "The Soul of the New Exurb." *New York Times Magazine,* March 27, 2005. LexisNexis Online.

Marx, Karl, and Friedrich Engels. *The Communist Manifesto.* Arlington Heights, IL: Harlan Davidson, 1955.

Marx, Karl, and Friedrich Engels. *The Communist Manifesto.* Translated by Terrell Carver. In *The Communist Manifesto: New Interpretations,* edited by Mark Cowling. Edinburgh: Edinburgh University Press, 1998. http://web.a.ebscohost.com.ezproxy2 .library.colostate.edu:2048/ehost/ebookviewer/ebook/bmxlYmtfXzk3NjdfX0FOo ?sid=c46b1d89-d2b4-4291-8fbb-cab2d6b7eb42@sessionmgr4002&vid=1&format =EB&lpid=lp_III&rid=0. Accessed February 25, 2014.

Marx, Leo. *The Machine in the Garden: Technology and the Pastoral Ideal in America.* New York: Oxford University Press, 1964.

Massey, Doreen. *For Space.* London: Sage Publications, 2005.

Massumi, Brian. "The Autonomy of Affect." *Cultural Critique* 31 (1995): 83–109.

——. *Parables for the Virtual: Movement, Affect, Sensation.* Durham, NC: Duke University Press, 2002.

Mayes, Frances. *Under the Tuscan Sun.* San Francisco: Chronicle Books, 1996.

Mayol, Pierre. "Living." In *The Practice of Everyday Life.* Vol. 2, *Living and Cooking* by Michel de Certeau, Luce Giard, and Pierre Mayol, 5–130. Translated by Timothy J. Tomasik. Minneapolis: University of Minnesota Press, 1998.

McAlister, Joan Faber. "Domesticating Citizenship: The Kairotopics of America's Post-9/11 Home Makeover." *Critical Studies in Media Communication* 27 (2010): 91.

——. "Figural Materialism: Renovating Marriage through the American Family Home." *Southern Communication Journal* 76 (2011): 279–304.

——. "Material Aesthetics in Middle America: Simone Weil, the Problem of Roots, and the Panoptic Suburb." In *Rhetoric, Materiality, and Politics,* edited by Barbara A. Biesecker and John Louis Lucaites, 99–129. New York: Peter Lang, 2009.

McCabe, Janet, and Kim Akass. *Reading Desperate Housewives: Beyond the White Picket Fence*. New York: I. B. Taurus, 2006.

McFarland, Lee. "What to Tell Your Gay Friend." http://www.radiantchurch.com /media/messages/audio/70.mp3. Accessed October 23, 2006.

McKerrow, Raymie. "Critical Rhetoric: Theory and Praxis." *Communication Monographs* 56 (1989): 91–111.

McStain Colonial. http://www.mcstain.com/the_parks/countryhomes/aspen_house .htm. Accessed November 12, 2002.

Mendes, Sam. *American Beauty*. Universal City, CA: Dreamworks SKG, 1999.

Meinig, D. W. "Symbolic Landscapes: Some Idealizations of American Communities." In *The Interpretation of Ordinary Landscapes: Geographical Essays*, edited by D. W. Meinig, 164–92. New York: Oxford University Press, 1979.

Miller, Claire Cain. "Now at Starbucks: A Rebound." *New York Times*, January 20, 2010. nytimes.com. Accessed December 31, 2010.

Milun, Kathryn. *Pathologies of Modern Urban Space: Empty Space, Urban Anxiety, and the Recovery of the Public Self*. New York: Routledge, 2007.

Morris, Meaghan. *Too Soon, Too Late: History in Popular Culture*. Bloomington: Indiana University Press, 1998.

Morse, Margaret "An Ontology of Everyday Distraction: The Freeway, the Mall, and Television." In *Logics of Television: Essays in Cultural Criticism*, edited by Patricia Mellencamp, 193–223. Bloomington: Indiana University Press, 1990.

Muzzio, Douglas, and Thomas Halper. "Pleasantville? The Suburb and Its Representation in American Movies." *Urban Affairs Review* 37 (2002): 543–74.

Nakayama, Thomas K., and Robert L. Krizek. "Whiteness: A Strategic Rhetoric." *Quarterly Journal of Speech* 81 (1995): 291–301.

The National Center on Addiction and Drug Abuse at Columbia University. "The Importance of Family Dinners, VI," September 2010. http://www.casacolumbia.org /upload/2010/20100922familydinners6.pdf. Accessed July 6, 2011.

Negra, Diane. "Ethnic Food Fetishism: Whiteness, and Nostalgia in Recent Film and Television." *Velvet Light Trap* 50 (2002): 62–76.

Newton, Sam. "Suburban Infill—Solving Infrastructure and Financing Issues." Urban Land Institute, November 10, 2011. http://urbanland.uli.org/Articles/2011/Nov /NewbergMinnesota. Accessed February 6, 2012.

Nicolaides, Becky. "How Hell Moved from the City to the Suburbs: Urban Scholars and Changing Perceptions of Authentic Community." In *The New Suburban History*, edited by Kevin M. Kruse and Thomas J. Sugure, 80–98. Chicago: University of Chicago Press, 2006.

Oakes, Timothy. "Place and the Paradox of Modernity." *Annals of the Association of American Geographers* 87 (1997): 509–31.

Olive Garden. "Our Passion." http://www.olivegarden.com/ourpassion/CITbook_p2 .asp. Accessed October 18, 2005.

Olive Garden RevItalia. http://www.ramskiandcompany.com/portfolio/hospitality /olive-garden/. Accessed February 9, 2010.

Osteen, Joel. *Your Best Life Now: 7 Steps to Living your Full Potential*. New York: Warner, 2007.

Ott, Brian L. "The Visceral Politics of *V for Vendetta*: On Political Affect in Cinema." *Critical Studies in Media Communication* 27 (2010): 39–54.

Ott, Brian L., Eric Aoki, and Greg Dickinson. "Ways of (Not) Seeing Guns: Presence and Absence at the Cody Firearms Museum." *Communication and Critical/Cultural Studies* 8 (2011): 215–39.

Packer, Jeremy, and Stephen B. Crofts Wiley, eds. *Communication Matters: Materialist Approaches to Media, Mobility, and Networks.* London: Routledge, 2011.

Peiss, Kathy. *Cheap Amusements: Working Women and Leisure in Turn-of-the-Century New York.* Philadelphia: Temple University Press: 1985.

Pollan, Michael. *In Defense of Food: An Eater's Manifesto.* New York: Penguin Press, 2008.

———. *The Omnivore's Dilemma: A Natural History of Four Meals.* New York: Penguin Press, 2006.

Pringle, Patricia. "Spatial Pleasures." *Space and Culture* 8 (2005): 141–59.

Probyn, Elspeth. *Carnal Appetites: FoodSexIdentities.* London and New York: Routledge, 2000.

Pulido, Laura. "Rethinking Environmental Racism: White Privilege and Urban Development in Southern California." *Annals of the Association of American Geographers* 90 (2000): 12–40.

Radiant Church. http://www.radiantchurch.com/. Accessed October 18, 2006.

Radiant Church Adults. http://www.radiantchurch.com/adults.asp. Accessed October 26, 2006.

Radiant Church History. http://www.radiantchurch.com/history.asp. Accessed October 13, 2006.

Radiant Church Welcome. http://www.welcometoradiant.com/northcampus/default.htm. Accessed October 21, 2006.

Radiant Church Welcome Kids. http://www.radiantchurch.com/welcome/kids.asp. Accessed October 26, 2006.

Red Robin Food. http://www.redrobin.com/food/. Accessed February 4, 2010.

Relph, Edward. *The Modern Urban Landscape.* Baltimore: Johns Hopkins University Press, 1987.

Restaurant Industry Facts. http://www.restaurant.org/research/ind_glance.cfm. Accessed October 1, 2005.

Reunion. http://www.reunionco.com/index.php?c=56&d=57&a=39&w=2&r=Y. Accessed December 9, 2006.

Rosenfield, Lawrence W. "Central Park and the Celebration of Civic Virtue." In *American Rhetoric: Context and Criticism,* edited by Thomas Benson, 129–59. Carbondale: Southern Illinois University Press, 1989.

Ross, Gary. *Pleasantville.* Los Angeles: New Line Cinema, 1998.

Ross, Herbert. *My Blue Heaven.* Burbank, CA: Warner Brothers, 1990.

Rupert, Evelyn S. *The Moral Economy of Cities: Shaping Good Citizens.* Toronto: University of Toronto Press, 2006.

Russell, Daniel C. *Plato on Pleasure and the Good Life.* New York: Oxford University Press, 2005.

Rybczynski, Witold. *Home: A Short History of an Idea.* New York: Penguin Books, 1986.

Saunders, Joel. Introduction to *Stud: Architectures of Masculinity,* edited by Joel Saunders, 12–25. New York: Princeton Architectural Press, 1996.

Schivelbusch, Wolfgang. *Disenchanted Night: The Industrialization of Light in the Nineteenth Century.* Translated by Angela Davies. Berkeley: University of California Press, 1988.

Schlosser, Eric. *Fast Food Nation: The Dark Side of the All-American Meal*. Boston: Houghton Mifflin, 2001.

Seamon, David. "Gaston Bachelard's Topoanalysis in the 21st Century: The Lived Reciprocity between Houses and Inhabitants as Portrayed by American Writer Louis Bromfield." In *Phenomenology 2010*, edited by Lester Embree. Bucharest, Romania: Zeta Books, 2010. http://ksu.academia.edu/DavidSeamon/Papers/169389/Gaston _Bachelards_Topoanalysis_in_the_21st_Century_The_Lived_Reciprocity_between _Houses_and_Inhabitants_as_Portrayed_by_American_Writer_Louis_Bromfield. Accessed June 28, 2011.

Sedgwick, Eve Kosofsky. *Epistemology of the Closet*. Berkeley: University of California Press, 1990.

Sennett, Richard. *The Conscience of the Eye: The Design and Social Life of Cities*. New York: W. W. Norton, 1990.

Sheffield Homes Grand Opening. http://www.sheffieldhomes.com/grand_opening.htm. Accessed November 12, 2002.

Shepherd, Gordon M. *Neurogastronomy: How the Brain Creates Flavor and Why It Matters*. New York: Columbia University Press, 2012.

Shibley, Mark A. "Contemporary Evangelicals: Born-Again and World Affirming." *Annals of the American Academy of Political and Social Science* 558 (1998): 67–87.

Shome, Raka. "Space Matters: The Power and Practice of Space." *Communication Theory* 13 (2003): 39–56.

Shugart, Helena. "Sumptuous Texts: Consuming 'Otherness' in Food Film Genre." *Critical Studies in Media Communication* 25 (2008): 68–90.

Smith, Christopher P. "Translator's Introduction." In *The Idea of the Good in Platonic-Aristotelian Philosophy*, by Hans-Georg Gadamer, translated by P. Christopher Smith, vii–xxxi. New Haven, CT: Yale University Press, 1986.

Sorkin, Michael. "See You in Disneyland." In *Variations on a Theme Park: The New American City and the End of Public Space*, edited by Michael Sorkin, 205–32. New York: Noonday Press, 1992.

Spigel, Lynn. "The Suburban Home Companion: Television and the Neighborhood Ideal in Postwar America." In *Sexuality and Space*, edited by Beatriz Colomina, with Jennifer Bloomer, 185–217. New York: Princeton Architectural Press, 1992.

———. *Welcome to the Dream House: Popular Media and Postwar Suburbs*. Durham, NC: Duke University Press, 2001.

Squier, Susan M. "Reproducing the Posthuman Body: Ectogenetic Fetus, Surrogate Mother, Pregnant Man." In *Posthuman Bodies*, edited by Judith Halberstam and Ira Livingston, 113–32. Bloomington: Indiana University Press, 1995.

Standard Pacific Homes. http://standardpacifichomes.com/findhome/NeighborhoodIntro .aspx?NID=899. Accessed December 10, 2006.

St. Antoine, Thomas J. "Making Heaven out of Hell: New Urbanism and the Refutation of Suburban Spaces." *Southern Communication Journal* 72 (2007): 127–44.

Stevenson, Richard W. "Fed Reports Family Gains from Economy." *New York Times*, January 19, 2000, C1. LexisNexis. Accessed April 15, 2010.

Stewart, Jessie, and Greg Dickinson. "Enunciating Locality in the Postmodern Suburb: FlatIron Crossing and the Colorado Lifestyle." *Western Journal of Communication* 72 (2008): 280–307.

Stormer, Nathan. "Addressing the Sublime: Space, Mass Representation, and the Unpresentable." *Critical Studies in Media Communication* 21 (2004): 212–40.

Stone, Lawrence. *The Family, Sex, and Marriage in England, 1500–1800.* Abridged ed. New York: Harper Torchbooks, 1979.

Sturken, Marita. *Tourists of History: Memory, Kitsch, and Consumerism from Oklahoma City to Ground Zero.* Durham, NC: Duke University Press, 2001.

Swenson, Rebecca "Domestic Divo? Televised Treatments of Masculinity, Femininity, and Food." *Critical Studies in Media Communication* 26 (2009): 36–53.

Terkenli, Theano S. "Home as a Region." *Geographical Review* 85 (1995): 324–34.

Terdiman, Richard. *Present Past: Modernity and the Memory Crisis.* Ithaca, NY: Cornell University Press, 1993.

TGI Friday's "Good Things Happen in Threes." http://www.tgifridays.com/promos/3course.aspx. Accessed February 4, 2010.

Tiemann, Thomas K. "Grower-Only Farmers' Markets: Public Spaces and Third Places." *Journal of Popular Culture* 41 (2008): 467–87.

Trubeck, Amy B. *The Taste of Place: A Cultural Journey into Terroir.* Berkeley: University of California Press, 2008.

Tuan, Yi-Fu. "Images and Mental Maps." *Annals of the Association of American Geographers* 65 (1975): 205–13.

Twitchell, James B. *Branded Nation: The Marketing of Megachurch, College, Inc., and Museumworld.* New York: Simon and Schuster, 2004.

Uchittle, Louis. "Equity Shrivels as Homeowners Borrow and Buy." *New York Times*, A1. January 19, 2001. LexisNexis. Accessed April 15, 2010.

Vidler, Anthony. *The Architectural Uncanny: Essays in the Modern Unhomely.* Cambridge, MA: MIT Press, 1992.

——. *Warped Space: Art, Architecture, and Anxiety in Modern Culture.* Cambridge, MA: MIT Press, 2001.

Vileisis, Ann. *Kitchen Literacy: How We Lost Knowledge of Where Food Comes From and Why We Need to Get It Back.* Washington, DC: Island Press/Shearwater Books, 2008.

Villa Avignon Toast. http://www.brookhavenlane.com/va_default.htm. Accessed November 12, 2002.

Vivian, Bradford. *Public Forgetting: The Rhetoric and Politics of Beginning Again.* University Park: Pennsylvania State University Press, 2010.

Warf, Barney, and Santa Arias. "Introduction: The Reinsertion of Space into the Social Sciences and the Humanities." In *The Spatial Turn: Interdisciplinary Perspectives*, edited by Barney Warf and Santa Arias, 1–10. London: Routledge, 2009.

Warren, Rick. *The Purpose Driven Life: What on Earth Am I Here For?* Grand Rapids: Zondervan, 2002.

Watts, Eric King, and Mark P. Orbe. "The Spectacular Consumption of 'True' African American Culture: 'Whassup' with the Budweiser Guys?" *Critical Studies in Media Communication* 19 (2002): 1–20.

Wegner, Phillip E. *Imaginary Communities: Utopia, the Nation, and the Spatial Histories of Modernity.* Berkeley: University of California Press, 2002.

Wier, Peter. *The Truman Show.* Hollywood, CA: Paramount Pictures, 1998.

Wiese, Andrew. "'The House I Live In': Race, Class, and African American Suburban Dreams in the Postwar United States." In *The New Suburban History*, edited by

Kevin M. Kruse and Thomas J. Sugure, 99–119. Chicago: University of Chicago Press, 2006.

——. *Places of Their Own: African American Suburbanization in the Twentieth Century*. Chicago: University of Chicago Press, 2004.

Wood, Andrew. "'Are We There Yet?': Searching for Springfield and the Simpsons' Rhetoric of Omnitopia." *Critical Studies in Media Communication* 22 (2005): 207–22.

——. *City Ubiquitous: Place, Communication, and the Rise of Omnitopia*. Cresskill, NJ: Hampton Press, 2009.

——. "A Rhetoric of Ubiquity: Terminal Space as Omnitopia." *Communication Theory* 13 (2003): 324–44.

——. "'What Happens [in Vegas]': Performing the Post-Tourist Flâneur in 'New York' and 'Paris.'" *Text and Performance Quarterly* 25 (2005): 315–33.

Yakhlef, Ali. "Global Brands as Embodied 'Generic Spaces': The Example of Branded Chain Hotels." *Space and Culture* 7 (2004): 237.

Yates, Frances A. *The Art of Memory*. Chicago: University of Chicago Press, 1966.

Zita, Jacquelyn N. *Body Talk: Philosophical Reflections on Sex and Gender*. New York: Columbia University Press, 1998.

Žižek, Slavoj. "Looking Awry." *October* 50 (1989): 30–55.

——. *Looking Awry: An Introduction to Jacques Lacan through Popular Culture*. Cambridge, MA: MIT Press 1992.

Zukin, Sharon. *Landscapes of Power: From Detroit to Disney World*. Berkeley: University of California Press, 1991.

——. *Loft Living: Culture and Capital in Urban Change*. New York: Routledge, 1989.

Index